THE ELECTRONIC FUTURE OF BANKING

Succeeding in the New Electronic Age for Tomorrow's Financial Institutions

Floyd E. Egner, III

McGRAW-HILL BOOK COMPANY

London • New York • St. Louis • San Francisco • Auckland
Bogotá • Guatemala • Hamburg • Lisbon • Madrid • Mexico
Montreal • New Delhi • Panama • Paris • San Juan • São Paulo
Singapore • Sydney • Tokyo • Toronto

Published in the United Kingdom by
McGraw-Hill Book Company (UK) Limited
Shoppenhangers Road
Maidenhead, Berkshire England SL6 2QL

British Library Cataloguing in Publication Data
Egner, Floyd E.
The electronic future of banking : succeeding in the new electronic age for tomorrow's financial institutions.
1. Banking. Applications of computer systems
I. Title
332.10285

ISBN 0-07-707390-8

Printed and bound in the United States of America

10 9 8 7 6 5 4 3 2 1

ACKNOWLEDGMENTS

The Electronic Future of Banking is the product of opinions and insights developed during seven years of research into the impact of electronic delivery systems on financial services, most of which was conducted through various syndicated research programs for Payment Systems, Inc. (PSI) of Tampa, Florida. The opinions and recommendations, however, should be regarded as my own and do not necessarily reflect the opinions or recommendations of PSI or its parent company, JPT Holdings of New York.

That formality aside, this book would not exist without the efforts, thoughts and encouragement of many people with whom I have been associated during that period. Dale Reistad, who bears the curse of being credited with coining the phrase "the checkless society," was the first to challenge me to understand the impact that computers and electronic systems in general were having on banking. My first research in the area addressed home banking, an idea whose time had not yet come. However, I learned that electronics were dramatically changing finanical service delivery systems, change that was not as sudden as the early gurus of banking thought it would be, but every bit as profound.

This book represents a continuation of and expansion upon analysis that began with the realization that many bankers were misunderstanding electronic services as a series of products rather than as a delivery system. Its basic thrust is to argue that financial institutions lack a clear vision of why their future lies in electronic delivery.

I have written extensively on topics such as point of sale direct debit, automated teller machines and interactive computer-delivered services individually for numerous research reports, as well as for the *PSI*

Monitor and *Payment Systems Newsletter*, which I published for PSI. My associates as editors have included Diane Smith, Fonda Anderson and Barry Carroll. Researchers who contributed to the preparation and analysis of many research surveys include Martha Monk, John DeMarco, Jim Thayer and, especially, Veronica Bennett, who conducted the analysis of the 1988 PSI survey that is presented in chapters three and four.

Thanks also go to a host of people who have formally and informally reacted to my "Toward the Year 2000" projections, which I have presented at various conferences, seminars and meetings since 1986.

For permission to use PSI research data, I thank Al DeCotiis, president and CEO of PSI.

Floyd E. Egner, III

November, 1990

Table of Contents

CHAPTER

1

Electronic Delivery Strategies That Will Succeed

BANKING AS AN INFORMATION AGE TECHNOLOGY LEADER

Electronics have transformed the banking business to as great a degree as any of the industries that have been affected by computer technologies. The nature of banking has been revolutionized by electronics as profoundly as printed currency once displaced precious metals as a primary means of value exchange.

While the paper revolution took nearly a century, electronics are bringing change to banking literally at light speed. A conservative industry by nature, banking is in the uncomfortable role of a quintessential information age technology leader. Behind walls of regulation and tradition, financial institutions are struggling as electronics are restructuring banking's role as service providers and conservators of the most critical information about corporate and personal wealth.

While bankers have been leaders in applying computer technology to their operations (making the financial industry one of the largest users of computer and telecommunication services) bankers have encountered difficulties again and again in taking their vaunted technological expertise to the ultimate users — the consumers. In particular, efforts to introduce "home banking" — financial services electronically delivered to the home — repeatedly have resulted in massive expenditures and minimal market penetration. Instead of meeting the promises of ease of use and greatly expanded information and service choices, bankers have all too often introduced slow, awkward and expensive services which duplicate services offered in traditional form without adding significant advantage.

The reason for this lies in a failure to understand that the consumer household has not been revolutionized by computer technology in the same way that financial services have been. While consumers have eagerly embraced a variety of home electronic devices and are often enthusiastic about new high-tech toys, their purchase preferences are for entertainment devices and easy-to-use tools for routine and familiar tasks. Even the home computer, one of the most promising and versatile of electronic devices available to the home market, most often is used only for playing games or word processing.

The challenge is to develop electronic services that not only provide secure and efficient transaction capabilities, but also address needs for investment and credit information, including the ability to obtain instant access to such products. Automation of the full process of financial service delivery is the ultimate strategy, recognizing that partial automation introduces new inefficiencies and frustrations for both consumers and their financial institutions.

To adequately provide what consumers want, need and expect in electronic financial service delivery is costly in the short term and long term. But failing to adequately provide those things will be even more costly. Banking increasingly is transaction-oriented, a business highly prone to automation, while investment and credit services have become commodities. Automating transaction services is essential and cannot be dependent on decisions by the consumer to "buy into" the process. Ultimately, consumers pay the bill for the automation by doing business with those institutions that have most efficiently and effectively devised systems that deliver commodity priced services, wherever the consumer needs those services.

Electronic delivery services have come to dominate large dollar transactions for the very simple reason that time is money. The velocity of funds transfers is accelerating constantly. Much of traditional banking was built on intermediation, making money not only on the margin between interest paid by borrowers and to savers, but also on holding funds in transit, especially those in non-interest bearing transaction accounts. Float was inherent, unavoidable and a source of profit. But as computerized systems have allowed interest to be earned on large sums of money held even for a few hours, more and more players have recognized this opportunity. Electronics have been a double-edge sword, allowing ever swifter exchanges of funds and continually squeezing the opportunities for earnings from float.

Individuals and companies with the most money were the first to realize the possibilities and the first to use wire transfer services and electronic settlement. Banks repeatedly have seen corporate customers take back pieces of banking's traditional business, offering or creating their own financial services as electronic technology has assisted them in every arena from selling corporate paper to issuing consumer credit cards.

Electronic cash management services have become a critical element in any financial institution's services to corporate clients.Yet in the consumer market, financial institutions often plunge ahead with development of services that fit their needs rather than their customers. While technology is used on the corporate side to solve business problems, it has not been as well applied to consumer problems. Creative applications of technology to basic payment services by various entities could deprive conventional financial institutions of their basic franchise. Although banks have relationships with nearly nine out of every ten households, there are other single companies, not to mention industries, that have similar relationships, as AT&T has recently demonstrated in launching its highly successful credit card program.

The irony of this is that financial institutions have or are acquiring the means to provide the needed solutions, but a consistently piecemeal approach holds them back from achieving fully integrated, automated systems. Much of the blame can be laid at the feet of the guardians of the banking bureaucracies, which, for example, regard debit and credit as separate departments rather than the ying and yang, complementary parts of the whole that they are.

Another of the basic failings on the part of electronic banking advocates is to assume that any electronic system automatically is more convenient, rather than to examine whether a particular technology or application of electronics simplifies the process or complicates it. The home computer based and telephone based banking services of the past decade are largely examples of the latter. Services that are not completely integrated with existing automated consumer, merchant and financial institution systems are almost certainly doomed to failure.

In seeming contrast, the success of Automated Teller Machines (ATMs) in fact represents a very limited extension of banking service automation, primarily automating the basic functions of providing current account balance information and dispensing cash. Attempting to extend use of the ATM card to the merchant's point of sale immediately demonstrates the limitations of ATM system design and the importance of integrating systems. The ATM card is useful as long as it remains within the relatively closed environment of customer and financial institution transactions. But its use as a transaction card outside of that environment requires the installation of new communications systems, or integration with existing systems. The merchant generally does not have compelling reasons to do either, even though the merchant also is interested in automation of the payment process.

The assumption that the ATM card might function as a debit card or plastic check, facilitating purchasing convenience by substituting for cash or checks, is valid and logical. However, it suffers as a viable alternative because the financial industry's continual reality is that payment systems are only partially automated and cannot be transformed at a stroke. The ATM card as debit card immediately confronts the industry's structural separation of credit and debit operations. This separation generally excludes it from being used as an alternative payment device through rule-bound systems established to support use of credit cards at the point of sale.

Secondly, pricing structures for that existing credit payment system — even when highly automated — are based on a percentage of each transaction rather than on a flat fee per transaction such as developed in ATM systems. The discount or percentage approach makes sense when the financial institution accepting the credit transaction assumes inherently greater risk with an increase in dollar size of the transaction. But it makes no sense if the transaction is a debit of a verified account balance. In such a transaction, there is no additional risk with an increase in dollar value of the transaction.

For all of these reasons, the financial industry continues to stumble as it lurches toward a goal of developing a convenient means for a consumer to electronically debit an account balance to make a purchase. Point of sale debit, meanwhile, in some instances is being taken over directly by the merchant, who can issue its own cards and use a cooperative member of the automated clearinghouse association to directly dump batch ACH transactions into the banking system. The merchant collects funds as rapidly — or more so — as by accepting checks, likely avoids per check deposit fees and speeds customers through the check-out lines with no more risk than was entailed in accepting a paper check.

Partial automation leaves the financial industry vulnerable to many such end-around solutions to payment system automation. But completely automated, integrated delivery systems for financial services are unfortunately regarded by many as too expensive.

The financial industry is, in fact, continuing to invest heavily in technology. Some of those investments are encouraging in that they recognize that automation is an evolutionary process that must incorporate existing systems while moving as rapidly as possible to full automation. The pace of technological change also is allowing automation to behave in a more familiar fashion, so that automating a system increasingly does not require users to relearn basic functions and procedures.

Change In The Delivery System Infrastructure

Image processing and speech recognition are two of the most interesting of current technological developments that will shape the future nature of electronic banking. They share the common element of making existing systems work more like people do, rather than forcing people to adapt to the capabilities and mechanics of computer systems. Each represents a continuation of a process of infrastructure change that began with the introduction of the first computer tools for managing financial institutions' records. Electronic tools have been vital in allowing the financial industry to grow, providing both speed and accuracy for fundamental banking services. To a large extent, the changing capabilities of electronic information systems have defined what new services and delivery systems financial institutions could offer.

Image processing is addressing the need to cope with the volume of paper generated by today's transaction volume without completely eliminating paper as a part of the process. Speech recognition offers the potential to take automation of delivery and information systems to another level of efficiency while expanding the user market beyond those segments who are technically inclined or comfortable with gadgets.

Ironically, making systems behave more like people requires the application of more technology, not less. Indeed, applied technology often is most successful when it is least obvious. The current explosion of growth in telephone system automation is being fueled in part by the fact that better technology makes such systems literally easier to talk to and easier to understand. Image processing is important not only for the labor-saving potential it offers, but also because it allows both consumers and institutions to deal in the familiar forms of written communications via paper, while still recognizing many of the advantages of electronic automation.

The recent past has shown that the adoption of new financial service delivery vehicles and the systems that support them does not eliminate, but complements, existing systems. That has meant that the money-saving aspects of electronic financial services often have been oversold. Introducing or advocating new payment systems has come to be a sure means of shortening a promising career in many financial institutions. Nonetheless, the competitive pressures of the marketplace force institutions to constantly evaluate delivery alternatives and assess the possibility of income either from consumer or merchant fees as well as from potential operational savings.

Generational changes and ever-present consumer demands for convenience, control and cost-saving alternatives justify projections of substantial growth in usage of a variety of alternative payment vehicles. These alternatives have their roots in existing services and incorporate much of the current environment.

For example, take a look at what consumers call checking accounts. The banking industry more precisely refers to them as demand deposit accounts or DDAs. The use of paper checks has become a nearly universal transaction medium in the United States and the preferred means of obtaining access to the funds in such accounts. Despite what now has become more than two decades of predictions of a coming checkless society, paper checks are likely to remain dominant as a means of making payments through the end of the century, even though volume may decline. Although electronic payments through the automated clearinghouse system constituted about 2 billion items in 1989, paper check volume through the Federal Reserve system consisted of somewhere between 50 to 60 billion items. The volume, which includes business to business transactions, continues to be so great that there is even difficulty in finding agreement on how to measure the consumer portion of it.

The reason for that continued volume is that paper still has significant advantages for many users, even though the benefits of electronic payments are becoming evident. Electronic payments offer greater accuracy, greater security, less float and more rapid certainty of payment. Why shouldn't such attributes immediately be recognized and accepted? For many businesses as well as financial institutions the answer is that the benefits do not yet outweigh the expense and difficulty of converting from existing payment methods. Check processing costs, for example, have dropped steadily on a per item basis over the past three decades since the introduction of the first large-capacity check sorters and standardization of magnetic ink character recognition (MICR) usage. Check truncation, which has been implemented in a few areas of financial service and as a feature on some standard checking accounts, has the potential to add a bit more incremental efficiency, reducing the physical handling of paper. Image processing equipment may be combined with truncation to further increase the popularity of such services, while providing the consumer a facsimile of the returned checks now received.

For much of the public, including professionals and business people, reluctance to abandon paper also stems from the fact that we are far less sophisticated and comfortable with the electronic devices in our lives than we popularly perceive ourselves to be. Consequently, familiarity with old habits and reluctance to change established means of conducting business makes change occur much less quickly than the available technology could allow.

An additional reason, which is often overlooked, is that whether those characteristics of electronic payment — greater accuracy, greater security, less float and more rapid certainty of payment — are attributes or detriments may depend on which side of the transaction a particular party is on. The unequal distribution of benefits is especially common when systems are only partially automated. To an unfortunate degree, the implementation of electronic payment systems by financial institutions has been cautiously structured to first provide advantages to the institution, then secondly to share advantages with users — both consumers and business customers. If merchants or consumers want electronic payment systems, financial institutions say "Let them pay for them." The market is wise to such strategies and asks, "What's in it for me?"

While financial institutions certainly have obligations, both fiduciary and regulatory, to protect themselves and ensure that they pursue potentially profitable ventures, a failure to understand the critical role of fully automated electronic banking in future strategies is short-sighted and in the long term opens doors of opportunity for fleet-footed non-bank competitors. Ultimately, many financial institutions are likely to suffer the fate of companies bypassed by technologically superior competitors, gradually becoming less profitable as operations costs mount on dwindling volumes of the traditional business.

The delivery of financial services generally (and electronic delivery in particular), has become a commodity business, with one provider's offering virtually indistinguishable from another's. This trend makes it all the more critical for financial institutions to understand market preferences so that appropriate delivery system strategies are in place.

Financial services as commodities

While the paper check is inexpensive, flexible and easy-to-use, usage of checks is not likely to remain constant. Increasingly, the check is recognized as only one of a variety of means of conducting financial transactions from the home and at the point of sale. Segments of the consumer population, particularly younger and more affluent consumers, are likely to write far fewer checks than other segments have during the past two decades. They will do so not solely by their own initiative, but with the encouragement and assistance of merchants and bankers who will see growing advantages to the use of electronic forms of payment, whether by credit or debit card, preauthorized payment or through a customer-initiated electronic payment using a telephone or computer based device. While credit cards have taken on a larger role in payments and will contribute to this decline of checks, greater impact will come from the growing use of debit cards, preauthorized payments and new electronic payment forms using telephones and computers.

Use of credit cards at the point of sale has grown exponentially as merchant acceptance has grown and societal taboos about the stigma of "charging" have weakened. New ventures by fast food merchants that make credit card acceptance virtually instantaneous for small purchases are harbingers of efforts by the major card associations to penetrate the last remaining areas in which cash is a preferred means of payment. The long anticipated spread of debit cards for such purchases has been delayed by myriad issues, including the reluctance of financial institutions to pay for additional infrastructure or to promote an alternative to the highly profitable credit card business. Credit cards also have taken on a minor role in bill payment from the home, particularly for mail and telephone orders, but several other alternatives are likely to have greater impact long term on the use of paper checks.

Automated or preauthorized payments are not an innovation in themselves. Insurance companies in particular have made such payments a standard means of doing business, and sometimes a requirement. The automated clearinghouse system, through which such payments are routed, has reached a level of penetration and efficient, consistent operation such that virtually any payment recipient today — individual, merchant or financial institution — can receive automated payments without having to devise special procedures or exception processes that complicate accounting systems. The standardization of electronic information exchange formats has brought standard and inexpensive software that can be used on standard and inexpensive hardware. Furthermore, no credible financial institution today lacks such capabilities. Correspondent relationships are available to even the smallest and least automated of facilities.

The maturing of the automated clearinghouse system as a means of providing settlement between financial institutions is critical, because it coincides with the computerization of much of the business community. By the mid-1980s the accounting profession was one of the few standard industrial classifications that reported nearly complete penetration of computer usage. Much as banking was becoming a computerized information business, financial recordkeeping for even the smallest of businesses became a task for computers. Exchanging financial information through computers is commonplace among larger companies and their financial institutions, and similar services aimed at smaller businesses are just beginning to be marketed.

As the decade of the 90s begins, major corporations are routinely exchanging non-financial business information electronically in the process that falls under an umbrella called "Electronic Data Interchange" or EDI. Bankers have recognized the import and potential of EDI, addressing it through the Bankers EDI Council of the National Automated Clearinghouse Association, among other forums. Because EDI traffic consists largely of routine business correspondence such as purchase orders and invoices, providing business-to-business payments in the same electronic message is a natural next step.

The impact of EDI on consumer payments is indirect, but is likely to be equally substantial. The growing standardization of the ways in which businesses exchange information electronically suggests that business information systems have increasing flexibility to exchange information. Specifically, this flexibility opens opportunities for entrepreneurs or entrepreneurial institutions to devise cost-effective means of electronically collecting, processing and transmitting consumer payment information for a tremendous number of payments currently made from home. Aggressive institutions already encourage preauthorization for payments on loan products, ranging from mortgage and automobile loans to credit cards. However, the interesting growth potential lies in non-financial institution payments, particularly utility payments.

For example, a wide range of consumer payments are not truly elective payments. Payment is only a matter of timing. To not pay a bill one month risks the loss of a service such as gas, water, electricity, telephone or cable television. While the consumer fiercely wants to retain control of the timing of that payment, that control essentially is constrained to the period between receipt of the bill and the due date—or the date at which a late fee is imposed. With a financial institution as an intermediary, the payment recipient — the merchant — might be persuaded to consider a program accepting electronic payments. The timing of the payments could remain a consumer choice. Often the consumer needs no more incentive to cooperate than the assurance of an end to late fees.

The changing role of the financial institution is somewhat subtle, but becomes clear when the information role of the institution is understood. Where once the primary purpose of a financial institution was to provide a physical means of safekeeping wealth, that has become an antiquated role reflected today only in the relatively small volume business of providing cash on demand, either at the teller station or through an automated machine. Even the healthiest financial institutions today maintain no more than a tiny fraction of their assets in a liquid form. The role of a financial institution today is to be a safekeeper of information. That information must be accurate, current and accessible, which means it probably is maintained electronically.

Once information is maintained electronically, the process is the same whether the information concerns a database of telephone numbers associated with particular households or the flight and fare schedules of airlines. The entity that can meet regulatory requirements and boast the biggest, most efficient and most accessible databanks is likely to dominate. The primary distinguishing characteristics are generated by marketing strategies, which must incorporate considerations of delivery strategies.

Understanding the nature of a financial institution today as a marketing entity is important because automation, for all practical purposes, has made what were once called financial products into commodities. From the form of a paper check, which is regulated as to size, paper weight, type of ink used and positioning of identifying characters on its face and endorsements on its back, to credit cards that are distinguished by rate and fees rather than functionality, what were once regarded as financial products are today seen as interchangeable commodities. They differ only in their packaging and the quality of the service in their delivery and support.

PROVIDING ACCESS TO FINANCIAL SERVICES VIA ELECTRONICS

Rather than constituting a discrete product, paper checks are one of a number of means by which consumers may draw upon their relationship with an entity that holds information about their financial status. Checks are one way to make payments of all kinds. Cash is another. Changing notations in a computer database is yet another. The appropriateness of various alternatives depends on external factors that can be expressed by considering the full range of consumers' dynamic activities.

A consumer's relationship with a financial institution has at least three dynamic levels of access: mobile, stationary and automatic. In less esoteric terms, consumers increasingly use universal and multiple means of conducting transactions in person, from the home and automatically. Beyond the conventional means of conducting business face-to-face with a teller, cashier, check-out clerk, shopkeeper or other human being, consumers are accustomed to using the mail for conducting financial transactions and obtaining information. On occasion, pre-authorized payments result in a merchant or vendor being paid by a third-party on behalf of the consumer.

The account upon which paper checks are drawn is no longer the "simple" DDA nor is it likely that many checking accounts will long continue to be standalone financial products. Increasingly, they are part of a database of information about a particular consumer's financial behavior. The nature of that information defines the appropriate services and form of account for that consumer. Most institutions offer a diverse range of checking accounts, from "lifeline" accounts to accounts that are interest-bearing and may be tied to overdraft or personal lines of credit. Some, in fact, are credit card accounts providing easy access to cash advances or loans by a convenient and familiar means — writing a check.

Any of these accounts can offer access by checks that meet American Banker Association (ABA) processing format standards. Institutions participating in the ACH system, which for all practical purposes means all financial institutions, can use such accounts to make pre-authorized and automatic payments of various kinds or to accept direct deposit. Most can be tapped for cash by use of a plastic card at an ATM or at many retail points of sale.

Checking accounts are symbolic of a relationship with a financial institution. That relationship consists of information about the consumer. It isn't merely that the consumer has funds on account at the moment, but that the consumer has an ongoing value that might be expressed in the form of a balance sheet weighing both assets and liabilities. Just as banking can not solely be a matter of collecting deposits, a consumer is not only a source of funds, but a user of credit. With a range of products to offer, the financial institution has to recognize the range of opportunities a particular consumer represents. The amount of money the consumer has deposited in a particular account at a particular time is relatively meaningless without understanding how much potential that consumer represents. Consequently, the relationship hinges on information beyond holding a given balance and providing funds from that balance upon demand.

Checks began a process in the nineteenth century of providing and honoring inexpensive representations of wealth. In the late twentieth century, this process has been taken to a mass market, universal level with the advent of electronic banking. Instead of coins or currency being necessary for payment, a check makes a signature sufficient, provided the payor is willing to accept the risk that the signer has adequate funds on deposit to back up that signature. Telecommunications and computers allow a variety of remote means of providing that assurance of payment even beyond immediate certainty of identification. Direct telecommunication links to computer databases allow recipients of payments — or the receiving party in any financial transaction — to obtain a financial institution's guarantee that funds are available or to even make a simultaneous — or slightly delayed — transfer of funds to the recipient. Such systems in various forms support acceptance of credit as well as debit cards.

The poorly kept secret behind all of this has been that various compromises are made in the process. Almost never is there a truly instantaneous transfer of funds as occurs when cash exchanges hands. Delays ranging from hours to days take place. But that is the nature of the banking business. Financial services consist of providing a vehicle for transactions in which one or both of the parties pays for the privilege of delaying or hastening the actual exchange of funds.

In a credit card transaction, it may be that both parties pay. The consumer pays for an extension of credit and the merchant pays a discount for immediate crediting of funds. The wisest consumer deals with an institution that does not charge for 25 or 30 days for that extension of credit, then pays the balance in full by writing a paper check. Credit card issuers prosper because consumers are willing to pay annual fees to hold such convenience cards and the majority fail to pay the balance each month.

Checking accounts and paper checks will continue to be a dominant means of financial service delivery during this decade. However, the nature of their use and their handling will change. Volume of checks written is likely to decline on a per household basis and may begin to slacken on an absolute basis. The checking account increasingly will be defined as a relationship account from which other related services are derived, accessed through multiple service delivery vehicles. For example, upon opening an account, an ATM card, which also functions as a debit (and, possibly, credit) card, is likely to be issued automatically along with an automated telephone service access number, both using the same Personal Identification Number (PIN) to verify legitimate access.

By integrating services, financial institutions will be able to develop new kinds of financial product packages combining multiple means of access with multiple features. For example, the typical consumer account incorporating the primary access means discussed in this scenario might be a transaction account into which funds are directly, electronically deposited, whether from the government, an employer or third party. Distinctions between savings and transaction accounts increasingly are likely to blur, hindered only by regulation. At a deposit level determined by the financial institution's need for return, by competitive pressures or—possibly—regulation, the consumer would receive interest payments, which might increase at certain predetermined balance levels.

To facilitate use of debit cards and minimize the need for balance verification and purchase authorization, the institution might automatically accompany this account with a pre-approved credit line, which could be accessed via credit card (or the debit card functioning as a credit card in the instance of a low or negative balance) or as overdraft protection. The amount of this credit line could be determined in several ways utilizing the advantages of electronic record-keeping information. Besides such conventional measures as net worth and income, the line could be variable based on average monthly balances from the previous six months or year, information that is readily accessible to an institution from its computer systems and is likely to be used as a means of determining the profitability of individual customers. A customer implicitly would be encouraged to maintain a free balance to guarantee what would, in effect, be a collateralized credit line. In essence, this also gives the customer free float, which is a possible response to the consumer objection that use of a debit card eliminates float. Such systems also would encourage consumer consolidation of accounts to maximize availability of tiered services and return on balances.

Since consumers have shown a continuing desire to maintain multiple credit card accounts in order to have access to additional credit lines, such an account would not be likely to pose a significant threat to other credit card business. Furthermore, when the account credit line was used, it would carry an interest rate comparable to a credit card, yielding proportionate income with a possibly reduced risk of default.

In addition to such conventional means as walking into a branch or driving up to a window and writing a check or taking back cash while making a deposit, funds could be withdrawn from this account through ATMs or as cash-back on a debit card purchase. Payments could be made through any of a series of alternatives. These might carry an associated cost reflecting both the cost to the institution of offering the alternative, and the institution's market experience-based assessment of the value to the consumer of having the option available.

Today, the most basic of these options — and least expensive both to consumer and institution — is writing a paper check. Within the decade, a fully electronic transaction should not only be commonplace, but notably less expensive. That transaction might be initiated by the consumer through a voice telephone call, by preauthorization, by presenting a plastic card at an ATM or at a retail point of sale, or from home or office via a personal computer. Preauthorized or automatic payments from this account would be encouraged and fulfilled electronically. Such payments could be promoted to consumers as a means of obtaining greater security in the conduct of their financial affairs. Lenders, in turn, might trade reduced interest rates for the guarantee of an automatic, pre-scheduled payment. Telephone and computer access would be routine to make payment alterations, cancellations or additions. Again, if the account balance should be insufficient, the financial institution would profit from the consumer's use of the automatic credit line.

STRATEGIES FOR INTEGRATION OF DELIVERY SYSTEMS

Three crucial steps are necessary to developsuccessful strategies for full integration and automation of delivery systems. They must be directed from the most senior levels of a financial institution with a clear understanding that what is at stake is the future of the institution.

The first task for any financial institution evaluating electronic delivery systems is to consider the state of its current automation and the capabilities of systems already in place, a process that equipment vendors readily will join in conducting. The greatest immediate benefits may be in encouraging increased usage of existing systems and services.

The second task is to evaluate the current and target customer markets, particularly considering ways in which such markets differ from the overall market. Such considerations range from basic target market sizes to particular attitude or behavioral characteristics that may vary from the overall market. In addition to evaluating consumer markets, relationships with merchants also should be examined to seek partners for implementation of bill-paying services.

Thirdly is a weighing of the costs and benefits of providing various electronic delivery systems, given their likely impact on customer behavior. Such an analysis is by definition unique to each institution. Clearly, full automation carries the greatest potential benefits, but may not be immediately practical in all cases. When a state of partial automation exists and is likely to continue, some forms of electronic delivery may be better avoided because they will not operate effectively and will only cause customer resentment.

Some institutions may find strategies to serve niche markets most appropriate. Others may strive to be among the surviving, national providers of automated, commodity services. In either case, fully automated and integrated approaches are critical to success.

The following chapters will examine trends in consumer electronics behavior and explore the premise that the state of consumer automation is considerably less than it is often perceived to be; examine consumer market segments and their readiness to use automated, electronic financial services; and, further examine the specific market for direct delivery and use of financial services in the home.

CHAPTER

2

Consumer Trends in Home Electronics

DEMOGRAPHIC IMPORTANCE OF THE BABY BOOM

There is a very real bulge in the population, that phenomenon known as the Baby Boom. As has been noted many times, that unusually large, post-World War II generation has had dramatic impact on a variety of products and services. Its habits and desires, particularly in its youthful years, have influenced the rise and fall of entire industries during the past decades.

This influential group, however, is not exempt from the lifestyle changes that typically occur as any generation ages. Although the stages may vary for individuals, there tends to be a time to play, a time to be a parent, a time to prepare for retirement, and so forth. Those basic lifestyle stages strongly influence consumer behavior, which in turn determines what strategies are necessary to succeed in serving this market. The maturing and rising affluence of this especially influential generation is creating opportunity.

In 1995, census projections show that for the first time in many years, the largest portion of the entire U.S. population will be in the 35 to 49 age range. This range tends to be the lifestage in which persons are settled, productive and concretely preparing for the future. By the turn of the century, the majority of the Baby Boom population bulge will be in that age range with the leading edge of the bulge, combined with increasing lifespans, bringing about one of the largest populations of older persons that the nation has known. Among other consequences, this should mean a larger proportion of affluent households within the population. Aside from affluence derived from inheritance, most affluent households reach that status by virtue of years of productive work. Therefore, the 35 to 49 and 50 to 64 age lifestages typically have a high percentage of all affluent households.

Beyond the simple fact that there are likely to be larger numbers of affluent households, the significance of this aging factor will in several ways affect usage of financial service delivery systems. First, much of that generation is familiar with and favorably disposed toward consumer electronics of all kinds, as well as electronic delivery of financial services, such as through use of ATMs and card based services.

Second, this generation has matured during an economic period that primarily has been peaceful, stable and growing, despite the occasional recessions, cyclical shifts within various industries and minor regional wars. There consequently is less evidence of fear of the future and what it will bring, which leads to less concern about using credit, much in contrast to the fears of the Depression-era generation. Consumer debt continues at near record levels, with little sign of slackening.

Third, the aging of the population entitles a larger percentage to various government payments, which increasingly are likely to be delivered by direct, electronic deposit or tapped through an electronic means of access.

This generational effect is extremely important. It suggests that we should be seeking harbingers of future behavior among younger consumer segments and populations that demonstrate traits of such segments. In 1985, one of the studies conducted at PSI was an examination of the financial service habits and activities of the California and New York consumer markets as opposed to other states. California, especially, proved to live up to its image of being a leading edge state with a strong youthful orientation. Besides owning and using greater numbers of consumer electronic devices, its consumers were more likely to use electronic financial service delivery methods of all types than any other state and were notably more inclined to ATM usage than consumers in other states. In 1987, PSI research showed that more than half of all California households were using ATMs as opposed to about a third of households in other states. Also notable was that nearly 40% of California households made deposits through ATMs, double the percentage in other states.

By 1990, the rest of the nation was catching up with California in ATM usage as more than 50% of all U.S. households used an ATM at least once a month. Deposit acceptance hasn't proven to be a strong point for ATMs. Many banks currently are reevaluating accepting deposits at ATMs because of concerns about meeting the regulatory requirements for timely access to funds. Furthermore, efforts to explain the benefits of direct deposit — electronic crediting of payments to consumer accounts by employers, federal agencies and other financial institutions — are having a clear impact, which is beginning to decrease the need for consumers to make a trip to deposit checks, whether in the branch or at the ATM. Yet, in still another electronic payment area, California is again leaping ahead, leading the nation in acceptance of direct debit at the point of sale.

Trends in the California market . . . assessments of likely technological developments . . . consideration of the impact of the aging of the population . . . and an understanding of the needs of the financial service industry . . . these are all factors contributing to this effort to find means of segmenting the consumer market in a useful fashion.

COMMUNICATIONS, ENTERTAINMENT, WORK AND CONVENIENCE

Consumers can be classified as falling into several relatively distinct segments defining their orientation toward technology (as statistical analysis demonstrates in the next chapter). These classifications tend to support the argument that there are several discrete functions within every consumer household that are currently being affected by technological change. Consumer likelihood to use particular alternative delivery systems may be related to where both they and a particular delivery system stand in terms of complexity of use and ability to deliver complex products.

The consumer functions being affected by technological change are related to entertainment, communications and controls. These changes provide greater convenience and affect how work is done in the home, whether that work is part of maintaining and operating the home or work done for someone else from the home. These areas of concern are so intermingled that many of the technological devices involved in this milieu may play a role in more than one, if not all, of those areas. It is important to understand, however, that the three functions of entertainment, communications, and controls are relatively compartmentalized in the consumer's mind and frequently are literally separated within the home. Although thereis overlap, consumers tend to have activity areas designated, particularly separating entertainment from communications and controls.

Affecting this is a significant trend today toward multiple ownership of various consumer electronic devices, particularly televisions and telephones. The Electronics Industry Association says the average U.S. household now owns three television sets. At least one of those televisions is highly likely to be a color set. In addition to the basic universality of telephone ownership, PSI research shows two-thirds of all households say they specifically own a touch tone telephone. Sales of telephone instruments suggest most households have several, but data is not available on how many of those instruments may be unused. Nonetheless, multiple ownership of these two particular devices, the most widely owned devices of all, suggests overlap in the areas of communications and entertainment.

Estimates of Home Electronics Products Household Penetration

All TVs	98%
Color TVs	94%
B&W TVs	58%
VCRs	52%
Camcorders	4%
Audio systems	89%
Compact disc players	8%
Home computers	20%

Source: Electronic Industries Association, 1988

Entertainment is highly individualized, which is a factor behind the plethora of entertainment devices and delivery channels. Enormous sums of money are spent on entertainment, but the market can be volatile, shaped by fads more than by technological change. For example, remember the spectacular rise of the cable home shopping business. An innovative idea created the concept of displaying merchandise in a talk show format while listeners called 800 telephone numbers to place orders for merchandise displayed on air. After nearly three dozen companies entered the business, a shake-out has left the original Home Shopping Network and a single major competitor formed by the merger of its surviving competitors. A similar meteoric rise and decline occurred in the early 1980s with the home video game business, which also now is making a resurgence as more sophisticated, yet less-expensive hardware and software is available.

While common sense says that an individual may only "look" at one thing at a time, our culture bombards us with information, which increasingly is "browsed," "grazed," "scanned" and "zapped." Sound, image and the written word may be delivered by multiple means. The natural inclination is to seek tools as well as products that assist in coping with the volume of information available.

In print, the trend is toward concise messages accompanied by strong visual images, à la *People Weekly* magazine and the newspaper *USA Today*. Broadcast television is using the 15-second commercial as one of the weapons against attention spans that will not tolerate a full minute-long commercial message. Television viewers armed with remote controls have invented a new pastime in armchair viewing, simultaneously watching programs on several channels. So, television manufacturers utilize digital technology to feed the "flipping" habit by offering PIP (picture in picture), which allows one or more "windows" within the screen area to show another channel — whether broadcast, cable, VCR or laserdisc output — while the main program remains on screen.

Our response to a multiplicity of information and entertainment sources is predictable. Less time is spent with each source, the pie is cut in smaller slices and there is less patience with unpopular products. Yet this multiplicity offers opportunity as well. The public demonstrates an incredible appetite for entertainment technology, opening new delivery channels for a variety of non-entertainment services.

TELECOMMUNICATIONS AND A MOBILE POPULATION

There is a popular image of the home of the future being a place in which one talks to the walls. Like life in a television commercial, people wake up to the smell of coffee brewing without concern for where the grounds came from nor how they are disposed of. One simply says, "Make the coffee and turn on the news," and unseen automation does our bidding like an obedient butler. Voice controls don't work very well in the home because we are mobile — both a microphone and a speaker are necessary wherever the user is. People are not likely to consent to constant wearing of headsets or implantation of such devices in their skulls. The very idea illustrates some of the things wrong with many scenarios of how consumers will change their behavior to cooperate with the limitations of technology rather than technology changing to allow consumers to behave much as they currently do.

For example, the automobile that we may see before the 21st century begins, although perhaps still fossil-fuel powered, will incorporate technology to assist in navigation and communications as standard features. Both Japanese and American automakers include such features in virtually all of their current prototypes. Purchasinga car with a telephone will seem as ordinary as having an FM radio. Hands-free, voice-control operation of such telephones are likely for safety reasons.

By contrast, few homes readily lend themselves to being retrofitted for voice controls without extensive and expensive rewiring. Furthermore, despite the frequency with which Americans change homes, homes do not wear out and face the scrap heap as rapidly as automobiles. Already, some luxury automobiles are sold with a cellular telephone as standard equipment and various kinds of onboard navigation systems have been proposed. Inexpensive satellite receivers are being developed that could allow an automobile's onboard computer system to display its position with a high level of accuracy, much as today's fishermen can check their coordinates by glancing at a digital LORAN display.

Consumers do not have to be in automobiles to have mobile telecommunications. Prices for personal mobile telephones—portable cellular telephones — have plummeted, although monthly usage charges generally remain fairly steep. Nonetheless, in certain areas of the country, such as Los Angeles, a cellular phone is regarded by many as not only a status symbol but a necessity. Cellular phones themselves also are going through a typical stage for consumer electronics, becoming smaller and lighter, which increases their portability and, consequently, their functionality.

Consolidation within the cellular business and availability of service within virtually every metropolitan area is preparing the stage for national marketing efforts that could dramatically increase usage. It also sets the stage for the potential emergence of the personal telephone number, a number unique to the individual that could be independent of geography.

Our society is increasingly mobile and telecommunications companies provide service seamlessly and conveniently, whether the consumer is at home, work, on the road or in the air. From 1980 to 1987, while the U.S. population grew by only 7%, phone use jumped by 25% to 3.754-trillion minutes, says the Federal Communications Commission. Some of the growth was due to facsimile and electronic mail, but a bigger factor was the growth of cellular telephone use. Mobility in use of telecommunications is one of the important trends in consumer electronics.

VIDEO QUALITY, EASE OF ACCESS AND CONTROL

Even in the home, mobility is a factor. A multi-function, portable remote control device may be a better alternative as a home control than omnipresent microphones for voice controls. That device may use some or all of the current technologies — infrared, sonic or FM — it could have voice recognition as well as a keypad and small screen built into it and be shaped to look like anything from Maxwell Smart's shoe to a microphone, keypad, wand, whatever...including a telephone handset or Captain Kirk's communicator.

The consumer is smart and quick to ask, "What does this do for me?" A device must be easy to use and easy to learn *how* to use. A miss on any one of those points is likely to mean commercial failure. Fundamentally, controls begin with on-off switches, instructions to do something or not do it. More sophisticated controls, which behave more like computers, deal with multiple sequences of events and continual input of new information, while retaining programmed information. Of increasing importance is the portability of the control device, literally the ability of the user to carry it. A multi-function, portable control device suggests interesting scenarios.

Various companies are now manufacturing sophisticated, universal remote control units that can be readily programmed to control any device that responds to infrared signals. These devices are aimed at the home entertainment center that has a VCR, CD audio player, cable television receiver and television set — all controlled by incompatible infrared remotes. Clearly, a device that can be programmed for such a variety of tasks potentially also could control lights, heating, security systems or any number of other systems. Building a portable telephone into the same instrument is feasible, creating a single device that brings together controls, entertainment and communications.

What telecommunications can bring to this high tech future is summed up in one word: interactivity. Passive reception of informa-tion already transcends time and space, bringing incredible images such as the worldwide witnessing of a revolution in Eastern Europe. However, until recently, the viewer's only control was to turn the image on or off. Now the consumer not only has a mind-boggling array of choices, but growing capability to select at will from a larger universe of choices, to obtain information on demand, whether that information is a motion picture or a weather report.

Although amazing high tech toys are available, price is a greater obstacle than familiarity to adoption by the general population. The public has an astonishingly high expectation level of what "should be" available. These high expectations for ease of use and completeness of function may explain the consistent willingness of consumers to tell researchers that they are ready, eager and willing to pay for computer-based, interactive services that fail dismally when brought to market. Consumer expectation levels are fed by movies and television programming that portrays the state-of-the-art — and beyond — in technology. In print and broadcast media and advertising, consumers are bombarded with high tech versions of the future. The problem is not conceiving of the services, but delivering them in a fashion that meets consumer expectations.

Adding interactive capability to the home media mix turns conventional advertising on its ear. Suddenly the consumer moves from the position of passive recipient of commercial messages to active procurer of information specific to his needs. Instead of flipping through endless specialty television channels of "narrowcasting," the consumer becomes the event scheduler, the selector of the messages he will see. The challenge is to provide easy means of getting information about what is available.

How will that be done? Again, consider the parallels in today's market. One of the most universally recognized means of quickly finding business information is to pick up the "Yellow Pages." The conventional printed pages today are being supplemented by services that provide touchtone access to expanded information delivered by computer-generated speech and prerecorded messages. The pipelines telephone companies are developing will allow an even greater flow of information. Instead of just a recorded voice reciting the times of the next screenings of a movie, the consumer may also request a preview of the film. If the timing or price offered by a particular theater aren't acceptable, the consumer might turn to another service provider to directly purchase a copy of the film, which might be delivered by mail in a hard copy, cassette form, or be immediately downloaded to the consumer's television receiver.

Consider that the capacity of this telecommunications pipeline opens such an overwhelming realm of possibilities that the first business opportunities will lie simply in providing guides to the information available. Indexing alone will require huge databases. Just as cable television programming requires entire magazine-size publications to list schedule times, so the peripheral businesses in interactive services will emerge, particularly publishing ventures that furnish printed guides to this plethora of programming. Of course, there also will be online versions of these guides.

While the growth of the cable entertainment market is an impressive thing to consider, take heed of the lesson it offers. Much of its growth has come at the expense of broadcast media. Although con-sumers devote phenomenal amounts of time to television viewing, that figure actually has declined somewhat as the range of choices has exploded. As interactive telephone services begin to compete with coaxial cable as a delivery channel, telephone companies potentially will join cable and broadcast as sources of video entertainment, further dividing the pie. The prospect should not be regarded as distressing, but only a progressive step. Displacement of some providers may occur, but the primary competition will be for new product to put in the distribution channels.

Interactive telephone services represent a complementary channel in the evolution of electronic delivery systems. Inroads will occur in other electronic media offerings and they will change, much as broadcast radio changed in response to television. A major difference may be the time frame during which this change occurs. It may be much more brief — and imminent — than many would imagine.

Interactive cable television services currently are being tested by several small companies, including Interactive Network Incorporated of

Mountain View, California, and ACTV of New York. The former has financial backing from NBC, United Artists Entertainment, A.C. Nielsen, Ameritech and Le Groupe Videotron, says the *New York Times*. ACTV's backers are reported to include General Motors, Coca-Cola and AT&T. In the tests, viewers can select among several camera angles or directly participate in programming, such as competing in a quiz show.

While the means of obtaining television programming become more diverse, another interesting trend is under way that could bring together television sets and computers in unprecedented fashion. Consumers soon will see a new generation of toys and tools that expand their powers over the ubiquitous television set. These tools are far beyond "Space Invaders" video games, first generation videotex graphics, VCR tapes or "programming-on-screen." In still and full-motion pictures, computers are melding with television to create a new visual language for entertainment, communications and controls. The "Picture-Phone" of the 60s was merely a hint of what lies ahead.

There has been extensive discussion of HDTV — High Definition Television. It has taken on particular importance in the fight for world market share in entertainment hardware. However, it is only an interim step toward true digital television. The ultimate result will be computers that can display television programming, perhaps in a separate window, just as today's more sophisticated computers can display multiple software programs in separate windows, and television sets that have computer capabilities. In the short term, this development may have interesting business applications.

Intel Corporation, the maker of the chips that IBM and the myriad compatibles use in their personal computers, in 1988 purchased a technology from General Electric Company called Digital Video Interactive (DVI). This technology, which originally was developed in the same RCA labs that pioneered the American versions of HDTV, allows a personal computer to read and manipulate digitized video, specifically using a five-inch laser disk that is virtually indistinguishable from a CD audio disk. (In fact, there are formatting differences, but the disks are otherwise identical.) This development may result in significant decreases in the cost of marrying video and computer technologies, which can be done now, but usually at a high price. One of the implications is that the ability to store full-motion video on a disk and call it up through a personal computer may make it much more economical and simpler to develop on-line delivery of video for advertising, catalogs, entertainment features, public affairs reporting or a host of other activities.

Like Americans and Britons, television and computer monitors share a common language separated by standards. Despite what commonly occurs in movies, a color monitor on a personal computer can not — yet—readily display the same picture as a television set using the same signal source. However, the reverse is sometimes true. Certain television sets can act as color monitors for computers. Even in that case, however, the set being used as a color monitor can not simultaneously display an ordinary television picture. Is it feasible to do so? Absolutely. In fact, hardware and software is available for certain computers that allows the display of a full-motion video image in a separate window on the computer screen. Professional television production equipment (the price of which typically runs 10 to 20 times more than the cost of expensive personal computer set-ups) can do just that. Such devices are used to place titles over video, to integrate text visuals with full-motion visuals and to create animated sequences and special effects such as dissolves, zooms and "tumbling" graphics.

Much as print publishing has been transformed by technology over the past two decades (reaching the "desktop" level during the last few years) so television production is being transformed. "Desktop TV" productions are as close today as desktop publishing was in the mid-80s, well within a five-year time frame. This development will have an impact on the television industry similar to the impact of electronics on the print publishing industry, allowing new entrants to create products rivaling those of established firms for substantially less overhead.

Harbingers of the tools that will create desktop TV are available in the form of graphics and animation software that are being used in desktop publishing today. Electronic devices allow still images to be captured digitally, integrated with text or other graphics and printed on toner-based printers such as laser printers or output on phototypesetting equipment. These same images also can be stored for display on a computer monitor. Seemingly exotic now, electronic image capture may soon be as commonplace as a "Walkman."

Sony Corporation, long a pioneer in bringing sophisticated consumer electronics to market, was first to introduce a color still video camera — intended for general consumer use — that requires no film. Although it has a fixed lens and electronic strobe flash like many conventional cameras, the "Mavica" is a $650 electronic still camera that captures images in digital form, much as some video cameras. It uses 2-inch diameter, magnetic-media floppy disks similar to those used in personal computers to take color pictures that are shown on an ordinary color television or recorded on a VCR by use of a special, $250-priced adapter. At a combined price of $900, it has barely made a ripple in a competitive market in which video cameras are similarly priced.

The electronic still camera also can provide hard copies of pictures, but they must be printed on an expensive, special printer. Sony expects the printer will be purchased by retail outlets such as drugstores that will offer electronic "film processing" when the camera goes into general distribution. Sony optimistically notes that because the images are electronic rather than photographic, they may readily be transmitted through telecommunications or integrated with computer software such as graphics, word-processing and page layout programs.

In a similar development, the company whose name is virtually synonymous with amateur photography, Eastman Kodak, has announced release in 1992 of a so-called hybrid imaging system, which transfers conventional film images to compact digital disks for display on television screens. Photofinishers are expected to make the equipment investment to enable consumers' conventional film to be digitally recorded on compact disks.

To view the disks, consumers will be offered an under-$500 device from Kodak and N.V. Philips of the Netherlands. The player, which will also play audio CD disks, will be controlled by a remote unit that allows viewers to zoom and crop photos on screen. Fuji Photo Film Company also has developed a unit that transfers negatives to computer floppy disks for display on television, but has never released the device in the United States.

The marriage of computer and video technologies make it much more economical and simpler to develop inexpensive systems for on-line delivery of full-motion or still video for advertising, catalogs, entertainment features, public affairs reporting or a host of other activities — literally anything that can be captured by a camera and might be of sufficient interest that another party would be willing to pay to receive or view it. Civic agencies, governments or businesses may make such video access available at no charge to distribute advertising or to provide access to public meetings and similar activities.

When the concept of computer video is better understood, it is certain to have a substantial impact on the relatively primitive interactive services that have so far been developed. It especially will place greater control of full motion video information in the hands of users than has ever before been seen.

The mass market the television networks once owned already is international, and now a senior fellow at the Gannett Center for Media Studies, on the subject of why the broadcast networks did not anticipate the combined effects of cable television, VCRs, independent stations and new networks and, consequently, lost their grasp of the mass market: "The networks closed their eyes to reality. They didn't fully comprehend the extent of technological changes," he says. Any industry that is complacent about technological change will one day open its eyes to the reality that new competitors are taking away its market. While broadcast television perhaps once thought its primary business was creating entertainment products, now it has discovered that it was a *delivery medium* for news, entertainment and advertising.

HOME OFFICE FUNCTIONS AND AFFORDABILITY

Entertainment plays a critically important role in shaping electronic delivery systems in the home. But there is another side to our daily home lives, "taking care of business." Sometimes, this is a matter of paying a bill; another time it may be ordering a product or service; or it may be a matter of feeling secure about our premises, safe from intrusion whether we are home or away. These "business" functions also have roots in today's environment.

In-home use of modem-equipped personal computers, cellular telephones, beepers and facsimile machines illustrated that distinctions between "business" and "consumer" products and services frequently blur. Small businesses and individuals are responsible for much of recent sales growth in facsimile machines, particularly as prices fall below $1,000, say retailers. "Send a fax," is quickly becoming a standard business request, taking a place beside overnight mail and package delivery, which exploded on the scene over the past decade. Fax has been a major factor in the decline in the United States of Telex traffic, which has dropped to less than half what it was in the mid-1980s.

It also soon may be commonplace to send a personal fax from home-to-home, freed from the uncertainty of leaving a message on an answering machine, yet also free of the delays of using the mail. Students in California already exchange homework notes by fax, says the *Los Angeles Times.*

Today, nearly 2 million facsimile machines are installed in the United States, but the world leaders are the Japanese with 3.4 million installed. Japanese not only use faxes in business, but send faxes from taxis and public phone booths equipped with the machines. The Japanese national telephone company, Nippon Telegraph & Telephone Corporation says half the telephone traffic between Japan and the United States is now fax.

In the United States today, fax machines are being used to place lunch orders and to request songs from radio stations. Various publishers, including Dow Jones & Company, the New York Times and Knight-Ridder, are experimenting with fax delivery of conventionally printed products. Public fax machines are appearing in hotels, airports and other high traffic locations in the United States. Several states are considering legislation to outlaw "junk fax." National directories of fax numbers are appearing, fax numbers are becoming commonplace on business cards and stationery and regulators are considering special tariffs for fax lines.

Facsimile Machine Shipments

Units	Average	Selling Price	
1982	64,000	$4,429	
1983	75,000	$4,195	
1984	89,000	$3,827	
1985	157,000	$3,170	
1986	188,000	$2,682	
1987	417,000	$2,200	
1988	785,000	$2,150	(est.)

Source: Dataquest

Link, a New York-based research company, released a study in 1987 that found more households with photocopiers (4.3%) than with personal computers equipped with modems (3.9%). Household purchases of fax machines do not yet compete with either, but the possibility is clear.

Other communications devices that once were only business tools are finding consumer applications, also. The sound of a beeper in a public location once indicated the presence of a doctor, fireman or someone else whose job kept them on call. Now it may be the babysitter calling. There are approximately five million electronic paging service subscribers nationwide. From their original incarnation as devices that did indeed beep, beepers or "pocket pagers" now shake, flash and speak. Some have small display screens that show the number of the party who wishes to be called. Others can display timely information such as a current stock quote. In Miami, public schools have banned beepers, saying drug dealers frequently use them to receive word of shipments.

Similarly, other tools currently used primarily for business may provide future links to consumers as they become more widely owned. Many potential applications are neither illicit nor trivial. Financial services, in particular, are "office" functions, even within the home. Very few households check an account balance for amusement purposes. However, a household that has a personal computer for other purposes, whether playing games, working at home or intellectual curiosity, may also be a prime candidate for use of that computer for electronic access to interactive services and information. Financial institutions may wish to encourage such links because that household is likely to be above average in income and education and have more complex financial needs than average. (The home computer, however, is not the only answer for home banking services, as is discussed in a later chapter.)

HOME AUTOMATION

A household that occupies a home of above average value or size tends to have a greater likelihood of interest in general interactive services that may provide controls for other functions, such as security systems, heating-cooling systems or information services. Such interactive control systems are becoming common among higher-priced new homes, where initial wiring may include fiber optic cable. Significant progress also is being made in the development of systems for retro-fitting existing homes. Experiments by various telecommunications companies have demonstrated possibilities that are now on the shelf almost exclusively for regulatory reasons. Eventual services include not only voice and video, but also security monitoring, meter reading, home energy management and access to on-line information services.

Home control technology has been relatively stagnant for several years after an initial burst of enthusiasm that coincided with the emergence of the first generation of home computers. The only significant advances have been in the development of a variety of independent control devices such as smart thermostats and sophisticated remote controls compatible with several types of infrared-controlled entertainment appliances such as VCRs, TVs and CD-audio players.

While the concept of integrated controls has languished, there have been some interesting projects such as the optical fiber "wiring" of Heathrow, a large, "new town" residential development in central Florida that combines efforts of entrepreneur Jeno Palucci's Heathrow Land and Development, Northern Telecom and BellSouth. The Heathrow development is pre-wiring each of 4,400 homes with telecommunications and video access through a single fiber optic cable, which also creates an infrastructure for additional in-home controls.

The development is specifically a large scale test of ISDN (Integrated Services Digital Network) standard services on a fiber optic line, the first such application in a residential environment, the developers say. Eventual services are to include not only voice and video, but also security monitoring, meter reading, home energy management and access to on-line information services.

Similarly, GTE is experimenting with a new phone switch in Cerritos, California, that will provide voice and video to a community of 56,000 that previously was not wired for cable television. Using both fiber optic and coaxial cables, GTE plans a five-year experiment to measure market demand for services such as pay-per-view video and video-on-demand. However, true video-on-demand is being tested in only five households. Others will be able to select pay-per-view programming channels, but not control when the programming appears, much like hotel room pay-per-view services.

Other experiments include an optical fiber test in Perryopolis, Pennsylvania, where Bell of Pennsylvania is using technology similar to that used in France for cable television, and in Princeton Gate, New Jersey, a new housing development, New Jersey Bell is wiring each home with optical cable. Ameritech has a test involving 100 house-holds in Tipton Lakes, Indiana, and Pacific Bell is conducting a test in Menlo Park,California. Most such tests rely on interest in cable television programming as a source of revenue with other services in test stages.

Another sign of the interest in the automation of home controls was the formation in 1988 of the Home Automation Association, a Bethesda,Maryland-based organization formed to "promote home automation by monitoring the current state of the art as well as the social, economic, legal and other effects" of related technology, says the newsletter *Interactivity Report*. The association defines home automation as comprising five areas: home entertainment, security, heating/cooling, plumbing and electrical.

Meter reading is an area in which there are strong economic arguments for the development of new home automation tools. The expense of in-person, monthly visits to residences to read meters is ready justification for installation of automated devices that can accomplish the same thing. In doing so, other services become feasible.

For example, 20 rural electric cooperatives in 12 southern, midwestern and western states are installing computers at customers' homes or farms that automatically read electric meters and transmit the information by telephone line to the co-op's central office for billing purposes. Using computers from Access Corporation, a Nashville, Tennessee, firm, the cooperatives are spending approximately $100 per customer to install a device that also can monitor security alarms and thermostats and provide pay-per-view television. Each of the additional services bears an additional charge, providing the cooperatives with new revenue opportunities while labor savings pay for the terminal installation.

SELECTION OF REPRESENTATIVE HOME ELECTRONICS DEVICES

Give us technology, say consumers, not for the sake of technology, but for the sake of doing a job more effectively. Research on consumer electronics shows no more strongly expressed sentiment. Analysis of the attitudes and desires of technology-oriented consumers, particularly the early adopters, suggests a high degree of pragmatism at work rather than a simple-minded willingness to try anything new. It is interesting and important to note, however, that high-end consumer electronics and low-cost business tools such as computers overlap, leading to increasingly sophisticated, low-cost devices being used in homes. These devices are reshaping the home environment.

Consumer trends indicate continuing overlap between business and home functions. We see this in the form of increasing home ownership of modem-equipped personal computers, cellular telephones, beepers and facsimile machines. Distinctions between "business" and "consumer" products and services frequently blur. Yet, understanding distinctions between home "business" and entertainment functions is critical to consideration of the future environment for interactive service delivery.

In the context of everyday consumer life, technological change in the home is affecting entertainment, communications and controls. But there is a conundrum. Consumers, time and again, demonstrate a willingness to be extravagant in their purchases of toys and amusements, even while scrimping on necessities. Those entertainment expenditures shape the infrastructure through which more utilitarian services, such as product information, interactive services and utility controls, may be delivered.

Also confusing the picture, consumers are likely to use services not only via devices they will own, but also by using devices that various businesses will choose to make available as an incentive to encourage usage, much as telephones once were distributed. Just as a recent gimmick in radio marketing is to give away small radios permanently tuned to a particular station, service providers will distribute low-cost, single purpose access devices to encourage sampling of their wares. That factor alone makes projection of current behavior difficult, because it is possible to force-feed a market and thereby stimulate demand.

What is clear is that these services will be used in multiple locations: offices, businesses large and small, retail locations, public locations, in automobiles and in the home. Public telecommunication networks will provide the communications connection, connecting to a wide variety of instruments through standards that have already been set by international agreement.

For the purposes of the research study that is detailed in the next chapter, ten consumer electronics devices were selected representing equipment that had sufficient consumer household penetration to make survey results meaningful and that also covered four areas of interest: equipment that was telecommunications-oriented, computer/home office-oriented, entertainment-oriented and household convenience-oriented.

The specific devices surveyed were:

- telecommunications-oriented — touchtone telephone and telephone answering machine;
- computer/home office-oriented — personal computer, computer printer and computer modem;
- entertainment-oriented — color television, video cassette recorder, video camera and compact disc player; and,
- household/convenience-oriented — the microwave oven.

The last item is particularly interesting because it has been the subject of several previous studies of consumer acceptance of home technology innovation. The microwave represents a significantly different means of conducting a routine household activity — cooking — yet has achieved remarkable household penetration. Although not yet as common as color television, it challenges touchtone telephones as standard household equipment. It was anticipated that there would be a correlation between use of a microwave and a favorable orientation toward technology.

INTENTIONS TO PURCHASE HOME ELECTRONICS

Perhaps then, we should consider what consumers tell us they plan to purchase next. Surveys of such purchase intentions demonstrate the influence of entertainment on consumer trends in home electronics. Highest on the lists are CD-audio players, video cameras and camcorders. Nonetheless, there are several communications-oriented devices that also appear high on consumer shopping lists. Telephone answering machines already are owned by one household in five, but consumer research shows that planned purchases could in- crease that market penetration by 50% if all intentions to purchase were exercised. Cellular mobile telephones and facsimile machines are more business-oriented, but both industries report a notable share of their current growth is occurring in the home market.

The home electronics devices consumers specifically say they plan to purchase in the next 12 months are videocassette recorders, video cameras, CD audio players and personal computers. VCR purchases would add only incrementally to market penetration that already represents a majority of households. VCRs are joining microwave ovens as nearly universal items in American households. Enhanced features in new VCRs include stereo sound and higher quality resolution, which provide reasons for replacement purchases. Just as with televisions, many households are beginning to boast of more than one VCR, which also facilitates copying of pre-recorded tapes.

Planned CD audio player purchases would increase penetration by about 25%, but to only 10 to 12% of all households, making the players one of the hottest selling of new consumer electronic devices with huge market growth still ahead. The recording industry has all but abandoned vinyl records. Classical music, in particular, is almost exclusively released in CD form today. Mini-CDs, tiny disks that fit in the palm of a hand, are taking the place in teenagers' hearts and budgets that once was occupied by the 45 rpm single.

Sony is the largest producer of CD audio players. It reported sales of 2.8 million CD audio players in 1987, which was estimated to be a 50% market share. It expected to sell 4 million CD audio players in 1988, while its market share slipped to 40% with competition from Matsushita, Pioneer and Yamaha.

While 20% of households already own personal computers, planned personal computer purchases could more than double ownership within the "mainstream" household segment described in the next chapter, which represents half of all households, where market penetration could go from 5% to 12%. That growth reflects both lower prices for personal computers and greater ease of use, which are introducing the machines to households that until now have been reluctant to invest time or money.

Technology-oriented segments of the market, where ownership already is common, will be responsible for a major share of purchases. Unlike CD audio, upgrading and replacement are major factors in person-al computer purchases. The ongoing change in computer hardware brought about by the availability of more powerful chips continues to push upward "minimum" requirements for personal computers.

Finally, video camera purchase intentions could bring an explosion in that market. Only 2% of the "mainstream" segment currently owns a video camera, but 13% plan to buy one within the next year. Given the $1,000+ price levels for such cameras, it should be noted that a significant share of the market may delay purchases while waiting for introduction of lower-priced devices. Furthermore, emerging alternatives such as electronic still cameras may compete with both video cameras and conventional photographic equipment as well.

Intentions should never be interpreted as absolute indicators of future behavior. As is the road to hell paved, so are product sales forecasts that are based on intentions. They merely indicate consumer interests and desires, which may be capitalized upon with the proper mix of product and marketing.

THE NEW MEDIA HOUSEHOLD

The challenge to planners and marketers studying future directions in the market is to anticipate how new products will fit in this new media environment, how consumers will use new media products and how existing products can be enhanced through use of these new media channels. The evidence suggests that new delivery channels do not in themselves create new products, but provide alternatives for delivery of successful products.

Clearly, the use of advanced technology in the home is as much, if not more, of a marketing question than an operations question. We know that telecommunications companies can provide a pipeline, a high-capacity channel that can deliver voice, data and video. The questions concern what products will fill that pipeline. It is inevitable that some of those products are things we haven't even dreamed of, yet many will be familiar products and services that will benefit by the availability of a new delivery channel. New entrants will appear in traditional service businesses, using technological advantages as a marketing weapon while not carrying the burden of outmoded systems.

For example, consider the change that has been produced by one of the forerunners of enhanced telephone line capability, the coaxial cable that delivers television programming to more than half of U.S. households today. Ten years ago, only one household in six subscribed to a cable service and that often was solely for the purpose of getting improved reception of local over-the-air broadcast stations. Today, A.C. Nielsen tells us every other household subscribes and specialty networks proliferate.

This has been a profitable development for many companies because consumers have demonstrated their willingness to pay for these services. Broadband fiber optic networks will take this to the next logical step in the evolution of home communications. They offer the ability to deliver specific programming on demand — whether video entertainment, data or general information. Current regulatory restrictions on such activity by telephone utilities will fade as the enormity of necessary capital investments, as well as the public interest, in allowing technological progress of this kind is recognized. Interactive capability will be key to distinguishing public telephone network delivery from existing, one-way coaxial systems.

Cable television brought a greater range of entertainment programming into the market, but has not played a significant role in interactive services, except by using a telephone line to provide a return communication channel. Nonetheless, its impact on the distribution of advertising expenditures for marketing has been substantial, without even considering the revenues of direct sales via 800 or 900 numbers advertised on cable channels. The emergence of special interest television programming has brought programming — and even entire networks — devoted to financial news, home shopping, weather, sports and other interest areas, all of which are supported by advertising.

To assist in the process of identifying likely markets for new technology-based services and quantifying the business value of such markets, we will next examine a market segmentation scheme based on today's consumer ownership of various electronic devices. Given that a major concern of this book is to establish the likely environment for future electronic banking services, this study also examines how consumers who fall into distinct segments differ in their economic backgrounds and usage of financial services.

CHAPTER

3

Consumers and Technology: Consumer Market Segments by Technological Orientation

A PARADOX IN DEFINING CONSUMER SEGMENTS

The development of electronic delivery systems for financial services depends heavily on advanced technology, but not necessarily on the technology used within the home. This apparent paradox emphasizes the importance of understanding the nature of segments within the consumer market.

In fact, serving households that are resistant to use of technology is likely to require development of more sophisticated, technology-dependent systems than are required for serving technologically literate households. Systems serving technology-resistant households must be the most transparent, least intimidating systems to use. Approaching electronic banking with a goal of developing an integrated delivery system for financial services requires a strategy that provides entry not only for the segments that are ready and willing to use electronic delivery systems, but also for those who have little or no interest.

Alternative delivery systems, meaning non-branch delivery, have been evolving for the past several decades, gaining capability while becoming easier to use. Technological advances are accelerating that evolution. Combined with the impact of generational change that is creating a large group of consumers familiar with such services, electronic delivery systems face a strong prospect for growth. However, there are still significant areas of resistance from consumers, who are not seeking such change in delivery of their financial services.

For a financial services provider, the key to developing a successful strategy is understanding the degree to which consumers are ready to use the cost-effective technological capabilities that are available today. Leapfrogging the market has proven both extremely difficult to achieve and expensive to attempt. Successful development and marketing of electronic delivery systems requires analysis of the willingness of various segments to change their behavior. Such analysis will un-cover alternatives to familiar ways of conducting business as well as a reasonable sizing of the market segments that readily will use new methods.

Many studies attempting to size the market for in-home financial service delivery have focused on personal computer ownership, as have the developers of such services. The efforts primarily demonstrate that only relatively small segments currently have either the inclination or the equipment to take advantage of computer based in-home financial services. The more difficult task is to identify automation related behavioral segments within the broader market that define a path for automating delivery systems for financial services. The automation will occur and must be designed in response to consumer behavior, particularly resistant to most forms of automation that require an active participation by the consumer.

While there is an obvious mass market alternative approach to direct electronic delivery — providing service through the nearly universal medium of the telephone — efforts to devise such services have been botched. The medium may be universal, but the quality of services developed has not been. Furthermore, consumer attitudes toward usage of it for electronic service delivery vary, and a significant number of households are not interested at all.

Evaluations of such services usually conclude that the market either doesn't exist or isn't ready for telephone delivery. Such dismissal misses the point that not only were the services mediocre at best from a consumer perspective, but were not truly automated from the providers' standpoint, which may have been a significant part of the problem. For nearly 20 years, large numbers of consumers have been offered telephone-based services that were cumbersome, awkward to use and expensive to support. The unsurprising result has been that relatively few consumers have taken advantage of telephone access to financial services and few institutions have found them profitable to continue with the important exception of services that evolve directly from automation of existing telephone answering systems.

In the case of computer based financial service delivery, financial institutions allowed in-home technological potential to define offerings and relied on consumers' enthusiasm to make up for shortfalls of the services. In the second instance, the service is widely available and somewhat easy to use, but only beginning to be supported with sufficient technology to make it viable for the institutions offering it.

The third area of electronic delivery system development is the automation of existing products and services or enhancement of such products and services through automation, which generally might be termed "indirect" electronic delivery. Examples include electronic authorization systems for credit cards, which has helped set the stage for online debit, and use of the automated clearinghouse for various debits or credits to checking accounts. Such internal automation constitutes the area in which most financial institutions should concentrate efforts and are likely to reap the greatest rewards.

Electronic delivery systems may be introduced or promoted as new products, but any success will quickly render them little more than expensive competitive necessities. Far more fruitful efforts would be aimed at improving existing systems. The strategy explored here argues that all of the various forms of electronic delivery must be linked to provide an integrated delivery system approach that addresses the entire market, while also having sufficient commonality that an individual's lifestyle may evolve from one market segment to another, whether through changes in lifestyle or by maturing, in a natural progression that doesn't require learning new systems or changing institutions.

FIVE CLUSTERS DETERMINED BY ORIENTATION TO TECHNOLOGY

The question, therefore, becomes how to segment the market in a useful fashion that allows insight into likely future behavior, specifically regarding financial services delivery system usage. The-approachtaken here is to examine ownership and usage of home electronics as a means of identifiying orientation to technology. Although there are general perceptions that consumers purchase and use a wide variety of home electronics equipment, identifying characteristics that certain segments of the consumer market hold in common offers insight as to financial service strategies that are likely to fit their needs, and whether there is reason to expect that targeting certain segments is worthwhile. For example, this analysis demonstrates that households holding the greatest dollar value of investment products also are the most favorably inclined toward home electronics, which is partly a result of being able to afford such devices, but also points out that segments with the highest assets and highest usage of credit products are the most prepared to use electronic delivery alternatives.

The theory, which this analysis supports, is that any household falls into one of several broad categories that may be defined by the type of home electronic devices owned or planned to be purchased by that household. By identifying these broad categories, it is possible to recognize appropriate approaches in electronic financial service development to serve those categories.

In a special analysis of national consumer survey data gathered by Payment Systems, Inc. (PSI) in 1988, as part of a larger study of delivery systems, cluster analysis techniques were used to classify respondents according to the level of technology they currently use or aspire to use. The questionnaire from which this data was obtained also addressed usage of financial institutions, household point-of-sale payment habits and financial service attitudes. Classifications for the cluster analysis were based on responses to questions concerning whether respondents owned or planned to purchase 10 specific consumer electronic devices, ranging from color televisions and touchtone telephones to computer modems and compact disc players. The items were selected to be representative of several types of activity that take place within the home: communications, entertainment and household management. For purposes of the analysis, respondents who currently own these devices and those who currently own and plan to purchase additional products of the same type during the next 12 months were combined. Ownership was considered to be the critical indicator.

The analysis identified five distinct market segments. This chap-ter presents a profile of each of these and discusses strategies for targeting the segments. Tables presenting summary statistics on all five segments are included as an appendix. No segmentation effort can be perfect because there always will be overlap, households that do not neatly fit in a single segment. However, the distinctive nature of these segments suggests there are some general attitudes and behavior that are held in common by large portions of the population.

There are at least two very important findings from this analysis that may seem contrary to expectations. The first is that consumers who tend to purchase above average amounts of home electronics equipment fall into two quite distinct segments that have some very different characteristics. Combined, these two segments represent more than a quarter of the market, but the segment oriented to entertainment is four times the size of the segment oriented to computers. These two technology-oriented segments differ in important demographic characteristics as well as behavior.

The second finding is that fully half of the population is likely to have no more than four items of home electronics equipment and those items are a color television set, a microwave oven, a video cassette recorder and a touchtone telephone. Although 10% of this segment intends to purchase another of the ten devices surveyed, the top preferences are for an additional video cassette recorder or a video camera.

These findings support the thesis that entertainment is and will continue to be a more significant force driving home electronics purchases than demand for sophisticated electronics, such as home computers and similar devices that automate routine household functions. For routine functions, convenience is the driving force.

Consumer Electronics Ownership by Segment and Segment Size

(% of all Households)

Techies 5%	Gadgeteers 22%	Mid-America 51%	Procrastinators 10%	No-Tech 12%
Color TV (99%)	Color TV (97%)	Color TV (99%)	Color TV (81%)	Color TV (59%)
PC (87%)	VCR (36%)	Microwave (92%)	Microwave (88%)	TouchPhone (69%)

Consumer Electronics Ownership by Segment and Segment Size (Cont.)
(% of all Households)

Techies 5%	Gadgeteers 22%	Mid-America 51%	Procrastinators 10%	No-Tech 12%
Microwave (86%)	Microwave (92%)	VCR (68%)	TouchPhone (65%)	Ans. Machine (18%)
PC Printer (85%)	TouchPhone (84%)	TouchPhone (64%)	VCR (43%)	Microwave (9%)
VCR (82%)	Ans. Machine (50%)	Ans. Machine (19%)	PC (21%)	VCR (5%)
Modem (70%)	PC (49%)	CD Player (9%)	Ans. Machine (20%)	PC (2%)
TouchPhone (67%)	PC Printer (38%)	PC (5%)	PC Printer (17%)	CD Player (1%)
Ans. Machine (44%)	Video Camera (30%)	Video Camera (2%)	CD Player (10%)	Video Camera (1%)
CD Player (27%)	CD Player (9%)	PC Printer (1%)	Video Camera (9%)	PC Printer (0%)
Video Camera (2%)	Modem (8%)	Modem (0%)	Modem (7%)	Modem (0%)

The sizing of the market rendered by this approach to segmentation demonstrates the appropriateness of the argument that automation of financial service delivery requires that the automation be institutionalized rather than developed as a means of responding to automation occurring within households. Although home automation is allowing opportunities for development of niche services, the basic thrust of electronic service delivery continues to be to provide convenient financial service access for non-technologically inclined consumers.

Incidentally, this analysis will demonstrate that the technologically inclined market segments are valuable and represent above average opportunity, but not as a focus for standalone businesses given the expense of supporting such efforts.

THE MID-AMERICA SEGMENT

The largest segment is labeled Mid-America because of its demographic characteristics. At 51% of the consumer market, its demo-graphic profile is almost indistinguishable from that of the entire market. A majority of households in this segment own only 4 of the 10 consumer electronic products listed in the questionnaire:

Color television	99%
Microwave oven	88%

Video cassette recorder	68%
Touchtone telephone	64%

In addition, 10% or more of these households indicated plans to purchase one or more of the following products during the next 12 months:

Video cassette recorder	14% (68% own)
Video camera	13% (only 2% own)
Compact disk player	12% (9% own)
Personal computer	12% (5% own)
Telephone Answering Machine	9% (19% own)

Personal computers and peripherals are at the bottom of the projected ownership list with both low rates of current ownership and low purchase intentions. Relatively little interest is shown in telephone answering machines among those who do not already have one. The nearly one in five already owning an answering machine reflects the general level of ownership of such devices and is not significantly greater than the levels of ownership reported in the segments that are not positively inclined to technology.

It appears that this market segment is somewhat timid in its dealings with technology; comfortable with products that do something for the owner such as providing convenience in food preparation or increasing access to entertainment, but reluctant to tackle devices that require more effort to be useful. The data suggest this segment has a rather passive orientation toward advanced technology.

Familiarity With Personal Computers

The low level of personal computer ownership in this segment should not be mistaken for computer illiteracy, however. In fact, nearly half of Mid-America households (45%) have used a personal computer, and 36% report that they have access to a microcomputer at work.

And the finding that only 12% of respondents who own or plan to buy a personal computer report that someone other than the male and/or female head of household will use it would seem to dispel the notion that the few mainstream American households that purchase computers do so for their kids.

Nor is there any indication that the segment perceives personal computers to be mainly for men. Although a plurality (42%) indicated that the male head of household is or will be the computer user, 16% said the female head of household uses or will use it, and 30% indicated it is or will be used by both. Thus there are or will be female users in 46% of Mid-America households that own or plan to buy computers.

Demographic Characteristics

Demographically, Mid-America households are representative of all households nationwide. Median age in this segment is 45. Median household income is $26,100 per year. Sixty-three percent of the heads of households in this segment are employed full time; 45% have attended college, 23% have one or more college degrees (11% did post graduate study). In short, this group *is* demographically the norm.

Analysis showed no statistically significant differences between the percentage of Mid-America households in any age, income, or education category, and the percentage of the total sample, weighted for representativeness, in the corresponding category.

Financial Holdings of the Mid-America Segment

Financial product and service usage rates and mean and median balances for users and for all households in the Mid-America segment are displayed in the Mid-America Balance Sheet (included in the Appendix as well as an exhibit in the next chapter) detailing financial service usage and behavior.

Approximately two out of three households in this segment have a regular checking account (67%), a regular savings account (66%), and/or an automobile loan (61%). Between 40% and 50% have an interest checking account, first mortgage, Visa credit card and one or more whole life insurance policies. About one-third (30% to 34%) own at least one certificate of deposit, a MasterCard credit card, and an IRA. Aside from retirement and insurance products, real estate and individual stocks are the most popular investment vehicles among the Mid-America segment with about 20% of respondents reporting ownership of these.

Because not all households own each of the products listed, it is necessary to spread the balances for each product over the entire segment base in order to arrive at an estimate of per household holdings. A comparison of the mean and median balances shows the extent to which balances are skewed. While the average net worth of all Mid-America households is $59,579 ($13,952 in deposits plus $69,303 in investments minus $23,675 in liabilities),

50% of the households have net worths of less than $31,312 ($7,028 deposits, $44,475 investments, and $20,190 outstanding balances on mortgages, credit cards and loans).

THE TECHIES SEGMENT

The Techies segment is so named because computer ownership is the most distinguishing characteristic of the group. However, not all households in this segment currently own personal computers; nor were all households that own personal computers classified as Techies by the cluster analysis.

The cluster analysis procedure classified respondents according to a pattern of responses to survey questions regarding consumer electronics ownership. The response *pattern* that characterizes this segment is average or above average current ownership of all consumer electronic devices listed in the question and average future purchase plans. In other words, this segment, which comprises about 5% of all U.S. households, represents early purchasers of consumer electronic devices. Most households in this segment have already fulfilled their desire to own the products listed in the survey instrument, and unmet demand is at about the same level as it is for Mid-America

Techie households are as likely as Mid-America households to own touchtone telephones (67%), color television sets (99%) and microwave ovens (86%). They are more likely to own video cassette recorders (82%), but only half as likely to plan to purchase one in the next 12 months. They are also more likely to own telephone answering machines (44%) and compact disk players (27%). And they are overwhelmingly more likely to own personal computers (87%), printers (85%) and modems (70%). The only device listed in the survey that has no appeal to this group is a video camera. Only 2% of Techie households already own one of these, and 93% claim they have no plans to buy one.

Techie households appear to be much more likely to view computers as serious machines belonging to the male domain. Almost three-fourths of the households in this segment that already own a computer (87%) or plan to purchase one (11%) claim that the value of their computer is or will be more than $1,000. And 55% claim that the computer user is or will be the male household head. Only 4% say the user is/will be the female head of household; 25% claim both use or will use it, and in 16% of the households the user is or will be someone else.

Demographic Characteristics

Demographically, Techies are middle-aged and upscale. The median age for the segment is 44 years, one year lower than that of the Mid-America segment. A plurality (31%) are in the 35-44 age bracket, and 80% are between the ages of 25 and 54. The median household income for the segment is $42,500, and 37% earn $50,000 or more a year. Eighty-two percent are employed on a full-time basis. More than half (56%) are college graduates. And more than a third (34%) have done post graduate work.

Financial Holdings of the Techies Segment

The median net worth of Techies is approximately twice that of the Mid-America (See Techies Balance Sheet). The average (mean) net worth per household in this segment is $85,723.

Of course, the segment's product and service usage patterns are also significantly different from those of Mid-America. Techies are significantly more likely to have interest bearing checking accounts and money market deposit accounts and significantly less likely to be users of regular checking accounts. They are more likely to have first mortgages, unsecured personal loans, unsecured personal lines of credit, and Visa and MasterCard credit cards. And they are significantly more likely than Mid-America households to own all types of investment products covered by the survey except bond mutual funds, government securities, insurance products and Keogh accounts.

THE GADGETEERS SEGMENT

Households whose consumer electronic ownership patterns and plans suggest a very favorable attitude toward advanced home electronics technology—particularly video technology—make up the second largest segment identified by the cluster analysis. The selection of entertainment-oriented home electronics suggests a different basic attitude within this group. These households appear to be less business minded than Techies, younger and yet equally affluent. This segment is labeled Gadgeteers because a majority of the households in it either own or indicate plans to purchase all of the consumer electronic devices listed in the survey except modems and, surprisingly, compact disk players.

In particular, Gadgeteer households own video cassette recorders (92%) and video cameras (30%) at far higher levels than Mid-America (68% and 2%, respectively). They also have much greater purchase intentions. With 92% already owning a VCR, only 2% have no plan to buy one. In Mid-America, 19% say they have no plan to buy. While 30% of the Gadgeteers have video cameras, an additional 34% intend to purchase one within the next year. By comparison, Mid-America's appetite for video cameras is relativley modest. Only an additional 13% plan a purchase within the next year.

Gadgeteer households also are significantly more likely than households in the Mid-America segment to own touchtone telephones (84%), computers (49%), printers (38%), modems (8%), and telephone answering machines (50%). Furthermore, ownership of touchtone telephones, VCRs and video cameras in this segment is significantly greater than Techies' ownership of these machines. And while there is a high level of computer equipment ownership relative to Mid-America, it is far lower than in the Techies' segment. However, almost one out of three Gadgeteer households indicated plans to purchase personal computers (35%), printers (35%) and modems (28%) sometime during the next year, suggesting there is an inclination toward such devices, but not one that is strong enough to actually bring a purchase.

The vast majority of households in the Gadgeteers' segment are computer literate, with 80% reporting that they have used a personal computer and 51% reporting that they have access to a microcomputer at work. And half of the 84% that own or plan to buy a personal computer say that the value of their systems is or will be in excess of $1,000.

Finally, Gadgeteer households are less sexist than either Techies or Mid-America households in their ideas about who computers are for. Thirty-five percent of Gadgeteer households that own or plan to buy a computer indicated the main user is or will be the male head of household. Twenty-two percent indicated the user is or will be the female household head. And both male and female heads of households are or will be co-users in 31%.

Demographic Characteristics

The demographic variable that best characterizes the Gadgeteers market segment is youth. Sixty-eight percent of the respondents in this segment are under 44 years of age. The median age is 41. Although slightly less well-educated than the Techie segment — 39% of Gadgeteer households graduated college with at least a bachelor's degree compared to 56% of the Techies group — the median annual household income among Gadgeteer households is a healthy $41,600.

Financial Holdings

Financial product and service usage rates and balance data for the Gadgeteer segment are presented in the Gadgeteers Balance Sheet. A majority of these households have regular checking accounts, interest checking and regular savings accounts. More than half have a first mortgage, and the median balance for mortgage users in this group is $62,500, compared to $37,500 for both Mid-America and Techie segments. This probably is a reflection of Gadgeteer household youthfulness. Fewer households in this segment purchased their homes before the relatively recent skyrocketing of real estate values.

More than half of Gadgeteer segment households also have an automobile loan (median balance $6,250), MasterCard and or Visa credit card (median balance $500) and whole life insurance policies (median value $62,500). Forty-four percent have individual retirement accounts, and about one in four have stocks, real estate investments and/or 401 (k) savings plans. The average net worth of a Gadgeteer segment household is $74,039; the median is almost $50,000.

THE PROCRASTINATORS SEGMENT

Procrastinator households account for 10% of households nationwide. Overall, this segment's ownership of consumer electronic devices is in line with the ownership rates of the sample as a whole:

Touchtone telephones	65%
Personal computers	21%
Computer printers	17%
Modems	7%
Compact disk players	9%
Video cameras	9%
Telephone answering machines	20%

These figures show that this segment is significantly more likely than Mid-America to own personal computers and peripherals. But it is significantly less likely to own the more common products such as VCRs (43%), color TVs (81%) and microwave ovens (69%). Thus there appears to be an element of independence in this segment's selection of technological devices. Households in this segment appear to choose those devices that meet their specific needs. They do not simply follow the crowd.

This is also the interpretation placed on the high level of non-response found in the Procrastinator segment. (See Appendix Table 2.) One could argue that failing to respond to this question is the same thing as a "do not own, have no plans to buy" response, and this may well be the case. But the data show that households in this segment did not check this alternative, which was on the survey instrument. Instead, they chose to ignore the instructions and respond in their own way.

The Procrastinator segment is the least computer literate segment — defined as having ever used a personal computer — of the five produced by the cluster analysis. Only 31% of this segment have ever used a personal computer, and only 25% have access to a personal computer at work. Also, the segment appears to be attracted to lower priced machines. Of the 21% of households in this segment that own personal computers and the 4% that plan to purchase one within 12 months, only 13% claim that the value of their system is more than $1,000. Current or planned computer users are:

Male head of household	29%
Female head of household	23%
Both heads of household	31%
Someone else	17%.

Demographic Characteristics

The Procrastinator segment tends to be considerably older and less affluent than any of the segments examined up to this point, although it is still a mixed group. The median age of this segment is 61. Forty-five percent of the respondents are 65 or older, although only 38% are retired. Fifty percent of the heads of these households have full-time employment, but the median income is only $18,600 per annum, and 40% earn less than $15,000 per year. The educational attainment of the segment is similar to that of Mid-America. A majority have only a high school diploma or less, but 11% graduated college and 16% have done post graduate work.

Financial Holdings

While the Procrastinator segment's median household income is substantially lower than that of Mid-America, the typical Procrastinator household has a somewhat higher net worth, reflecting that older households tend to have assets such as paid-for homes. (See Procrastinators Balance Sheet in the appendix.)

The types of accounts owned and the mean and median balances indicate that investment income is more important to this older segment than to Mid-America and that credit and life insurance products are less so. In the deposit account section of the balance sheet, Procrastinator households are significantly less likely than Mid-America to have regular checking and regular savings accounts and significantly more likely to own money market deposit accounts.

Households in this segment are also significantly less likely to have first mortgages, automobile loans and Visa and MasterCard credit cards. And while those households that do have bank cards appear to have higher average (mean) balances than MasterCard and Visa account owners in Mid-America, the average balance of Mid-America home equity line of credit users is about four times as great as the average for Procrastinator households that have this type of account.

Procrastinator households tend to hold all types of investment products except whole life insurance policies in about the same proportions as Mid-America households, but the balances in the accounts of Procrastinators that own these are higher, on average, than those of the mainstream. Not surprisingly, given the median age of the segment, Procrastinators are significantly less likely than Mid-America households to own whole life insurance policies.

THE NO-TECH SEGMENT

The remaining 12% of U.S. households fall into a segment labeled No-Tech. The only consumer electronic device that a majority of households in this segment (59%) currently own is a color television. Thirty-six percent of the No-Tech respondents to the survey own a touchtone telephone, and 18% own a telephone answering machine, but fewer than 10% own any of the other items listed in the questionnaire.

Furthermore, a majority of households in this segment report they have no plans to purchase technological devices. The item most likely to be purchased by No-Tech households is a microwave oven. Twenty-one percent of the segment said they planned to buy one during the 12 months following the survey. Nine percent indicated plans to purchase a personal computer. The same proportion planned to buy a compact disk player, and 8% planned to buy a VCR.

In short, this segment lags even the Mid-America segment by a substantial amount in home electronics interest. Only 33% have ever used a personal computer. Even fewer (17%) have access to a microcomputer at work. And of the 2% that currently own and 9% that plan to buy a computer this year, only 9% say that the value of their system will be more than $1,000. About the most positive thing that can be said about this segment's orientation toward advanced technology is that it is not sexist. Three out of four current and proposed computer owners said both heads of households do or will use the machine.

Demographic Characteristics

The most outstanding demographic characteristic of the No-Tech segment is its low income. The median annual income per household in this segment is only $13,100. Fifty-seven percent earn less than $15,000 per year, and another 24% earn between $15,000 and $24,999 annually.

Given the low level of consumer electronic ownership and the low median household income, it should come as no surprise to learn that the No-Tech segment has a median age of 61. Thirty-four percent of respondents in this segment are retired, and 23% are 65 and older with incomes between $10,000 and $25,000 per year. Thirty-five percent are households with less than $10,000 income, regardless of age.

But the entire segment is not without potential. Householders below the age of 25 are significantly more likely to be classified as No-Tech households than to fall in any of the other segments, and in fact 11% of the No-Tech segment are younger than 25. But when the educational attainment of the No-Tech segment is compared with that of Mid-America, larger percentages of No-Tech households report that they attended college, graduated from college, and/or did post graduate work. A larger proportion (13%) also are engaged in part-time jobs. Thus it is not unreasonable to speculate that perhaps as much as 5% of the respondents in this segment may be college students or recent graduates whose low level of consumer electronics ownership is temporary and simply reflects a different set of priorities rather than a different attitude toward technology per se.

Financial Holdings

When it comes to the use of and balances held in deposit accounts, the No-Tech segment is very similar to Mid-America. In fact, the mean and median deposit account balances of No-Tech households ($14,927 and $7,995, respectively) are somewhat higher than those of Mid-America

($13,952 and $7,028). And like Procrastinators households, with which they share a common median age, No-Tech households are significantly more likely than the Mid-Americas to have money market deposit accounts. But No-Tech households are much less likely than Mid-Americans to own many types of investment products or to use several types of credit products.

Specifically, No-Tech households are less likely to have:

First mortgages	22%
Automobile loans	13%
Secured personal loans	7%
MasterCard credit cards	25%
Visa credit cards	29%
Individual stocks	14%
Real estate investments	10%
Whole life insurance policies	35%
Universal life insurance policies	3%
Insurance annuities	6%
Individual Retirement Accounts	20%
401(k) savings plans	6%

The net result is an estimated net worth of only $42,655 (mean), which is about $24,000 less than that of Mid-America ($66,488). (See No-Tech Balance Sheet in the appendix.)

STRATEGIES FOR SERVING EACH SEGMENT

Beyond the general strategy of developing integrated electronic access to product and service information (as is discussed in more detail in the chapter specifically addressing home banking), the nature of the segments suggest particular strategies for electronic banking service development.

As the largest segment, behavior of Mid-America households sets the stage for the continued development of services for the entire market. Many of these households already use some aspects of elec-tronic delivery systems and the immediate opportunity is to generate greater usage of existing services before addressing new systems.

Consider cash access, for example. An average Mid-America household obtains $337 in cash monthly, although half of the households obtain less than $250 each month. Within the segment, 40% of the households obtain cash on at least a monthly basis from an ATM. However, 72% say they also obtain cash while making a deposit and 57% cash a personal check while visiting their primary financial institution. When ATM usage is adjusted for consideration of whether the respondent's institution offers such service, the usage level jumps to 57%, exactly the same number as walk into the branch to write a check. Since 30% of this segment currently is not aware of being offered ATM service, and the whole segment essentially was neutral concerning usage of ATMs, there is an immediate potential to shift non-users of ATMs to at least some ATM usage by increasing awareness, and then by increasing usage among current users who now also cash a check while at the branch.

Increasing ATM usage has had drawbacks for some institutions that had anticipated such transactions would directly offset teller transactions, and justified equipment investments on that basis. The industry experience seems to point to approximately a two-to-one offset. In other words, two visits to an ATM are generated to replace one visit to a teller. The good news for financial institutions has been that even the imposition of fees for ATM transactions has not greatly affected this ratio. The convenience of ATMs tends to encourage expectations that a machine will be available when needed, which actually creates new transactions and generates new fee revenues while usage of tellers does not.

ATMs have become a competitive necessity for institutions that provide retail consumer financial services. Usage continues to grow and now exceeds the levels reported in this 1988 study. ATM networks report transaction volume is growing at double digit rates, even allowing for the impact of network mergers. With the number of ATMs installed in the U.S. nearly stagnant at 80,000 machines, per machine volume in 1990 was estimated by the newsletter *Bank Network News* at 7,750 transactions, up 40% from 1989 volume of 5,516 transactions per machine. Although it is likely some of that increase also reflects double-counting as consumer transactions are routed from one network to another, the usage trend is still strongly upward.

The apparent success story of ATMs, however, is diminished as they become a commodity service that most institutions offer. A decade ago

ATMs provided competitive advantage to the institutions that first offered them. A few institutions, notably Citibank, clearly were able to shift market share by promoting the convenience of exclusive ATM services. Exclusivity is no longer an issue and ATM sharing has minimized competitive advantage. With the recent agreement to honor one another's transactions between Plus and Cirrus, the two largest of the national shared ATM networks, the vast majority of ATM cardholders have access to virtually every ATM in the market. Consumers have been persuaded of ATM convenience and demonstrate their willingness to use the machines. To maximize the advantages of offering ATMs requires further offsetting of routine traffic in the branch, particularly at peak periods when any possibility of cross-marketing is eclipsed by the need to keep lines moving.

An integrated approach to electronic delivery offers an immediate example of how to provide rational incentives to consumers to increase ATM usage without simply driving up volumes by reducing individual transaction size. If 72% of the Mid-America segment is obtaining cash while making a deposit, financial institutions are not obtaining the volume of direct deposit of payrolls that is possible. A significant share of those deposits are payroll checks, as any teller can affirm. Increasing use of direct deposit encourages consumers to visit an ATM at their convenience rather than make a trip to the branch on payday when many others are likely doing the same. The financial institution, particularly one that has branches with significant numbers of accounts held by employees of major nearby employers, not only evens the flow of traffic in the branch but also may see higher average balances as funds remain on deposit until needed. The trade-off is that instead of taking cash back while making the in-branch deposit, the consumer may make two transactions at foreign ATMs before the next payday, which results in the financial institution paying interchange fees. But between reduced staffing expense, fee income and increased earnings on higher average balances, the institution is a net winner.

However, as with many aspects of electronic delivery, this is not simply a matter between the consumer and the financial institution. In the vast majority of cases, the consumer does not control access to direct deposit service. The employer determines whether direct deposit will be offered to employees.

Encouraging direct deposit services requires cooperation between financial institutions that serve commercial customers and those serving consumers. Ironically, that cooperation sometimes is no easier to obtain when both the employer and employee are served by the same institution than when competitors are involved. Too often, the bureaucracies of financial institutions leave the potential parties antagonists rather than partners. An integrated strategy may be logical, but it runs against the grain of the corporate culture in many institutions.

Even with turf battles settled, there still are difficulties in implementing direct deposit because the industry is not uniformly automated. The process should be very straightforward. On payday, the employer's account should be debited and the employee's account credited. If both parties have accounts with the same institution, a ledger notation—computerized or not—is made and the process is complete. However, even when the automated clearing house system is used to exchange funds information electronically between institutions, the process is rarely as simple nor as timely as it should be.

Since the ACH system must allow for institutions that are not able to receive electronic notifications, several days of lag time are introduced between the time funds are debited from the employer's account and credited to the employee, complicating the situation for all involved. For the employer, the first disadvantage is that the lag time has a clear price in interest income lost once the funds have been placed in a non-interest-bearing transaction account or are in transit. For a large employer, that lost interest income may be significant. The second disadvantage is that the paper payroll check provided the employer with a bonus from the float generated between the time the check was written and the employee could place it in deposit. Although that interest income may be regarded as something the employer was not entitled to in the first place, there is no denying it was real.

But those disadvantages aren't the worst problems created by the limitations of a partially automated system. As with most payments, the process of automation becomes more complicated when the payment amount varies, such as may be the case with hourly employees. For the employer who has hourly employees, direct deposit may mean that paychecks will not lag the end of the pay period merely by a day or two as is common today, but by four or five days because of the extra time that is required to generate the ACH transactions! Not surprisingly, few employers are willing to tell employees that hourly wages will be delayed so that they can be offered the "convenience" of direct deposit.

Even with salaried positions, the direct deposits must be scheduled as ACH transactions two or more days in advance of payday, so that the employer's financial institution can execute the appropriate debits in time to ensure funds are credited to the employees' accounts at other institutions on payday. Again, the lag is necessary to accommodate non-automated institutions.

Such oddities of dealing with a partially automated system introduce further obstacles. It is possible, for example, that an employer's payroll account will not actually contain funds to cover the payroll until the day paychecks are actually to be credited to employees. However, to make the transaction electronically, the financial institution initiates the process prior to the actual payday. Consequently, it faces two choices. Either debit the account in advance and likely incur the wrath of the employer, who may wish to retain payroll funds in an interest-bearing account, or assume the risk that the employer will have funds sufficient to cover the transaction on that settlement day. Because on settlement day, the employer's financial institution has for all practical purposes already transferred the funds. By contrast, the financial institution would not have faced a similar risk if the employer simply wrote checks. If funds were not in the account on pay day, the institution would not transfer any funds. Pay checks would bounce, but it would be the employer's problem, not the financial institution's.

These inefficiencies could be reduced or eliminated if the auto-mated clearinghouse system were truly all-electronic, but the need to accommodate non-automated institutions at times actually reduces ACH transactions to a poorer degree of timeliness than checks processed through the Federal Reserve system. Portions of the ACH systems are all-electronic and the National Automated Clearing House Association is on record as urging the Federal Reserve to mandate an all-electronic system. Until that occurs, the financial industry's chronic state of partial automation limits its ability to achieve the efficiencies electronic delivery systems offer.

Automating other payments from the home raises similar concerns. Although one in five of the Mid-America households uses an automatic bill payment service for at least one payment, it isn't surprising that such services have made minor inroads except when automatic payment was the only alternative to prepayment, such as is the case with many insurance policies that offer automatic payment plans. With conventional preauthorized debits of consumer checking accounts, financial institutions again may debit an account prior to actual settlement on the due date to allow for delays in the ACH system. The situtation also exists with many telephone bill payment programs and reduces their attractiveness. Institutions do so not to obtain extra earnings on such funds, but to accommodate the same system of partial automation faced by the employer attempting to offer direct deposit services. To the consumer, such policies not only seem unfair, but can trigger a cascade of returned check charges, overdraft charges and general financial confusion if the consumer anticipated that debits should occur on the due date.

The short-sighted attitude from the financial community has been that the responsibility is fully on the consumer to assure that funds are in place. To ensure cooperation, sometimes severe penalties are enforced for overdrafts. Such a coercive approach ignores the reality that in the vast majority of cases, the consumer has the funds or adequate credit and has the intention of making the payment, but through oversight has not deposited the funds appropriately. If the consumer also is a user of direct deposit as well as automated debits, the timing may be completely out of his control, which becomes a major disincentive to using either service.

A more positive approach is possible when the institution can use its electronic information capabilities to consider information about the consumer's payment history and creditworthiness. Rather than charging a penalty, an instant credit extension might be made, particularly if an overdraft was created by an automated debit. Such an approach wouldn't necessarily mean that the institution would charitably forego income from penalty fees, but that it would build usage of all other fee-generating products and services, which well might offset the $15 or $25 penalty income. Greater fee income potential lies in additional product sales (such as for an account that guaranteed certain bills always are paid) than might be derived from even the most punitive overdraft charges that were intended to keep free balances at a high level in non-interest bearing accounts. To see why, consider the following example drawn from figures in the household balance sheets included in the Appendix.

The average balance of credit products held by a Mid-America household was $23,675 in the survey examined here. Such households also held an average of $5,131 in liquid funds and had an estimated average net worth of $59,577. However, half of the 67% of the segment who were holders of regular, non-interest bearing checking accounts reported a current balance of less than $750, identically to holders of such accounts in all other segments except the Gadgeteers, who were both more affluent and more liquid. Maintaining such relatively low balances in non-interest bearing accounts is fiscally prudent. The institution that penalizes a customer for an oversight in a transaction account is likely reducing its chance of seeing any of the credit products income potential that is represented by that household. Furthermore, if the household had any of its $12,849 in interest-bearing balances with the institution, then such penalties not only could chase those funds away, but those funds were overlooked as a potential guarantee on the credit extension.

This is not to suggest that there are not deadbeats nor bankrupts. However, a system designed to penalize such miscreants tends to treat every accountholder as a potential miscreant rather than as a valued customer.

Electronic delivery strategies for the Mid-America segment basically are mass market strategies and should be derived directly from automation of basic banking services. Each of the other segments may be targets for niche market strategies as well, using devices in the home to enhance access to those same basic services as well as specialized products. The two most attractive segments to a financial institution are Techies and Gadgeteers, both of which are more affluent than the general market and represent the heaviest users of credit services. In differing fashion, they also may be the best targets for interactive electronic services provided directly to the home.

The No-Tech households have the lowest income and net worth, but represent a group that is becoming critical in electronic delivery strategies because they are most affected by government efforts to shift various entitlement payments to electronic transfers from paper checks, as is discussed in more detail in a later chapter. These are the households least likely to have a life insurance policy that offers automatic payment options, but most likely to receive Social Security funds by direct deposit. They are the most opposed to levelized utility billing plans and least interested in a service providing a household income statement/balance sheet or in using financial decision programs on public information terminals.

In short, No-Tech households are the audience that financial institutions and the govenrment would most prefer to deal with through low-cost electronic delivery methods, but are likely to be the most resistant to taking an active, cooperative stance. Services for this segment must be among the least complicated and easiest to use.

Procrastinators, who represent 10% of the market, have a higher estimated net worth than Mid-America, but are low users of credit services, reflecting that they tend to be older and consequently less likely to have a home mortgage or other major loans outstanding. Procrastinators are likely to be least responsive to any effort to encourage direct usage of electronic financial delivery systems. Although the average age of this segment makes them above average recipients of Social Security and pension benefits, direct deposit is the electronic delivery system they are most likely to use.

While a larger percentage of Procrastinator households say they use ATMs than do Mid-America households, 46% to 42%, only 80% of the ATM users say they obtain cash from ATMs. Among Mid-America, Techie and Gadgeteer households, percentages using ATMs and those obtaining cash from ATMs are nearly identical. This would suggest that the ATM is more frequently used as a source of an account balance by this segment than among more affluent households. A similar pattern among No-Tech households seems to support that argument. This pattern further suggests that easy-to-use, telephone-based account balance information services will garner more usage.

Gadgeteers, who have high net worth and active usage of credit products, particularly should be targeted for services using new technology such as automated telephone information services. This segment, one in five households, has the least resistance to dealing with computerized voices on the phone and the highest level of comfort with telephone answering machines. The segment also has the highest interest in the concept of levelized utility billing and a household income statement/balance sheet service, while being the most likely to say they are time-pressed.

Above average usage of existing alternative delivery systems suggests this segment is inclined to convenience-oriented services and combined with its orientation toward home electronics generally, would be most receptive to considering usage of a device such as a telephone with a screen that would display a transaction in progress. This assumption is supported by the segment's relatively high level of agreement with a statement that they would be "more likely to use telephone bill payment if they could see the transactions on a TV screen."

Additionally, the fact that this segment is not particularly oriented to computer hardware suggests that any such device should be preprogrammed and ready to plug-in and use when purchased or received. Gadgeteers also may be most receptive to a financial service provider who offered a device that also provided investment information such as stock prices. Nearly a third say they own stocks and their average household holdings of investment products is more than 50% greater than Mid-America households, second only to the Techie households.

Finally, the 5% of the market that falls in the Techie segment is potentially a strong target for electronic delivery services that can interact with a home computer system, particularly if the service supports use of financial management software on that system rather than simply making the home computer act as a dumb terminal. Supporting such software means that the service should allow quick access to current account balances across the full range of the customer's product usage as well as access to all recently cleared items. Historical information also could be available and users are more likely to find separate fees for such information to be acceptable than fees for current information.

Bill-paying services for this segment should generate electronic transactions that conform to bank processing formats so that the activity is completely automated from the institution's standpoint. The financial institution, in its role as the holder of information, could act as the official repository for records of the financial activity of the service user. In such a capacity, the institution could verify the authenticity of transactions and accuracy of records to the Internal Revenue Service or to outside auditors.

Such services also would be useful in this segment's investment activity, which is significant. At least one in four holds some type of mutual fund, nearly four in ten own stocks and more than half have whole life insurance policies. With $122,860 in average household ownership of investment products, the segment has nearly twice the investment holdings of the average Mid-America household.

To summarize, more than half of the market already has access to all of the electronic delivery services that they are likely to use, but those services can be made much more efficient from the financial institution's perspective by full automation of industry systems. Such increased efficiency will encourage greater marketing, which will bring more usage.

New services should be developed for the two extremes of the market, the technology-oriented segments and the anti-technology segments. In the first case, the services will be investment and financial management oriented and will be profitable as movers of market share and, ultimately, fee generators. In the second case, the services will be designed to automate delivery of public benefits. Financial institutions will be paid by government agencies, who will find the expenditures worthwhile as a means of reducing the overall expenses of such programs.

The following chapter details the banking and financial behavior characteristics of the segments before we return to a general examination of electronic delivery directly to the home.

CHAPTER

4

Technological Orientation and Banking Behavior: The Financial Behavior Characteristics of Different Technological Segments

MARKET SEGMENTATION

One of the great advantages of electronic information tools is the capability they offer to look at large masses of data in new ways. In financial services, the power of the computer allows service providers to look at current and potential markets with new insight. The following discussion expands on the market segments identified in the previous chapter. The data used throughout this chapter is from a nationwide consumer survey conducted in 1988 by Payment Systems, Inc. (PSI), the Tampa-based financial services research and consulting company. This analysis used electronics ownership to uncover the characteristics that could predict the extent and speed with which households will accept various forms of electronic automation of financial services delivery.

Among the financial behavioral characteristics being detailed in this chapter are the current

Financial Product/Service Usage and Balances
MID-AMERICA SEGMENT

	% Own	Mean Bal/ Owner	Median Bal/ Owner	Mean Bal/ Household	Median Bal/ Household
Deposit Accounts					
Regular Checking	67%	$1,647	$750	$1,103	$503
Interest Checking	49%	$3,153	$1,500	$1,545	$735
Regular Savings	66%	$3,167	$1,500	$2,090	$990
Certificate of Deposit	30%	$29,402	$15,000	$8,821	$4,500
Money Market Deposit Account	4%	$9,822	$7,500	$393	$300
				$13,952	$7,028
Credit Products					
First Mortgage	42%	$37,845	$37,500	$15,895	$15,750
Second Mortgage/ Home Equity Loan	5%	$18,532	$12,500	$927	$625
Home Equity Line of Credit	5%	$27,383	$12,500	$1,369	$625
Automobile Loan	61%	$5,497	$3,750	$3,353	$2,288
Secured Personal Loan	16%	$3,296	$1,750	$527	$280
Unsecured Personal Loan	8%	$3,429	$1,750	$274	$140
Unsecured Personal Line of Credit	9%	$2,393	$500	$215	$45
MasterCard Credit Card	34%	$1,425	$500	$485	$170
Visa Credit Card	45%	$1,126	$500	$507	$225
Broker Margin Account	1%	$14,506	$5,000	$123	$42
				$23,675	$20,190
Investment Products					
Money Market Mutual Fund	8%	$18,339	$7,500	$1,467	$600
Stock Mutual Fund	10%	$19,554	$7,500	$1,955	$750
Bond Mutual Fund	5%	$26,090	$17,500	$1,305	$875
Other Mutual Fund	5%	$25,226	$7,500	$1,261	$375
Stocks	20%	$22,547	$7,500	$4,509	$1,500
Corporate or Municipal Bonds	3%	$36,740	$37,500	$1,102	$1,125
Government Securities	7%	$15,500	$7,500	$1,112	$538
Real Estate Investments	20%	$65,315	$37,500	$12,952	$7,436
Whole Life Insurance Policies	47%	$54,440	$37,500	$25,587	$17,625
Universal Life Insurance Policies	11%	$63,674	$62,500	$7,004	$6,875
Insurance Annuities	8%	$38,591	$37,500	$3,087	$3,000
IRAs	31%	$15,682	$7,500	$4,861	$2,325
Keogh Accounts	1%	$28,446	$17,500	$284	$175
401 (k) Savings Plans	17%	$16,554	$7,500	$2,814	$1,275
				$69,300	$44,474
Estimated Financial Net Worth				**$59,577**	**$31,312**

Source: Payment Systems, Inc. (1988)

financial services delivery system usage patternswithin the segments. This includes main transaction account usage, usage of various accounts for bill paying, obtaining cash and making purchases at the point of sale. Attitudes toward financial services also are detailed by segment, including attitudes toward delivery system alternatives to the conventional paper check.

The balance sheet for each segment applies survey respondent's reported balances in various accounts and ownership incidence to calculate average and midpoint balances for households in each of the segments. These figures encompass balances held in all types of financial institutions, including banks, thrifts and credit unions, as well as credit and investment products in non-institution specific fashion. Consequently, a more complete view of consumers' overall financial behavior is obtained.

MID-AMERICA SEGMENT CHARACTERISTICS

The largest segment, Mid-America, reflects a slight majority of the entire population and is very similar in characteristics to the population considered as a whole. More than any other segment, the following describes the typical financial holdings and attitudes of an average American household.

Main Financial Institution

Mid-America households are primarily commercial bank customers, with 61% of respondents in this segment identifying a commercial bank as their main financial institution. About one-fourth said their main institution is a savings and loan association or savings bank, and one-eighth see their credit unions as their primary Depository Financial Institution (DFI).

Branch Location Use

In fact, a plurality of respondents seem to consider the branch they use to be their bank. Three out of four Mid-America households reported they regularly use only one or two branch locations, with 42% using only one. Virtually all households in this segment (90%) visit their main depository financial institution once a month. The average (mean) number of visits per month is six, and the median is 4. The mean and median number of visits per month by function is as follows:

To night depository	mean = <.5, median = 0 (9% use monthly)
To inside teller	mean = 3.0, median = 2 (80% use monthly)

To drive-in teller	mean = 2.0, median = 1 (60% use monthly)
To other staff	mean = <.5, median = 0 (14% use monthly)

Main Transaction Account and Usage

As noted in the balance sheet for this segment, 67% of Mid-America households own a regular checking account. The vast majority of regular checking account holders apparently use them as their main transaction account. When asked, "From which... account do you usually pay most of your household's expenses," 62% of this segment indicated a regular checking account. Only 28% of respondents usually pay household expenses from an interest bearing account (22% from NOW or share draft accounts and 6% from SuperNOWs), although 49% report holding such an account. Three percent reported paying expenses from a regular savings account, 4% from some other type of account, and 3% reported having no type of transaction account.

On average, Mid-America households write 18 checks per month (type of account not specified). The median monthly check volume in this segment is 17. The mean and median monthly check volume by transaction type for this segment is:

At stores for purchases	median = 3, mean = 5
At home for bills	median = 8, mean = 10
To obtain cash	median = 3, mean = 1
For other purposes	median = 3, mean = 2

Bill Paying and Budgets

The mean and median number of household bills paid each month for this segment are 10 and 8, respectively. Since these are identical with the mean and median number of checks written to pay bills, it is obvious that the segment uses virtually no alternative bill-payment media. And in the majority of Mid-America households (59%), the female head of household usually pays the bills. The male head of household is the primary bill payer in 26% of these households, and the job is shared in 14%. Only 24% of Mid-America households have a written budget that is used to manage spending.

Sources of Cash

Mid-America households report obtaining an average of $337 cash each month to meet their routine cash needs. The median value is $250. Nearly three-fourths of these households (72%) obtain at least some of this cash via split deposits (deposits with cash back); 57% cash personal checks at their primary financial institutions to obtain cash; 40% get cash back when paying for supermarket purchases by check; and 40% obtain cash from ATMs.

Payment Media Used at the Point of Sale

The median amount of cash obtained monthly is estimated to represent approximately 15%-20% of the Mid-America's monthly after-tax income. Nevertheless, this segment is quite cash-oriented at the point of sale. Eighty-eight percent of Mid-America households who have shopped at a convenience store during the past 12 months reported paying for their purchases in cash; 77% of those who ate at local restaurants paid cash; and 70% of those who ate at non-local restaurants used cash as the payment medium. Other locations in which a majority of Mid-America shoppers pay in cash include gasoline stations (63%), drug stores (56%) and supermarkets (55%). Of the 13 shopper locations that PSI's consumer survey inquired about, only one — medical and health services — was a location where a majority of Mid-America household users (65%) last paid by check. And two types of purchases were usually paid by credit card:

Airline tickets - 45% by bank credit card, 15% by another type of card

Hotels/motels - 51% by bank credit card, 11% by another type of card

At department stores, Mid-America shoppers were about twice as likely to use a store card as a bankcard even though bankcard ownership is not that much lower than store card ownership in this segment (69% and 76%, respectively). At service stations they were three times as likely to use a gasoline company card as a bankcard (43% of this segment owns gasoline company cards). But at other locations (i.e., furniture/appliance stores, discount department stores, clothing stores and local and non-local restaurants) Visa and/or MasterCard were clearly preferred over other types of credit cards. (See Appendix Table 5.)

General Banking and Financial Attitudes

One financial attitude that appears to characterize Mid-America households almost universally is price sensitivity. When asked to rate the importance of various financial institution attributes on a five-point scale ranging from very unimportant (1) to very important (5), 81% of respondents in this segment gave "reasonable service charges on checking services" a score of 5. Fifteen percent rated this attribute "somewhat important" (4), and 3% gave a neutral (3) response. The weighted average score for the segment, then, is 4.8.

The only other attribute that achieved such a high weighted average score was accurate bookkeeping, with 89% considering this very important, 8% somewhat important, 1% neutral and 1% very unimportant. The other bank attributes whose weighted average importance scores put them in the very important category for this segment were easy to read statements, courteous personnel, branches close to home or work and quick teller service. All of these achieved a weighted average importance score of 4.5. (See Appendix Table 7.)

None of the attributes tested in the survey earned a low enough average importance rating to put them in the somewhat or very unimportant categories for the Mid-America segment. The lowest average score was a 3.0 (neutral). Attractive facilities and branches or offices in other states were the attributes that earned this score.

This analysis also computes weighted average agreement scored for the 19 general banking and economic attitude statements contained in the questionnaire. Respondents could either agree (score = 1), disagree (score = -1), or indicate a neutral position (score = 0) with each of these questions. The weighted average scores for all of the statements are presented in Appendix Table 7. Statements with which Mid-America households tended to agree were:

My bank generally resolves errors quickly and easily (weighted average score of .58).

Most tellers at banks and savings and loans are competent and well-trained (weighted average score of .51).

Financial institutions should provide low cost basic services to the economically disadvantaged (weighted average score of .36).

Given my current income and future expectations, I am comfortable with my current level of debt (weighted average score of .30).

It doesn't matter who provides the service as long as I can conduct my banking quickly (weighted average score of .30).

The deductibility of interest expense from my taxable income is not a major consideration in my use of credit (weighted average score of .30).

Consistent with the importance the segment attaches to reasonable checking account pricing, the statements with which the largest proportion of Mid-America respondents disagreed concerned their willingness to pay more for financial services:

I would be willing to pay $25 more per year for basic checking account services in exchange for improved service (weighted average score of -.76).

If a financial institution opened a branch or office that was more conveniently located than the institution I currently use, I would strongly consider moving my accounts even if I paid more for basic banking services (weighted average score of -.71).

I do not mind periodic reasonable price increases for financial services (weighted average score of -.46).

However, the weighted average agreement score for the statement, "I feel that I am paying too much for financial services" was -.08, well within the neutral range, as were the scores for all but one of the remaining nine statements.

The segment tended to disagree with the statement "I prefer using an Automated Teller Machine for the majority of my banking needs," although when considered as a financial institution attribute, convenient ATMs received a "somewhat important" average importance rating of 3.5. The apparent inconsistency suggests many respondents were reacting to the word *prefer* in the attitude statement. That is, a substantial percentage of Mid-America households probably do not care whether they conduct their routine banking transactions via human teller or ATM, but they do not *prefer* ATMs.

Alternative Delivery Systems Usage and Attitudes

Analysis of specific questions in the survey instrument concerning ATM usage reveals that 40% of all Mid-America households use these machines. However, only 70% claim that one or more of the financial institutions they deal with offers ATM services. Thus ATM usage among Mid-America customers of ATM providers is about 57%. The median number of cash withdrawals among ATM users in this segment is four per month. The median number of deposits is two.

Forty-two percent of Mid-America households whose financial institutions offer ATM services also reported that they could access ATMs in retail locations; and of this 42%, 39% use these machines to obtain cash before they shop while only 21% use them to check their account balances before shopping.

Similar percentages reported that their financial institutions participate in shared ATM networks (46% of Mid-America households whose institutions offer ATM services) and that they use local shared ATMs one or more times per month (40% of the 46%). Thirty percent of those with shared ATM service available to them use non-local machines monthly.

Financial Product/Service Usage and Balances
TECHIES SEGMENT

	% Own	Mean Bal/ Owner	Median Bal/ Owner	Mean Bal/ Household	Median Bal/ Household
Deposit Accounts					
Regular Checking	54%	$1,973	$750	$1,065	$405
Interest Checking	61%	$3,610	$3,500	$2,202	$2,135
Regular Savings	67%	$2,919	$1,500	$1,956	$1,005
Certificate of Deposit	33%	$25,174	$15,000	$8,307	$4,950
Money Market Deposit Account	14%	$8,925	$7,500	$1,250	$1,050
				$14,780	$9,545
Credit Products					
First Mortgage	61%	$63,024	$37,500	$38,445	$22,875
Second Mortgage/ Home Equity Loan	9%	$26,104	$12,500	$2,349	$1,125
Home Equity Line of Credit	10%	$20,928	$12,500	$2,093	$1,250
Automobile Loan	55%	$7,587	$6,250	$4,173	$3,438
Secured Personal Loan	11%	$6,951	$6,250	$765	$688
Unsecured Personal Loan	18%	$2,703	$1,750	$487	$315
Unsecured Personal Line of Credit	19%	$2,814	$1,750	$535	$333
MasterCard Credit Card	50%	$1,784	$500	$892	$250
Visa Credit Card	65%	$1,112	$500	$723	$325
Broker Margin Account	8%	$18,294	$5,000	$1,457	$398
				$51,919	$30,997
Investment Products					
Money Market Mutual Fund	19%	$24,829	$7,500	$4,718	$1,425
Stock Mutual Fund	25%	$16,616	$7,500	$4,154	$1,875
Bond Mutual Fund	10%	$34,156	$17,500	$3,416	$1,750
Other Mutual Fund	14%	$7,787	$2,500	$1,090	$350
Stocks	38%	$28,154	$7,500	$10,699	$2,850
Corporate or Municipal Bonds	9%	$31,918	$37,500	$2,873	$3,375
Government Securities	11%	$8,809	$7,500	$935	$796
Real Estate Investments	34%	$101,490	$75,000	$34,129	$25,221
Whole Life Insurance Policies	53%	$58,274	$37,500	$30,885	$19,875
Universal Life Insurance Policies	13%	$94,917	$87,500	$12,339	$11,375
Insurance Annuities	11%	$25,248	$12,500	$2,777	$1,375
IRAs	53%	$16,632	$17,500	$8,815	$9,275
Keogh Accounts	5%	$18,758	$17,500	$938	$875
401 (k) Savings Plans	36%	$14,145	$2,500	$5,092	$900
				$122,860	$81,317
Estimated Financial Net Worth				**$85,721**	**$59,865**

Source: Payment Systems, Inc. (1988)

Overall, the most popular locations for ATM users in Mid-America segment are:

Financial institution branches	86% use, 14% would like to
Drive-in branches	38% use, 18% would like to
Shopping malls	31% use, 33% would like to
Supermarkets	26% use, 34% would like to

Only 7% currently use ATMs at work, 12% at airports, and 14% at convenience stores; however, 20% would like to have ATM access at each of these locations.

Other alternative delivery systems are not so popular among Mid-America households. About one-fourth (22%) use automatic bill payment services, 18% bank by mail, and about 10% use direct deposit of salary, direct deposit of social security, and payroll deduction payment plans. Eight percent reported using a bank-by-phone service, but only 2% use pay-by-phone; and no household in this segment reported using a computer-based home banking service.

Finally, based on the weighted average agreement scores for 15 attitude statements concerning alternative delivery systems, the conclusion must be that it will take time and some powerful incentives to get Mid-America households to adopt electronic delivery of financial services. The segment displays an apparent aversion to telephone-based services, with the statement "I would prefer to be able to use the telephone for more of my financial transactions" receiving a weighted average agreement score of -.42 and the statement "I dislike telephone answering machines" receiving a score of .41.

The segment also exhibits a degree of suspicion with regards to computer based services. The statement "Computerized bill-paying services give institutions too much information about a person's financial affairs" received an average agreement score of .31. As well as suspicion, there was little awareness of innovation in telecommunications technologies. The statement "I am familiar with the delivery of services electronically, such as services provided through data bases, videotex, and home banking projects" had a weighted average agreement score of -.31.

And, Mid-America households apparently do not perceive a great need for more convenient or efficient ways of handling their financial affairs, giving an average agreement score of -.32 to the statement "It's hard to find time in my busy schedule for routine chores like paying bills." With the segment even being more likely to disagree than to agree with such a non-threatening statement as "I would prefer to use the mail for routine financial transactions such as deposits, loan payments, etc." (score = -.31), it is difficult to imagine how any electronic system for delivery of financial services could generate a positive response from Mid-America if initiative for its use were left solely to demand.

If the inertia of the Mid-America segment in its financial service behavior, which essentially represents the mass market, is not persuasive, consider that the potentially most amenable segment is not much more enthusiastic.

TECHIES SEGMENT CHARACTERISTICS

The Techies segment is the smallest of the segments identified, representing only 5% of the overall market. It is male-dominated, tends toward middle-age and is more affluent than average. Consumer electronics ownership is highest in this segment, particularly reflecting ownership of computer hardware. As a segment, investment and credit usage activity are both high, running nearly double the average levels in the Mid-America segment. While it is a small segment, its level of financial activity makes it very interesting to financial institutions.

Main Financial Institution

Techies are not significantly different from Mid-America households in their choice of a primary financial institution. Fifty-nine percent claim their main institution is a commercial bank, 25% use a savings bank or savings and loan association, and 16% deal primarily with a credit union. However, households in this segment are much less likely to say they use only one branch. While 29% do make this claim and 33% say they use only one or two branches, 11% state that they regularly use multiple locations and 15% indicated they "rarely use any location because I prefer Automated Teller Machines." Nevertheless, the mean and median number of visits to the primary financial institution each month (exclusive of visits to use an ATM) are the same (six and four, respectively) for Techies as for Mid-America.

Main Transaction Account

Not surprisingly, in view of the account ownership data reported in the balance sheets included in the Appendix, Techies are significantly less likely than Mid-America to use a regular checking account as their main transaction account and significantly more likely to use an interest-bearing transaction account. Main transaction account usage figures for the segment are as follows:

Regular checking	47%
Interest checking	39%
SuperNOW	8%
Regular savings	4%

It is also not surprising to find that these more affluent households write a substantial number of checks. The mean number of checks written per month by Techies' households is 26; the median is 22. Of these, the mean and median number written at stores to pay for purchases is 8. The mean number written to pay bills is 12 (median 8), and in 46% of these households the male head of household usually pays the bills. The mean and median number of checks written to obtain cash are 2 and 3, respectively; and for other purposes they are 4 and 3.

Sources of Cash

Techies have significantly higher monthly cash needs than Mid-America. The average for this computer-oriented segment is $420 per month, and the median is $350.

Almost two out of every three Techie households (65%) who write checks to obtain cash present them for cashing at financial institutions. A majority (51%) also write checks for more than the amount of purchase at supermarkets and take the difference in cash, and 61% get cash back when making a deposit. But the one method of obtaining cash used by more households in this segment than any other is the ATM. Sixty-seven percent of this segment reported making ATM cash withdrawals at least once a month. However, the mean and median numbers of cash withdrawals per ATM user (5 and 4, respectively) are the same for this segment as for ATM users in all other segments except the group labeled No-Tech. In short, Techies are significantly more likely than any other segment to be ATM users, but not to use them more often than ATM users in most other groups.

POS Payment Media

Despite the higher than average value for monthly routine cash needs noted above for the Techies segment, this segment is less cash oriented than Mid-America households when paying for purchases at the point of sale. At the supermarket, Techies are more likely to pay by check

(57%) than by cash (40%). And at the following locations Techies shoppers are significantly less likely than Mid-America households to pay cash, opting instead for credit cards:

Department Stores	Cash 12% Bankcard 22% Other card 37%
Discount Department Stores	Cash 29% Bankcard 28% Other card 4%
Clothing Stores	Cash 8% Bankcard 32% Other card 14%
Gasoline Stations	Cash 56% Bankcard 6% Other card 27%
Local Restaurants	Cash 57% Bankcard 24% Other card 8%
Non-local Restaurants	Cash 54% Bankcard 29% Other card 10%

Of course, this preference for credit cards as a POS payment medium is complemented by the finding that Techies are significantly more likely than Mid-Americas to own department store cards (85%), gasoline cards (54%), bankcards (85%), other general purpose cards such as Discover or Choice (30%) and T&E cards (31%).

General Banking and Financial Attitudes

Despite the above behavioral differences — which also are a reflection of the Techies segment's greater affluence — when it comes to attitudes about banking, financial services and the economy in general, Techies are not very different from Mid-America. The two financial institution attributes that this segment gave the highest average importance ratings to were the same as Mid-America's top two — accurate bookkeeping and reasonable service charges on checking accounts. Even the scores were the same, 4.8 on a 5-point scale.

Techies did tend to attach less importance than Mid-America to the attribute of having friendly tellers (weighted average score 3.9 versus 4.4), and to attach more importance to an institution's having convenient

ATMs (3.8 versus 3.5). But the scores for both segments put both of these attributes in the "somewhat important" range.

There were also few notable differences in the weighted average agreement ratings for selected statements concerning financial services and the economy. Like Mid-America households, Techies were virtually unanimous in their disagreement with the statement "I would be willing to pay $25 more per year for basic checking account services in exchange for improved service" (weighted average score = -.75). And they were more likely than Mid-America households to disagree with the statement "I do not mind periodic reasonable price increases for financial services" (score = -.55).

Techies did agree with two statements that Mid-Americas were more ambivalent about. "The need to borrow funds would override any tax considerations on the deductibility of interest expense," and "Given the general condition of the economy, this is a good time to buy a house" earned weighted average agreement scores of 3.5 each among Techies while Mid-Americas rated them .17 and .20, respectively.

And, perhaps paralleling a recent Gallup Poll finding that affluent households are less altruistic than households that are less well off, the statement "Financial institutions should provide low cost basic services to the economically disadvantaged" achieved a weighted average agreement score of only .19 among Techies, who were less likely than any other segment to agree with this statement.

Alternative Delivery Systems Usage and Attitudes

A substantial percentage of Techies households currently use electronic methods of managing and transacting their financial business, suggesting not only that their financial needs are greater because they are more affluent, but also that they may be more sophisticated in their awareness of the advantages of electronic delivery methods.

As noted earlier, 67% use Automated Teller Machines; and this represents 89% of the 75% of households in this segment that deal with institutions that offer ATM services. More than half (58%) of those Techie households that deal with ATM providers say that they have ATM service available to them in retail locations. And households in this segment are more likely than their counterparts in Mid-America to use these ATMs to obtain cash before shopping (58% and 39%, respectively). ATM provider customers in the Techies segment are also more

Financial Product/Service Usage and Balances
GADGETEERS SEGMENT

	% Own	Mean Bal/ Owner	Median Bal/ Owner	Mean Bal/ Household	Median Bal/ Household
Deposit Accounts					
Regular Checking	65%	$2,195	$1,500	$1,427	$975
Interest Checking	56%	$3,323	$1,500	$1,861	$840
Regular Savings	75%	$3,906	$2,000	$2,930	$1,500
Certificate of Deposit	30%	$30,020	$15,000	$9,006	$4,500
Money Market Deposit Account	15%	$12,466	$7,500	$1,870	$1,125
				$17,094	$8,940
Credit Products					
First Mortgage	58%	$64,361	$62,500	$37,329	$36,250
Second Mortgage/ Home Equity Loan	12%	$22,089	$12,500	$2,651	$1,500
Home Equity Line of Credit	7%	$56,930	$12,500	$3,985	$875
Automobile Loan	51%	$7,207	$6,250	$3,676	$3,188
Secured Personal Loan	18%	$4,069	$1,750	$732	$315
Unsecured Personal Loan	12%	$4,223	$3,750	$507	$450
Unsecured Personal Line of Credit	12%	$2,989	$1,750	$359	$210
MasterCard Credit Card	53%	$1,718	$500	$911	$265
Visa Credit Card	62%	$1,235	$500	$766	$310
Broker Margin Account	4%	$15,058	$5,000	$629	$209
				$51,545	$43,572
Investment Products					
Money Market Mutual Fund	12%	$14,971	$2,500	$1,797	$300
Stock Mutual Fund	14%	$17,566	$17,500	$2,459	$2,450
Bond Mutual Fund	6%	$15,057	$7,500	$903	$450
Other Mutual Fund	6%	$11,499	$7,500	$690	$450
Stocks	29%	$20,379	$7,500	$5,910	$2,175
Corporate or Municipal Bonds	3%	$32,189	$7,500	$966	$225
Government Securities	9%	$7,037	$2,500	$650	$231
Real Estate Investments	24%	$94,699	$62,500	$22,270	$14,698
Whole Life Insurance Policies	51%	$69,948	$62,500	$35,673	$31,875
Universal Life Insurance Policies	21%	$96,597	$87,500	$20,285	$18,375
Insurance Annuities	11%	$42,391	$37,500	$4,663	$4,125
IRAs	44%	$17,620	$17,500	$7,753	$7,700
Keogh Accounts	3%	$26,655	$17,500	$800	$525
401 (k) Savings Plans	26%	$14,119	$2,500	$3,671	$650
				$108,490	$84,229
Estimated Financial Net Worth				**$74,039**	**$49,597**

Source: Payment Systems, Inc. (1988)

likely to say that their institution participates in a shared ATM network (62% versus 46%) and to have used local and non-local shared ATMs (57% and 49%, respectively). Interestingly, Techies are significantly less likely than Mid-America ATM users to use ATMs at drive-in branches —only 25% do this—and significantly more likely to use ATMs at work — 24% say they do. There are no significant differences between the percentages of Techies and Mid-America ATM users who would like to use ATMs, however.

Other alternative delivery systems that Techies are more likely than Mid-America households to use include point of sale debit cards (17%), direct deposit of salary (37%), and payroll deduction plans (25%).

Techies show considerable variability in their attitudes toward alternative delivery systems. There was no delivery system attitude statement in the survey instrument that a majority of Techies either agreed or disagreed with. The net result is, of course, that the weighted average agreement scores for these statements (Appendix Table 9) are all in the neutral range (-.25 through .25).

The statements that drew the greatest level of agreement were "It's hard to find time in my busy schedule for routine chores like paying bills" (score =.16, 46% agree) and "I dislike telephone answering machines" (score=.25, 44% agree). More than 40% also agreed with the statement "I wouldn't mind using a public terminal, similar to an ATM, for bill-paying." But 21% were neutral and 37% disagreed, resulting in a weighted average agreement score for the segment of .05.

The statement that drew the greatest level of disagreement was "I generally do not leave messages on telephone answering machines" (score = -.21, 47% disagree). It seems, then, that although this segment may not *like* these devices, they accept the necessity of dealing with the machines. And this may well be the segment's underlying attitude — technology, not for the sake of technology, but for the sake of doing a job effectively.

GADGETEERS SEGMENT CHARACTERISTICS

The Gadgeteers segment is just over one-fifth of the market. It has a very high level of consumer electronic equipment ownership, heavily weighted toward entertainment devices. In part, this ownership may be a result of above-average affluence. Its usage of credit is nearly identical to the Techie segment, but it holds less in investment products. That lower holding may also be a reflection of the younger age profile of this segment. Members of this segment include the young, emerging affluent households, those that have above average annual incomes and are more consumption oriented at this point in their lives than savings oriented. It is a highly attractive segment for financial institutions and its apparent love of gadgetry and demands for convenience make it a prime target for a new generation of financial service delivery devices in the home.

Main Financial Institution

Gadgeteer households are not significantly different from Mid-America in their choice of a primary financial institution. Fifty-five percent named a commercial bank as their main institution, 28% named a savings bank or savings and loan, and 15% named a credit union. Neither were they significantly different in the number of branch locations they usually use. Thirty-seven percent reported using only one branch location, and 38% said they used one or two. They were not even significantly more likely than Mid-America households to answer that they rarely used any location because they preferred ATMs. Nine percent of Gadgeteer households made this claim, as did 5% of the Mid-America segment.

What distinguishes the Gadgeteers segment's use of the traditional branch delivery system is the frequency with which they visit their main institution each month. The mean and median number of monthly visits is seven, compared to a mean of six and a median of only four for Mid-America and Techies segments. It should be noted that for all segments the number of visits to a main financial institution does not include visits to use an ATM.

Main Transaction Account

Gadgeteer households are more like Techies than Mid-America households in the type of account they usually use to pay most of their household expenses. About half (52%) of the Gadgeteers respondents named a regular checking account as their main transaction account. But nearly one third (31%) said theirs was a NOW or share draft account. And 9% usually pay their expenses from a SuperNOW account.

Also like Techies, Gadgeteer households write a lot of checks each month (mean and median = 27). The distribution of these checks by function is as follows:

To pay for purchases at stores	mean = 9, median = 8
To pay bills from home	mean = 13, median = 13
To obtain cash	mean = 1, median = 3
For other purposes	mean = 4, median = 3

In these households the female head is less likely than female heads in Mid-America households to be the primary bill payer, although she still serves this function in 50% of the cases. And the Gadgeteers segment is significantly more likely than any other segment to say that they have a written budget that they use to manage their spending. Thirty percent of the households in this segment make this assertion.

Sources of Cash

The fact that only 9% of Gadgeteer households claim they rarely use any branch locations because they prefer ATMs does not mean that Gadgeteers' households are not ATM users. In fact, 59% of all respondents in this segment, or 69% of the 85% of this segment that deals with ATM providers, claim they obtain cash from ATMs at least once a month. As in all segments except the No-Tech, the mean number of cash withdrawals made by Gadgeteers ATM users is five, and the median is four per month.

Other sources of cash explored by the survey instrument and the percentages of Gadgeteer households that use them are:

Cash back with deposit — 75%

Cash personal checks at financial institutions — 57%

Cash third-party checks at supermarket — 17%

Cash back from personal checks for purchases at supermarket — 46%

Cash personal checks without purchase at supermarket — 17%

Cash third-party checks at other retailers — 7%

Cash back from personal check for purchase at other retailers — 11%

Cash personal check without purchase at other retailers — 5%

Cash third-party checks at work — 6%

Cash personal checks at work — 14%

Receive pay in cash — 4%

On average, the typical Gadgeteer household uses about $357 in cash to meet its monthly routine cash needs. The median figure is $250 per month.

Payment Media Used at the Point of Sale

Gadgeteers are also more like Techies than like Mid-Americas in their ownership of credit cards and their choice of payment media at the point of sale. The vast majority of these households own department store credit cards (86%) and bank credit cards (85%). Nearly two out of three (60%) own gasoline company cards. More than a third have other general purpose cards (38%), and about one in four have T&E cards (27%).

The locations where a plurality of bank credit card owners are most likely to use their cards include airline ticket counters (55%), hotels and motels (50%), furniture and appliance stores (40%), and clothing stores (31%).

At the supermarket, Gadgeteers are less cash oriented than Mid-America and more likely to pay by check (57%), which is similar to the behavior of Techies. But when paying for medical or health services, the segment is less likely than either Techies or Mid-America to reach for their checkbook, although 57% do. Complete statistics on the kinds of POS payment media Gadgeteers shoppers use are presented in the Appendix.

General Banking and Financial Attitudes

Like Techies and Mid-America households, Gadgeteer respondents put accurate bookkeeping and reasonable service charges on the top of the list of important bank attributes. Although the weighted average scores that each of the three segments gave these attributes put them in the "very important" range, the weighted average score was only 4.6 in the Gadgeteers segment, whereas the scores for the other two segments were 4.8 on a 5-point scale. On average, the Gadgeteers segment attached as much importance (score = 4.6) to quick teller service as to bookkeeping accuracy and reasonable costs. Other than this, there were no notable differences between the importance Gadgeteers households attached to specific bank attributes and the weighted average importance scores computed for the other segments.

When it came to agreeing or disagreeing with the 19 attitude statements concerning financial services and the economy, Gadgeteers households were like Techies and Mid-America in almost unanimously disagreeing with the statements about being willing to pay $25 more per year for improved checking service (77% disagree) or to switch institutions for more location convenience if it meant higher fees (74% disagree).

However, this segment was significantly less likely than the other two to disagree with the statement "I do not mind periodic reasonable price increases for financial services." This is also the segment that was most likely to agree that they would switch financial institutions for better service at the same price (47% agreed) and least likely to agree that "most tellers are competent and well trained" (46% agreed). Thus, even though this segment's weighted average agreement score on the statement "The quality of service is basically the same among all banks and savings & loans" is a neutral -.01, there is some evidence that the segment is somewhat more sensitive to service quality than the other groups.

Finally, the Gadgeteers segment is like the Techies segment in its overall, lower than average propensity to disagree with the statement about preferring ATMs for routine financial transactions (weighted average agreement score = -.24) and its overall lower propensity to agree with the statement that financial institutions should provide lifeline services for the economically disadvantaged (weighted average agreement score .25). These scores put the Gadgeteer and Techie segments in the neutral range on these two issues while the other segments show a clear tendency to agree with the statement about lifeline banking and disagree with the statement about ATMs.

Alternative Delivery Systems Usage and Attitudes

The Gadgeteer segment is significantly more likely than Mid-America consumers to use automated teller machines (59%) and direct deposit of salary (19%). These percentages are significantly lower than the percentages of Techies that use these two alternative delivery systems; however, Gadgeteers are significantly more likely than Techies to use drive-in windows when they visit the branch. (See Appendix.)

Of the 85% of Gadgeteers respondents that deal with financial institutions that offer ATM services, 53% claim that they have ATM services available to them in retail locations. And of these, 43% use the machines to obtain cash before shopping while only 25% use them to check their account balances before they shop.

The figures for shared ATMs are similar. That is, 56% of Gadgeteers customers of ATM service providers say their financial institution participates in a shared ATM network, while 44% of those with shared services available use local shared machines and 28% use them out-of-town.

Overall Gadgeteer ATM user usage by location is as follows:

Financial institution branches	91%
Convenience stores	19%
Drive-in branches	29%
Supermarkets	32%
Shopping malls	41%
Airports	13%
Work	6%

The percentage of Gadgeteer ATM users who take advantage of ATMs in shopping malls is significantly greater than the percentages of other segments that use this location. And ATM users in this segment are significantly more likely than users in other segments to say they would like to use ATMs at convenience stores (28%) and supermarkets (46%).

While the distribution of the Gadgeteer segment's responses to the attitude statements concerning electronic delivery systems concepts were such that the weighted average agreement scores for all but one were in the neutral range (-.25 — .25), they differed significantly from Mid-America on many of the issues explored. Specifically, Gadgeteer households are significantly more likely than Mid-America households to agree that:

"I would be more likely to use the telephone for bill-paying if I could see my transactions on my TV screen at the same time" (48% agree).

"I would like to have access to easy-to-use programs on public information terminals to help me make decisions such as when to invest in an IRA, or which type of mortgage is best" (39% agree).

"I would be interested in an information service that would regularly produce an income statement and balance sheet for my household" (37% agree).

"I wouldn't mind using a public terminal, similar to an ATM for bill-paying" (37% agree).

"It's hard to find time in my busy schedule for routine chores like paying bills" (36% agree).

"I am familiar with the delivery of services electronically, such as services provided through data bases, videotex, and home banking projects" (26% agree).

This segment is also significantly less likely to disagree that:

"I am using offices or branches of financial institutions much less frequently than two years ago" (36% disagree).

"I would prefer to be able to use the telephone for more of my financial transactions" (44% disagree).

"I would prefer to use the mail for routine financial transactions such as deposits, loan payments, etc." (45% disagree).

And Gadgeteer households are more likely than Mid-America to disagree that:

"I feel uncomfortable when I hear computer-synthesized voices over the telephone" (37% disagree).

"I dislike telephone answering machines" (34% disagree).

"I generally do not leave messages on telephone answering machines" (52% disagree).

The last statement was the only one that drew a majority response. Like Techies, 44% of Gadgeteers agree that they dislike telephone answering machines. But most of them leave messages anyway. As noted in a previous report, it seems possible that individuals who respond this way may not "dislike telephone answering machines" because of the technology, but because a message on a machine usually means having to wait for someone to call back before the purpose of the original call can be achieved.

PROCRASTINATORS SEGMENT CHARACTERISTICS

At first glance, one might dismiss the Procrastinators segment as unimportant because it is only 10% of the market and clearly is reluctant to respond quickly to any innovation. However, there are reasons to examine this segment, nonetheless. For one, it is more affluent than average, although not dramatically so. This segment undoubtedly contains a high number of "Depression-era" households. These are older consumers of moderate income and moderate education, who have a generally conservative approach to all aspects of their financial activities. They have relatively high levels of usage of direct deposit, probably reflecting that many are Social Security recipients, and relatively low levels of transaction account activity, suggesting that they are not consumption-oriented households like Gadgeteers or Techies. While preferring the personal service of in-branch personnel, these consumers offer opportunities for financial institutions because they are not costly to serve and retain investment balances that are above average.

Financial Product/Service Usage and Balances
PROCRASTINATORS SEGMENT

	% Own	Mean Bal/ Owner	Median Bal/ Owner	Mean Bal/ Household	Median Bal/ Household
Deposit Accounts					
Regular Checking	58%	$2,150	$750	$1,247	$435
Interest Checking	44%	$2,958	$1,500	$1,302	$660
Regular Savings	47%	$3,670	$1,500	$1,725	$705
Certificate of Deposit	29%	$27,234	$10,000	$7,898	$2,900
Money Market Deposit Account	16%	$11,225	$7,500	$1,796	$1,200
				$13,968	$5,900
Credit Products					
First Mortgage	34%	$38,508	$37,500	$13,093	$12,750
Second Mortgage/ Home Equity Loan	5%	$25,870	$12,500	$1,294	$625
Home Equity Line of Credit	6%	$6,447	$0	$387	$0
Automobile Loan	32%	$4,060	$1,750	$1,299	$560
Secured Personal Loan	12%	$4,744	$3,750	$569	$450
Unsecured Personal Loan	9%	$4,001	$3,750	$360	$338
Unsecured Personal Line of Credit	5%	$3,791	$500	$190	$25
MasterCard Credit Card	22%	$1,764	$500	$388	$110
Visa Credit Card	29%	$1,575	$500	$457	$145
Broker Margin Account	6%	$32,018	$5,000	$1,940	$303
				$19,977	$15,306
Investment Products					
Money Market Mutual Fund	10%	$24,824	$17,500	$2,482	$1,750
Stock Mutual Fund	11%	$29,800	$17,500	$3,278	$1,925
Bond Mutual Fund	6%	$38,157	$17,500	$2,289	$1,050
Other Mutual Fund	3%	$23,556	$17,500	$707	$525
Stocks	19%	$36,762	$10,000	$6,985	$1,900
Corporate or Municipal Bonds	5%	$46,895	$62,500	$2,345	$3,125
Government Securities	6%	$23,918	$2,500	$1,329	$139
Real Estate Investments	18%	$78,384	$62,500	$13,856	$11,048
Whole Life Insurance Policies	40%	$53,399	$37,500	$21,360	$15,000
Universal Life Insurance Policies	9%	$48,313	$12,500	$4,348	$1,125
Insurance Annuities	9%	$42,616	$12,500	$3,835	$1,125
IRAs	31%	$19,051	$17,500	$5,906	$5,425
Keogh Accounts	2%	$39,608	$17,500	$792	$350
401 (k) Savings Plans	14%	$21,325	$7,500	$2,986	$1,050
				$72,498	$45,537
Estimated Financial Net Worth				**$66,489**	**$36,131**

Source: Payment Systems, Inc. (1988)

Main Financial Institution

Procrastinator households are like Mid-America and Techie households in the types of institutions they name as their main source of financial services. Fifty-nine percent deal primarily with a commercial bank, 23% with a savings bank or savings association, 14% with a credit union, and 2% with some other financial service provider. The number of branch locations they use is not different from Mid-America either. Forty-three percent say they use only one location, and 27% say they use one or two. The only notable difference between this segment and the three segments already discussed is the mean number of visits Procrastinators make each month to their main financial institution, which is only 4. However, the median number of visits for this segment is also 4, the same as the median for Techies and Mid-America households.

Primary Transaction Account

Similarly, there is no significant difference between the percentage of Procrastinator households and the percentage of Mid-America households that use each type of transaction accounts listed in the survey as their main transaction account. Fifty-eight percent use regular checking, 18% use a NOW or share draft account, 6% use a Super NOW, and 3% use their regular savings accounts to pay most of their household expenses. Five percent of Procrastinator households have no checking account.

Again, however, their level of account usage, measured as monthly check writing volume, is significantly lower than Mid-America's. Procrastinator households write, on average, only 9 checks per month, and the median monthly volume is 11. The mean and median numbers of bills paid from home each month — 10 and 8, respectively — are the same as the numbers reported by Mid-America households. But Procrastinators write fewer checks to pay for purchases at stores and for other purposes.

Also in this segment the bill paying chores are more likely to be shared by the male and female heads of households. Twenty percent of Procrastinator respondents reported they shared bill-paying chores with their spouses, compared to 14% in Mid-America. In Mid-America, females are more likely to be the primary bill payers in 59% of the households, while the proportion among the Procrastinator segment is only 45%.

Sources of Cash

Procrastinator households are significantly less likely than Mid-America to regularly obtain cash in connection with making a bank deposit. Sixty-three percent of this segment does so, compared to 72% of Mid-America. On the other hand, 66% of Procrastinators get their pocket money, which averagse $349 per month, by cashing personal checks at financial institutions, while only 57% of Mid-America households reported doing this. The factor underlying these differences appears to be age. Procrastinators are more likely to be Social Security direct depositors. Thus the option of getting cash back with a deposit is less likely to be available to them, and cashing a personal check at their financial institution is the alternative they choose to obtain cash. Aside from these differences, and the Procrastinators segment's being less likely to cash personal checks at work, the percentages of Mid-America and Procrastinator households using alternative sources of cash are roughly the same.

Payment Media Used at the Point of Sale

While it was noted earlier that Procrastinators write significantly fewer checks at stores to pay for purchases than the other segments discussed to this point, the data suggest that the reason is not that Procrastinators prefer other alternatives (Appendix Table 5). In fact, this segment is more likely than Mid-America to pay by check when shopping at discount stores, and as likely to pay by check at other locations where they are less likely to pay by cash (i.e., drug stores, gasoline stations, local and non-local restaurants). Furthermore, the kinds of purchases that this segment is less likely than Mid-America to pay for by check (medical and health services and airline tickets) are not what one would expect a respondent to think about when asked how many checks they write at stores. Given this evidence, it may be concluded that Procrastinators probably write fewer checks to pay for purchases at stores simply because they shop less frequently.

Similarly, the Procrastinators segment is significantly more likely than Mid-America households to own gasoline company, travel and entertainment, and other general purpose credit cards (Appendix Table 4). However, they are not significantly more likely to use credit cards at gas stations or other locations. The only difference is that while Mid-America households tend to use their bankcards to pay for airline tickets and hotel or motel rooms, Procrastinators are more likely to use their T&E cards.

General Banking and Financial Attitudes

The financial institution attributes that are most important to Procrastinator households are generally the same as those Mid-America considers important. The two attributes that ranked highest on this segment's list are accurate bookkeeping and easy to read statements, both of which achieved a weighted average importance score of 4.5 — very important. These are followed closely by reasonable service charges on checking and courteous personnel, which achieved weighted average scores of 4.4 each. On average, Procrastinators attach slightly less importance to branches that are close to home or work and to quick teller service. The Mid-America's weighted average scores for these two attributes were 4.5 each, putting them in the very important range, while the Procrastinators scores for these were 4.1 and 4.2, respectively, which places them in the somewhat important range. And this segment gave convenient ATMs a weighted average importance score of 3.3 (neutral) compared to the 3.5 (somewhat important) rating ATMs received from Mid-America.

Overall, the segment does seem to be slightly less price sensitive than Techies and Mid-America households. The weighted average agreement scores for Procrastinator responses to statements about being willing to pay $25 more for better basic checking service (-.67) and being willing to consider switching to a more convenient institution even if it cost more (-.55) indicate that overall the segment is less likely than any other to disagree with these ideas.

Personal relationships with financial institution staff also seems to be somewhat more important to the Procrastinator segment than to others. It was the only segment whose average scores on the statements about being reluctant to switch financial institutions because of having a comfortable relationship with a staff member (.03) and preferring to deal with the same individual even if that meant waiting (.06) were on the positive rather than the negative side of the neutral range.

Alternative Delivery Systems Usage and Attitudes

The Procrastinators segment differs significantly from Mid-America in alternative delivery system usage in only two ways. It is significantly more likely to use direct deposit of payroll (20% versus 11%), and significantly less likely to use drive-in windows (38% versus 52%). Despite the substantial difference in the median ages of the two segments, there is only a 3 percentage point difference (not statistically significant) between the proportion of Procrastinators' households that are ATM users (37%) and the proportion of Mid-America households that use ATMs (40%).

Nevertheless, the segment's weighted average responses to the electronic delivery system concept statements contained in the survey

Financial Product/Service Usage and Balances
NO-TECH SEGMENT

	% Own	Mean Bal/ Owner	Median Bal/ Owner	Mean Bal/ Household	Median Bal/ Household
Deposit Accounts					
Regular Checking	68%	$1,654	$750	$1,125	$510
Interest Checking	49%	$3,095	$1,500	$1,517	$735
Regular Savings	60%	$2,442	$750	$1,465	$450
Certificate of Deposit	34%	$27,194	$15,000	$9,246	$5,100
Money Market Deposit Account	16%	$9,844	$7,500	$1,575	$1,200
				$14,928	$7,995"
Credit Products					
First Mortgage	22%	$26,319	$12,500	$5,790	$2,750
Second Mortgage/ Home Equity Loan	2%	$9,247	$12,500	$185	$250
Home Equity Line of Credit	5%	$6,881	$0	$344	$0
Automobile Loan	13%	$4,107	$1,750	$534	$228
Secured Personal Loan	7%	$3,091	$1,750	$216	$123
Unsecured Personal Loan	3%	$3,870	$500	$116	$15
Unsecured Personal Line of Credit	5%	$2,481	$0	$124	$0
MasterCard Credit Card	25%	$1,209	$500	$302	$125
Visa Credit Card	29%	$667	$500	$193	$145
Broker Margin Account	3%	$9,586	$5,000	$275	$143
				$8,079	$3,779
Investment Products					
Money Market Mutual Fund	13%	$14,552	$2,500	$1,892	$325
Stock Mutual Fund	8%	$17,006	$5,000	$1,360	$400
Bond Mutual Fund	5%	$35,426	$17,500	$1,771	$875
Other Mutual Fund	2%	$20,686	$7,500	$414	$150
Stocks	14%	$23,044	$10,000	$3,226	$1,400
Corporate or Municipal Bonds	3%	$50,796	$62,500	$1,524	$1,875
Government Securities	6%	$12,652	$2,500	$778	$154
Real Estate Investments	10%	$35,619	$12,500	$3,649	$1,281
Whole Life Insurance Policies	35%	$39,126	$37,500	$13,694	$13,125
Universal Life Insurance Policies	3%	$61,882	$37,500	$1,856	$1,125
Insurance Annuities	6%	$35,551	$12,500	$2,133	$750
IRAs	20%	$11,422	$7,500	$2,284	$1,500
Keogh Accounts	2%	$15,990	$2,500	$320	$50
401 (k) Savings Plans	6%	$15,092	$7,500	$906	$450
				$35,807	$23,460
Estimated Financial Net Worth				**$42,656**	**$27,676**

Source: Payment Systems, Inc. (1988)

instrument indicate that Procrastinatorshouseholds are less negative toward many of the ideas than Mid-America. For example, the segment's weighted average score vis à vis the statement "I would prefer to be able to use the telephone for more of my financial transactions" was only -.35 compared to Mid-America's -.42.

The respective scores on the statement "I would prefer to use the mail for routine financial transactions such as deposits, loan payments, etc." were -.21 (Procrastinators) and -.31 (Mid-America). And the Procrastinators segment's weighted average score on the statement about being familiar with videotex was -.17 (neutral) while Mid-America's was -.31 (disagree). On average, the older Procrastinators segment was even less likely than the younger Mid-Americans to agree with the statement "I dislike telephone answering machines" (weighted average scores were .30 and .41, respectively). Thus the Procrastinators segment's usage rates on electronic delivery systems are interpreted in much the same way as data about the segment's ownership of consumer electronic devices. That is, individuals in this segment are reasonably comfortable with advanced delivery system concepts, but they use only those products that fit their unique personal needs.

NO-TECH SEGMENT CHARACTERISTICS

The No-Tech segment, which is 12% of the market, is the least wealthy and least financially active of the segments. A color television set essentially defines the extent of its consumer electronics ownership. The demographic averages for this segment somewhat distort its profile, because it tends to contain households that fall at the older and younger ends of the age spectrum. The younger households have higher education levels, which suggest that their "No-Tech" status is more reflective of a student lifestyle in which lack of income prevents consumer electronics ownership, not lack of desire. At the other end of the spectrum, the majority of these households are older retired households whose holdings of various investment products pull up the average balances of the segment more than might be anticipated based on income alone.

Main Financial Institution

No-Tech households differ significantly from Mid-America in their choice of primary financial institutions. Although a majority (51%) say that their main source of financial services is a commercial bank, this proportion is 10 percentage points lower than the 61% of Mid-America households who deal primarily with a commercial bank. Most of this difference goes instead to savings banks and savings and loan associations, which 30% of No-Tech households name as their main DFI. Fourteen percent say their primary institution is a credit union, and 3% say it is some other type of financial service provider. Whether this difference results in No-Tech households having fewer branch location alternatives available to them or not cannot be determined from the data. However, a significantly larger than average proportion (55%) claim they usually use only one branch location. Twenty-five percent use only one or two.

Primary Transaction Account

Despite the difference in choice of primary institution, the percentages of No-Tech households that say they pay most of their household expenses from regular checking and other types of accounts are substantially the same as the percentages reported by Mid-America. Fifty-eight percent indicate that regular checking is their primary account. Twenty-three percent say it is a NOW or share draft account, and 6% pay most of their household expenses from a SuperNOW account. Five percent say they have no checking account of any type.

The No-Tech segment is more like Procrastinators in its average monthly check writing volume. Both the mean and the median number of checks written by No-Tech households are 11, and in this segment the male head of household is significantly more likely to be the principal bill payer than he is in Mid-America households.

Sources of Cash

In keeping with their having the lowest median income and lowest average household net worth of all the segments identified by the cluster analysis, No-Tech households also report the lowest monthly routine cash needs. On average (mean), No-Tech households spend about $253 per month in cash. The median value for the segment is $150.

The various methods of obtaining this cash that were listed in the survey are used by fairly typical proportions of No-Tech households. Like other segments that are above average users of direct deposit of payroll (Techies) and Social Security (Procrastinators), No-Tech households are significantly less likely than Mid-America to obtain cash in conjunction with making a deposit at a financial institution. Nevertheless, this is still the cash access method used by the largest percentage of households in this segment (61%), and it is followed closely by cashing personal checks at financial institutions, which 57% of the segment reports doing at least once a month. The most outstanding aspect of the No-Tech segment's cash access behavior, however, is the very low percentage who cash personal checks at supermarkets without making a purchase. Only 7% of this segment reports doing this regularly, while 12% to 17% of the other four segments regularly take advantage of supermarket check cashing services.

Payment Media Used at the Point of Sale

Although households in the No-Tech segment typically use only about $250 per month to meet their routine cash needs, they are much more cash oriented than other segments when paying for purchases at the point of sale. For example, 70% of No-Tech respondents who had shopped at a supermarket during the 12 months that preceded the survey reported that they paid for their last supermarket purchase in cash. In contrast, only 40% to 55% of other segments last used cash at the grocery store. Other types of locations where No-Tech shoppers are significantly more likely than Mid-America to pay cash are:

Local restaurants — 85% of diners in this segment last paid cash

Drug stores — 65% of shoppers in this segment last paid cash

Discount department stores — 54% of shoppers in this segment last paid cash

Department stores — 32% of shoppers in this segment last paid cash

In department stores and discount department stores, the above average level of cash usage was offset by No-Tech household's below average usage of credit cards. In other locations (specifically, furniture/appliance stores and clothing stores), their cash usage was in line with that of Mid-America, but the percentage paying by check was above that norm. Fifty-six percent of No-Tech shoppers at furniture and appliance stores paid for their last purchase in cash, and 39% of No-Tech shoppers at clothing stores did so. And at these locations No-Tech households were once again less likely than Mid-America to use credit cards.

Of course, given their household incomes, the low usage of credit cards should come as no surprise. Table 4 in the Appendix shows that the No-Tech segment is significantly less likely than Mid-America to own all types of credit cards except T&E cards. (Twelve percent of households in both segments own T&E cards). An anomaly that No-Tech households share with the Procrastinators segment is an above average level of ownership of "other" types of credit card accounts. However, no single "other" type of card was mentioned by enough respondents (i.e., >.05%) to be specifically identified in the data analysis.

General Banking and Financial Attitudes

The weighted average importance ratings for financial institution attributes that were derived from the responses of the No-Tech segment are approximately the same as those of other segments. The two attributes whose scores put them in the very important range were accurate bookkeeping (score = 4.6) and reasonable service charges on checking (score = 4.5). Most attributes were rated, on average, as somewhat important, although the weighted average scores for quick teller service (4.2) and convenient drive-through windows (3.6) were lower than those for the Mid-America segment, which gave quick teller service a very important rating of 4.5 and convenient drive through windows a somewhat important 3.9. And the segment was neutral toward "branches all over town" (score = 3.4), convenient ATMs (score = 3.2), attractive facilities (score = 3.0) and branches or offices in other states (score = 2.9).

Although the No-Tech segment was the segment most likely to disagree that they would pay $25 a year more for basic checking service in exchange for better service (82% disagreed), it was least likely, and significantly less likely than Mid-America and Techies segments, to disagree with the statement "I do not mind periodic reasonable price increases for financial services" (50% disagree). Furthermore, the No-Tech segment was the one most likely to agree that "Switching financial institutions is just too much trouble" (48% agree).

Overall, the segment's responses to the general banking attitude statements contained in the survey leave one with the impression that to No-Tech households, banking is just a necessity that they have to pay for, and as long as they can accomplish their banking quickly (62% agreed that "It doesn't matter who provides the service as long as I can conduct my banking quickly" compared to 51% to 57% of the other segments), they are not going to move their accounts.

The segment is also significantly different from Mid-America, Techies, and Gadgeteers households when it comes to the question of lifeline banking. Sixty-four percent of No-Tech households agree that "Financial institutions should provide low cost basic services to the economically disadvantaged." The comparable percentages for the other segments are:

Techies	43%
Gadgeteers	48%
Mid-America	52%
Procrastinators	61%

Thus, there appears to be an inverse relationship between technology ownership and a positive attitude toward lifeline banking, which undoubtedly reflects relative income differences.

Alternative Delivery System Usage and Attitudes

When the No-Tech segment's usage of electronic financial delivery systems is examined, the responses are as the data already discussed would suggest. This is the segment least likely to use ATMs (35%). Interestingly, it is not significantly less likely than Mid-America (40%) or Procrastinators (37%) households to do so, confirming that ATMs are no longer an innovative service but a commodity and, to financial institutions, a competitive necessity.

The No-Tech segment is also the one most likely to use direct deposit of social security, (23% do) but is not significantly more likely to do so than the Procrastinator segment, which has the same median age. And, like the Procrastinator households, the No-Tech segment is significantly less likely than the remaining three segments to use drive-in windows regularly. Again, these are delivery systems that have been around a long time and are no longer considered innovative products. Usage of direct deposit may not be as much a reflection of attitudes toward technology as it is a reflection of attitudes relating to the issue of control.

Finally, the No-Tech households are less likely than any other segment to use automatic bill payment services. Only 13% do so. This, of course, also follows naturally from the earlier finding that the No Tech segment segment is less likely to have many types of loans or to own life insurance products.

Turning to the segment's responses to the statements concerning electronic delivery systems concepts, the No-Tech segment has the lowest weighted average agreement scores of the five segments with regard to the following statements:

"I would prefer to be able to use the phone for more of my financial transactions" (score = -.44, 59% disagree).

"I am familiar with the delivery of services electronically, such as services provided through data bases, videotex, and home banking projects" (score = -.44, 54% disagree).

"It's hard to find time in my busy schedule for routine chores like paying bills" (score = -.37, 50% disagree).

"I would prefer to use the mail for routine financial transactions such as deposits, loan payments, etc." (score = -.34, 52% disagree).

"I would like a payment plan for my utility bills that averages them so each payment is the same" (score = -.26, 50% disagree).

"I would be interested in an information service that would regularly produce an income statement and balance sheet for my household" (score = -.21, 44% disagree).

"I would be more likely to use the telephone for bill-paying if I could see my transactions on my TV screen at the same time" (score = -.21, 45% disagree).

"I would like to have access to easy-to-use programs on public information terminals to help me make decisions such as when to invest in an IRA, or which type of mortgage is best" (score = -.07, 45% neutral, 30% disagree).

And the segment has the highest average agreement score on the statement "Using an automatic payment service might result in my inadvertently overdrafting my account" (score = .26, 47% agree). All of this confirms the interpretation of this group of respondents as No-Tech individuals, people who have a low knowledge of, interest in, and perceived need for electronic delivery systems, not simply people who cannot afford to own the consumer electronic devices that are available today.

SUMMARY OF SEGMENT CHARACTERISTICS

This segmentation by consumer electronics ownership characteristics proves to also be somewhat of a lifestage segmentation. Observing the varying usages of credit and investment products suggests that marketing efforts can be better focused with understanding of the characteristics of the segments when particular delivery systems are being promoted in addition to particular financial products.

Overall, however, the most significant finding is that strategies for delivering financial services must concentrate on the financial institution's ability to integrate and automate its delivery systems.

Electronics ownership suggests some directions for the introduction of new in-home devices, but in the larger picture, that represents a small portion of the financial services market. Once again, this reinforces the argument that financial institutions must first look inward in examining delivery system automation. When such structures are in place, information on the consumer market can be used to effectively promote usage of various electronic delivery systems.

CHAPTER

5

ATMs: Electronic Delivery That Works

ATM MARKET TRENDS

At one time offering automated teller machines was seen as a means of using electronic banking automation to provide an institution with a competitive advantage. Now ATMs generally are seen as a competitive necessity. Services increasingly are generic and available from any machine anywhere, although fees may be involved, while cash access is the single unique function of an ATM that no other automated service provides. Nonetheless, they represent the clearest success in electronic delivery automation.

When ATMs were first introduced, it was felt that their use would decrease the burden on tellers, thereby paying for the machines and increasing the efficiency of banking operations. In most cases this did not occur. ATMs tend to generate two transactions for each teller transaction that is displaced, doubling the potential level at which any cost displacement occurs. Furthermore, there has been a belated realization that discouraging customers from entering the financial institution's premises means that opportunities for marketing of additional products and services is foregone.

Since turning back the clock is a nostalgic fantasy and ATMs are a competitive necessity, providers of ATM services must deal with the economic tradeoffsof using automation. Adding a fee to ATM transactions is becoming commonplace. It seems to result in an initial decrease in transactions, followed by a gradual return to earlier usage levels and a resumption of growth. Consumers demonstrate that they are willing to pay for the convenience of ready access to funds.

ATM users tend to be active users of a variety of financial services and are desirable customers in general. In fact, ATM usage itself is a likely indicator of a customer willing to consider other non-traditional financial products. This suggests possible success in the sales of other products through the ATM, such as postage stamps and travelers checks, or selling additional financial products and services to ATM users, such as automatic bill payment services and loan services. ATM users tend to express greater interest in various products such as automated bill payments, telephone bill payments and bank by phone, and tend to be the most likely prospects for loan services such as automobile loans and lines of credit.

The trip to an automated teller machine has become routine for many consumers, but the action that has transpired over the past few years among ATM owners and others involved in offering remote banking technology has been anything but routine. Consumer usage is on the increase, both in terms of households using machines and in transaction volume; mergers of networks have been proposed and some completed; new technologies such as satellite communications have been applied to ATM communications, and enhancements such as coin dispensing machines have been created. But that's not all. The government has tested using ATMs as part of its strategy to deliver various public benefits through electronic payments, and consumers have shown they will accept various new services from ATMs in a variety of new places. These are but a few of the most important changes over the past few years regarding ATMs.

ATM TRANSACTIONS INCREASING BY DOUBLE DIGITS

ATMs definitely have caught the attention of consumers. According to an estimate by *Bank Network News*, about 500 million transactions per month were made through ATMs in 1990. That's nearly 700,000 transactions per hour every day. It's more than double the 2.5 billion transactions estimated in 1984 and represents double-digit growth on an annual basis. Such news on the surface would seem pleasant to any business involved in ATMs, and it is. However, now that volumes are up, the focus on the machines is changing. Increasingly, profitability analysis is applied to ATMs.

How profitability is measured and how to improve that profitability is important in light of studies such as that recently issued by Speer and Associates. The Atlanta-based group reported in 1988 that ATM operations of U.S. financial institutions would have an aggregate loss of $1.3 billion after total earnings of $856 million. That nets out at a loss of 68 cents per transaction. The firm based its report on a survey of the 100 largest shared ATM networks and 308 largest proprietary ATM systems. Some machine owners already know that picture too well.

Efforts to offset some of those costs have begun in earnest. Growth in interstate banking, bankers' willingness to share once-proprietary networks to increase market share, increased significance of national networks and an increasing number of third-party processors have all been factors contributing to changes in regional network operations over the last few years. That change has been particularly noticeable through consolidation efforts designed to achieve economies of scale, stronger market presence and profitability.

On a small scale there have been agreements such as that between Eastman Kodak and Chase Manhattan Bank. In late 1988, the Eastman Savings and Loan Association took the opportunity to expand its own 24-ATM network by hooking up with one of Chase Manhattan Bank's subsidiaries in Rochester, New York, home of Kodak. With the Chase agreement, employees had access to another 130 machines. Several months later the machines were hooked into the PLUS and NYCE ATM networks and the conveniences were expanded. Company officials saw the move as another benefit to employees while the networks and other ATM owners saw an opportunity to broaden their bases.

An example of consolidation on a large scale was the proposed merger in early 1989 of four super-regional Southeastern ATM networks. The four—Honor in Florida, Avail in Georgia, MOST in Virginia and Relay in the Carolinas—in January signed a letter of intent to merge after studying the option for more than a year.

The owners of these networks believed their decision would provide economies of scale, greater consumer convenience and help speed up the introduction of other electronic payment services, presumably, debit at the point of sale.

Industry analysts said the merger was inevitable following the advent of regional banking that began in 1984. After many of the banks in the Southeast crossed state lines to expanding their banking base, they also were forced to join other networks. It was believed the merger would reduce the duplication that had been built into the networks' operations.

But in August 1989 MOST pulled out. MOST, the largest of the four networks with about 38% of the estimated 60 million ATM transactions per month that the new group would have handled, was satisfied to stay independent. A consultant had told the network it was sitting on a golden franchise, and there was no compelling need to merge or consolidate. Without MOST, the network is still expected to have a 14-million card base, 6,972 on-line ATMS and 40 million monthly transactions, according to figures from industry tracker *Bank Network News*.

Following the initial announcement in the Southeast, prognosticators speculated the action could spur other mergers such as a Midwest group comprised of Tyme, Cash Station and Shazam or an eastern group comprised of New York Cash Exchange and MAC.

Meanwhile, other prognosticators said regional networks could survive by being innovative and offering new products to increase revenue. One example is Metroteller, which runs a utility bill payment program for most of the major utility companies in New York state; sells home security systems with its staff that is already on board 24 hours each day; and offers a service to auto dealers to route credit applications and credit reports to financial institutions from the dealership. That added volume is critical to survival for some networks so they can provide lower transaction prices. Generally, transaction prices are in the 12-cent per transaction range and projections are that the fee will drop to 2 to 5 cents. Perhaps no better example of the emerging price war was Visa's offer to switch transactions for free for a period of time as part of a compensation package if several regionals would join the proposed super-regional network in the Southeast.

ATMs LINKED VIA SATELLITE

While the mergers might bring down transaction fees, other cost-cutting measures have been found. First Union Corporation, the five-state, 677-branch financial institution, went to the skies to reduce telecommunication expenses. By the end of the 1990 summer, more than 650 offices in the Carolinas, Georgia and Florida will be networked via satellite.

ATM activity at the First Union branches is beamed to GSTAR II, a satellite owned by GTE Spacenet Corporation, a subsidiary of GTE Corporation, and contracted to other businesses such as Kmart Corporation, Days Inn of America and Prudential-Bache. The system is rated as 99.6% reliable compared to 98% for land-based phone lines. It's faster, too. The bank calculates that for each 1% improvement in accuracy, its more than 500 ATMs will be available for an additional seven hours per month. In addition, if one second can be eliminated from each of the 500,000 customer transactions sent across phone lines, nearly 140 hours a day will be saved. The overall cost savings First Union is expected to gain is $3 million in the first five years of the operation.

Institutions such as First Union have looked to cut costs, and others such as the National Bank of Commerce have sought to increase income. The Memphis, Tennessee-based bank, in what is believed to be the first such arrangement, began to offer food coupons along with cash withdrawals from 50 ATMs on Memorial Day weekend 1989: 33 in Kroger supermarkets and 17 in bank branches. When ATM users received cash, they also received a money-savings coupon for one of eight food items. There were different food coupons for each of the eight weeks the pilot project was operated.

While the number of ATM transactions did not increase, the rate of decreased card use experienced in the months preceding the coupon giveaway slowed. Bank officials believed transactions did not increase because of limitations on the monetary combinations that could be received from the machine. Typically, the machines had $10 and $20 dispensers. Any monetary amount with a multiple of 10 could be received. When the coupons were inserted into the machines, the $10 dispenser was eliminated in lieu of the coupons. That meant neither $10 nor $50 could be withdrawn, two of the more popular cash choices of ATM users.

National Bank of Commerce had begun the project to provide an additional service for customers and to generate an anticipated 10% increase in foreign fees by attracting customers that held ATM cards from other institutions. The bank expense for the program was $35,000 for software modifications. Advertising expenses related to the coupon giveaway were paid by Campbell's, the distributors of the coupons.

Cuts in expenses by First Union and additional income sought by National Bank of Commerce were progressive and without controversy. But not all efforts to bring profitability to ATMs have been without argument. There has been the issue of surcharges. In October 1988, Valley National Bank of Nevada began charging $1 to ATM card holders other than its own at 63 Valley machines. Customers using the machines were informed about the charge through a message on the screen. At that point, they had the option of continuing the transaction with an automatic debit to their accounts or not. A couple of months after the practice began, the Plus network said it wouldn't accommodate such surcharges. Among the organization's concerns was how the surcharges might depress ATM volumes — and subsequently network revenue — and how surcharges would affect pricing. The Plus interchange, as most others, had all revenue flowing from the card issuer, not the ATM owner.

It wasn't the first such case in which a financial institution wanted to add a surcharge, however. In 1988, Transfirst Corporation in Texas sued the Pulse regional network after the network lowered its interchange fee. Transfirst, with more machines than card holders, knew the action would cut into its revenues, and it went to court. Eventually, the case was brought before an arbitrator, who decided Pulse was in violation of anti-trust laws by setting the interchange rate without allowing members to tack on surcharges. This "free-market" approach would allow customers to decide whether or not they wanted to incur various charges to use a particular machine. Theoretically, machine owners could then price the machines accordingly. The debate over whether consumers will pay fees is practically nonexistent. Fees for foreign transactions have become common, and the trend has turned to charging customers for using their own bank's ATMs. The surcharges provide a third scenario. The questions that haven't been answered except in research studies are: How much will consumers pay before bypassing the ATM; are they aware of varying fees; will fees cause transaction levels to fall; and, at what point?

Controlling the financial side of the ATM balance sheet has become much of the focus for machine owners, but consumers haven't been forgotten.

CONSUMER ATM USAGE REACHING MAJORITY

And who are those consumers? PSI research in 1987 showed 35% of U.S. households used ATMs at least once per month to get cash, which was the same as 50% of households who had the service available to them. By 1989, the percentage of all households using ATMs month-ly had climbed to 44%, which included usage within some younger, more affluent segments of as high as two-thirds or more of such households who had ATM service available from their primary institution.

Generally, users who visit an ATM more than five times a month are younger and have slightly higher average household incomes than those people that use the machines four or fewer times per month. Unlike 12 to 15 years ago when young, well-educated, upscale males almost exclusively were users of ATM services, high levels of usage are common across all household segments. However, the pattern of usage continues to show a decline as age increases.

This phenomena reflects potentially contradictory trends. While adoption of new service delivery mechanisms such as ATMs more readily occurs among younger segments of the population, it also is true that older population segments tend to have different types of financial needs and, in particular, are less transaction-oriented. For example, the household segments with the greatest levels of checkwriting activity tend to be those that both have children and are in peak wage-earning years. Older segments write fewer checks, but make more investments. To the extent that using an ATM offsets checkwriting, there may be a natural decline as households age. However, ATM usage most frequently offsets a trip to a teller to obtain cash, which suggests that it primarily is a convenience service. Such a time-saving service is of possible interest to all household segments, but to differing degrees depending on life cycle. Consequently, financial institutions must examine the behavior of various segments to identify key factors in increasing ATM acceptance.

To a great extent, the evidence suggests that ATM usage is a learned behavior that continues as an individual matures rather than representing a service to which the young have a particular affinity. In addition to the general expansion of usage of ATMs by all households, research shows steady growth within every age segment except the under-25 segment. (Fluctuations within that group are attributed primarily to research error, reflecting the low numbers of under-25 house- holds that respond to financial services research questionnaires.) These findings suggest that efforts to get consumers to use ATMs have been largely successful and supports the argument that the important issues now are the concerns of a maturing business.

TECHNOLOGY USED TO ENHANCE ATM ACCEPTANCE

ATM networks and financial institution owners have used technology enhancements to broaden consumer acceptance of ATMs. On the technological side, probably no institution has been as successful at wooing consumers as Citibank. In addition to its initial success in capturing significant market share by being one of the first institutions to offer ATMs, it has been a leader in ATM development. In particular, the consumer activated terminal, or CAT-2, which was introduced in 1987, has allowed the bank to increase its New York metropolitan area market share to 17% from about 10% when the machines were introduced.

Citibank says 1,100 CAT-2 machines were in service in 1989 including terminals in Florida, Illinois, Arizona, Washington, Puerto Rico and Hong Kong. More are being installed. Developed by Citibank's Transaction Technology Incorporated, the machine has a color screen, is private so only the user can see the screen and converses in language common to people. The machine prints on screen such statements as "What do you want?" when the menu of 55 different transaction choices are given, and "You got cash" after a withdrawal is 5made. The information that can be gathered and services rendered from the machine range from the standard balance inquiry and cash withdrawal to how much interest has been earned through that day on a certificate of deposit.

The CAT-2 is trilingual, conversing in English, Spanish or Chinese and is equipped with a 24-hour telephone in the event the user has a problem at the machine. Of all Citibank transactions occurring in metropolitan New York, 7 out of 10 are handled via the ATMs. After the original design, the machine was enhanced to have the ability to move up and down for easier use by wheelchair-bound people and by consumers who use the machines at drive-up locations and whose driver's window is not the same height as the machine.

International Business Machines also heightened the ATM technology competition in November 1987 when it introduced its 4730 personal banking machine. It not only provided deposits and cash withdrawals, but can read and cash a check down to the penny. Prior to its introduction, no other machine could issue up to five denominations of currency and dispense four varieties of coins. Officials with IBM said it had created a machine to handle the work of a teller just like a teller would handle it.

MARKETING USED TO ENHANCE ATM ACCEPTANCE

Another approach is attracting consumers to ATMs through the marketing side rather than the technology side, as Cash Station in Chicago is doing. The network began a $1-million promotion in September 1989 that included radio advertisements and direct mailings. Two $2 checks were mailed to non-users of ATMs who previously had been issued a card, but hadn't used them. The only way the consumer could be credited the money was to deposit it in a machine. The promotion was aimed at activating personal identification numbers issued to consumers that had not before used the ATM cards. Earlier in the year, a survey by Cash Station had showed only 36% of its member institutions were satisfied with transaction volume, and only 56% of Cash Station customers had used their cards.

Other efforts launched in recent years have attempted to make consumers feel more comfortable with the machines while broadening the utility of ATMs and income potential. University of Iowa students in Iowa City, Iowa, began paying tuition and other bills through the Shazam ATM network in the fall semester, 1988; Exxon added ATMs to its convenience stores; McDonald's Restaurants placed ATMs in its restaurants along the Connecticut interstate; Wendy's International did the same in the Dayton, Ohio, area; New Hampshire skiers purchased lift tickets through ATMs at participating ski areas; Vail Mountain began a similar program prior to that; Applied Communications developed software to allow America Express Travelers Cheques to be distributed through ATMs; the Washington Area Metropolitan Transit Authority installed ATM-like machines that dispense bus and subway tickets; and the U.S. Navy plans to equip 112 of its biggest vessels with ATM and point-of-sale terminals to streamline an archaic payroll process.

And then there are the many ATMs that have been installed in the work place and others that are portable machines moved to work sites. The idea has been that banks could strengthen their relationship with business and customers and at the same time cut down on line lengths back at the branch. Businesses gain increased productivity because employees are less likely to take long lunch breaks on payday. Mobile ATMs also began appearing at public gatherings such as fairs and races, where they offer opportunities for fee income for the owners of the ATMs as well as convenience for consumers.

The majority of ATMs, however, remain inside bank walls or on outside bank walls. A smaller percentage are nowhere near banks at all, although consumers have a high level of interest in more such machines. Research shows ATM users would like to use the machines at the supermarket, followed closely by shopping malls and the work place. As regulatory restrictions have eased in a number of states, less conventional siting has been explored with great success.

CONCERNS ABOUT ATM CRIME

While more and more consumers use ATMs and machine owners determine how to make the machines more productive, concerns are raised about the machines susceptibility to crime. In 1987, the Bank Administration Institute reported the most dangerous hours for ATM customers was between 7 p.m. and midnight and that one assault is committed per every 3.5 million ATM transactions.

Some have said the attention given to ATMs and crime is over- stated, but *Bank Network News* reported in July 1989 that many banks and networks are again reviewing physical security precautions in light of two highly publicized crime incidents. Among action taken has been the creation of task forces. Chicago's Cash Station and the Chicago City Council have combined Electronic Funds Transfer Association executives from around the country with local law enforcement officials. The national EFTA also created a task force with invitations to industry executives to scrutinize the issue of ATM-related crime. In California, legislators have drafted a bill that requires minimum security standards at ATM locations. The proposed law requires corrective action or removal of an ATM at a site with a history of violent crime, *BNN* reported. That corrective action includes putting in better lighting, removing objects that may hinder visibility, limiting hours of operation or relocating or removing the machine from the site.

The changes in ATMs and usage have been many and broad based. The numbers of transactions have increased, methods of profitability blueprinted, alternative cost-cutting operations found and economies of scale discovered. Most have been made for one reason: improve profitability of the machines. But the consumer variable hasn't been forgotten. Marketing efforts have been undertaken, machines made more user friendly and the government has begun to demand electronic payment systems. Machines were placed in new areas and more of them purchased. As new arenas are found, new avenues of profitability will be chartered. If ATMs can be placed on U.S. Navy ships, then it seems only a restrained imagination can limit the future potential of the machines.

THE EVOLUTION OF ATMs

With a 20-year history since the first installations, ATMs are no longer a new banking service. For many financial institutions they are a vital part of the total delivery system. ATM usage, in terms of household penetration—the percentage of all households using an ATM at least once each month—has reached its current level in half the time required by credit cards to reach a comparable point. Today, more than half of the households that have ATM service available use it. By that measure, ATMs can be considered an unqualified success. However, that does not mean that ATMs necessarily have been a profitable investment for every financial institution that has installed them. While transaction processing networks and hardware vendors have thrived, ATMs have been problematic for financial institutions. The automation of basic teller functions has evolved from a competitive advantage offering a marketing edge and possible cost savings, to a competitive necessity — an essential element in competing for consumer loyalty, no matter what the cost.

To reach this current status as a competitive necessity, ATMs have gone through an evolution that has exhibited three distinct phases. The first phase was the "operations phase." This period was from approximately 1969, when the first ATMs were installed in the United States, to 1976, when research showed approximately seven percent of households using them on a monthly basis. During that time, the basic mechanics of ATM operations were developed and a functional design of service features emerged that continues to represent the primary tasks that ATMs perform: provide account balances, allow transfers among accounts, take deposits and, most importantly, dispense cash.

The second phase was the "marketing phase," which was of slightly less duration. It ran from approximately 1977 to 1983 and represented the period during which ATMs could be—and were—successfully used by some institutions as a marketing advantage. The ATM offered a financial institution an opportunity to present a service that others did not, 24-hour convenience, as well as an opportunity to extend geographic reach faster and less expensively than by building physical branches. The institutions that most highly regard ATMs as a successful contribution to their operations primarily were those that launched or expanded ATM service during this period. During this phase, household penetration grew to just under a third of the market, a "wall" that was to persist for the next several years.

Although it was not widely recognized at the time, the slowing of growth in household penetration in the early 1980s also marked the beginning of today's environment, which is the "business phase." This phase represents a distinct stage during the life cycle of many products and services, a point at which the utility or popularity of a product or service has spawned a level of competition that effectively makes that product or service a commodity. No longer does the simple provision of the product or service represent an advantage. However, failure to provide this same product or service may represent a disadvantage. Because it is accepted and expected by consumers, the commodity has become a competitive necessity.

EVOLUTION MADE ATMs A COMPETITIVE NECESSITY

This evolution brings us to the current market, in which there is a general perception among financial institutions that is summarized by ATM researcher Linda Fenner Zimmer in the January 26, 1988, issue of *Funds Transfer Report*, "In most cases, it is very difficult to demonstrate that ATMs make money for the banks that own them." Of course, there are many caveats and qualifications to such statements. The first is the recognition of the competitive necessity factor. Much as with disarmament, the willingness on the part of one party to forego certain "weapons" means little as long as others are willing to use them. The concept of financial institutions meeting in a "summit" to negotiate the disposal of unprofitable portions of their arsenal is ludicrous, not to mention the certainty of antitrust action.

Beyond the simplistic level of recognizing competitive necessity, many institutions find that ATM users represent customers who may be very important in other ways. Research consistently has shown ATM users to be younger and more affluent than average, with ATM usage highest among the young affluent. There also is an understanding that ATM service is of such importance to some consumers that they would switch institutions to obtain it, or regard it as a critical factor in selecting a financial institution when relocating their primary residence.

Additionally, with the level of affinity for ATM usage that is demonstrated by younger segments of the population, it is a virtual certainty that usage levels will rise simply by virtue of population growth. Nonusers tend to be concentrated in older age segments. There is nothing to indicate that this phenomena reflects anything other than the fact that ATMs are still a relatively new service, which require a change in behavior on the part of persons with established habits. Therefore, it is likely that current users will continue their behavior as they age and younger-yet entrants to the population will adopt ATMs with enthusiasm.

ATM POTENTIALS AND STRATEGIES

ATM technology, a banker remarked, largely consists of putting a television screen on top of a safe. His remark was in jest, but makes an important point. Because the primary function of an ATM is to dispense cash, the design is largely dictated by the necessity of providing a secure means of protecting a large amount of cash as it is, nearly by definition, left sitting in a public place. A substantial portion of the expense of an ATM will continue to be that "armor" and the related hardware that actually dispenses cash.

Consequently, the "television" component of the ATM represents the primary area of likely change. However, to mistake the screen for the real technology of an ATM is as serious a misconception as forgetting that the ATM is primarily a safe. The video tube itself is only the visible part of an interactive communications system that consists of some limited "on-board" computer processing capability, a telecommunications link to a switching node (another computer), and the host computer that contains account data. While there has been attention to the possibilities of using color monitors and/or touch screens to make use of an ATM easier and more pleasing, these developments pale in significance to the underlying telecommunications changes that have enabled the creation and inexpensive operation of regional and national shared ATM networks.

NETWORKING THE CASH DISPENSERS

ATM service increasingly is a commodity. The linking of various separately owned ATM networks is both a consequence and a cause of the commodity status of ATMs. This trend is almost certainly irreversible, barring unforeseen legislative actions. The industry is rapidly approaching a time when any network will provide access to virtually all shared ATMs. It is possible — although perhaps not likely because of monopolistic concerns — that a single network will serve all ATMs. Such consolidation is a natural tendency resulting from efficiencies of scale in what is essentially a business of trading information in agreed-upon formats. Furthermore, while $1-billion-and-larger banks account for less than 5% of all ATM providers, they operate more than two-thirds of all installed ATMs and have about 20% of all consumer transaction accounts.

An indication that this consolidation trend is already in progress can be seen in the merging of regional networks, such as has occurred in the Midwest and is being discussed in the Southeast. Another indicator is the aggressive position taken by Visa in offering transaction processing for ATMs, as well as credit cards and POS direct debit, at prices in the automated clearinghouse arena competitive even with the Federal Reserve in its role as the nation's bank.

FUTURE TELECOMMUNICATIONS TECHNOLOGY

ATM communication links are one of the many business applications of telecommunications services that potentially will benefit by the movement of telephone service to Integrated Standard Digital Network (ISDN) service. Ultimately, such service could mean that data transmissions such as those generated by ATMs would be carried on the public switched telephone networks rather than by leased, dedicated lines. Not only would this mean lower operating expenses, but greater flexibility in placement of machines.

Data transmission is evolving rapidly even without ISDN implementation. For example, private networks such as those most major financial institutions operate can provide virtually all of the capabilities of ISDN while consolidating voice and other data traffic. Private networks also may include microwave or radio links that can reach a variety of remote locations more efficiently than public telephone networks. Despite concerns about the impact of deregulation, the base trend in telecommunications is similar to that of computers: more capability at less cost.

That suggests one of the potential threats to ATM profitability will be new communications-based payment systems that reduce consumer demand for cash or provide alternative sources. Because such systems — with the possible exception of point of sale direct debit — remain on the distant horizon, changes in telecommunications systems appear to primarily mean that ATM service providers will see continued declines in the expense of online links, one of the major cost elements of providing ATM service. And, even with point of sale direct debit, ATM cards seem well-positioned to play a major role in successful direct debit programs.

ATM CARDS AND POS DIRECT DEBIT

This trend in ATM services, which in fact is only minimally technological, will be affected by the increasing variety of card devices that potentially may be used to initiate a transaction at an ATM or to duplicate functions of an ATM. Recognizing the expanded cash access that is provided by interconnection of ATM networks, new issuers of cards are likely to seek alliances to allow their cardholders to obtain cash, account balances, etc. In addition to non-bank credit cards that have such potential, there are a variety of new, merchant-issued non-bank debit cards. As POS direct debit becomes more common, cards issued by merchants, as well as those issued by banks and other credit providers, may be capable of accessing cash or account balances from ATMs — or at the point of sale — at the customer's request. Politicaland business decisions will determine the extent to which this actually occurs.

ATM cards already may be used as POS direct debit cards in many areas of the country. At least three parties are involved in such developments: financial institutions, processing networks and merchants. Dual purpose cards that can pay for a purchase at the point of sale as well as obtain cash from an ATM particularly depend on agreements between bankers and merchants, each of whom may see advantages in maintaining the database of information associated with the card. The banker wishes to retain a proprietary identity for the card, but merchants increasingly recognize the possibility of using such cards as part of "frequent shopper" programs that offer discounts or other incentives for repeat business. Frequent shopper card programs are being described as the "trading stamps" of the 1990s.

Such dual purpose cards also raise the possibility of providing ATM functions at the point of sale. This next step in the evolution is occurring as the merchant who can accept an ATM card uses the same online authorization equipment to offer the customer cashback service, consolidating purchases and cash access, just as is commonly done with a paper check. Potentially, such services will displace ATM transactions and reduce the need for standalone machines.

BASIC ATM CONFIGURATION EVOLUTION

While a variety of issues that are only partly related to technology set the stage for evolution of ATMs, basic advances in computer and computer related technologies suggest some directions for the physical configuration of the machines.

There have been a variety of machines introduced during recent years that offered higher quality graphic images to the user, as well as touch screen options that eliminate or reduce the need for a keyboard or keypad. Touch screens also offer the service provider the flexibility of being able to change the screen display through software, suggesting, for example, that a "soft" keyboard can be added for a particular function or promotion, then removed when not needed.

Another basic component of ATMs is the printer. Reliability and dependability of printer operation is essential, perhaps as important as that of maintaining telecommunications links. In part, that dependability has been needed to meet regulatory requirements for provision of printed receipts. It also is necessary to meet consumers' perception that they should walk away from the machine with a printed confirmation of their actions. Interestingly, a visit to nearly any ATM location reveals that there is a sizable segment of the ATM-using population that has no interest in retaining such receipts, nor in disposing of them properly.

Although mechanical printers, usually dot-matrix style, have dominated in terminal design, printer design in general is shifting to various forms of toner-based printing, as is used in copying machines. Such printers offer greater speed and variety in the images produced. To date, toner-based printing has been more expensive and less reliable than dot-matrix printers, but rapid improvements are occurring on both counts.

Higher quality printers are not needed to produce a slip of paper that is likely to be discarded immediately. However, quality improvements may assist in development of ancillary services that may be provided through an ATM, such as statement printing. A number of financial institutions are finding success in providing the ability to generate a statement on demand—for a fee. In some instances, the institutions are scoring a double hit by both charging customers a fee for printing their statements and canceling the printing and mailing of the usual monthly statement, if the customers got their own statements within a certain period prior to the usual mailing.

Beyond printing a statement, such sophisticated printers also introduce the possibilities of offering products such as airline or other transportation tickets, stock quotes, loan calculations, investment option calculations, insurance product information and a host of other financial service information products. However, with each addition of a function, the ATM moves a step away from its basic function — providing cash (remember, it's a safe with a TV on top!). While some of these added functions may be appropriate in particular situations, an institution exploring such possibilities is likely to determine quickly that it is more cost effective and clearer to customers to separate such functions by placing them on another machine, which may sit side-by-side with the cash dispensing ATM.

Finally, one last technology related development that may be of importance is the development of the portable ATM. While there is an inherent contradiction in such a concept (a money filled safe that is easily moved!?), technology clearly allows the development of a cash dispenser that may be placed in a particular location on a temporary basis. Such a portable device might be useful for providing cash access at an event likely to draw large numbers of people, such as a fair, race or other sporting event; or to provide cash access at a manufacturing plant on pay day.

If the goal is, as it should be, to provide convenience and ease of use no matter where the individuals being served are located, then even a portable ATM makes sense.

BASIC ATM STRATEGY

With ATMs recognized as a competitive necessity, the primary effort should be to maintain simplicity and achieve efficiency, both in terms of operation and usage. Enhancements should focus on convenience of location and ease of use for the consumer, while functional elements of the machine are reliable and easy to maintain. Analysis of the functions of an ATM reveals that only its cash dispensing function is unique. The important questions are: how many consumers are able to use this machine (have an appropriate card), and how many are likely to use it because its location is convenient.

It is possible to generate profits by dominating prime locations and thereby obtaining fee income from "foreign" transactions. However, such fee based profit generally is minimal. Other fee based services, such as statement printing, can result in profits, but efforts to build such businesses are not yet supported by case histories.

Efforts to develop ancillary services are best focused on co-location of specialized terminals that may be enhanced through use of full-motion, broadcast-quality video from videodiscs; interactive programs that allow the collection of marketing information, and provision of a telephone handset to allow immediate connection to a human operator.

The role of the telephone and the familiarity of its usage by consumers offers an opportunity. Basic account balance and related information can be provided on a dial-up basis from any telephone. Additionally, a variety of telephone based information services may be added to the service, which can be cross-promoted at the ATM, as well as through the printed statement each month.

Finally, consideration should be given to the possibility that the ATM's basic cash dispensing role may be challenged by retailers' point-of-sale services. Given the history of evolution of delivery systems, however, this should be regarded as yet another likely parallel system, not a development that will significantly displace the need for public, cash dispensing terminals.

The delivery of financial services is not likely to witness dramatic change over the next five years. Applications of technology will continue to primarily function as a means of coping with increasing transaction volumes without increasing staff or physical locations. The ATM will continue to play a major role in that effort as a part of the electronic delivery that has demonstrated that it works.

CHAPTER

6

Direct Debit at the Point of Sale

Will consumers use Point of Sale Direct Debit services? Absolutely. In all the markets where it has been introduced, the result has been the same. There is a significant segment of the population that will use POS direct debit if it is available and if marketing makes consumers aware of that availability. However, that is not, and has not, been the important question for most of the firms that are likely to be offering or otherwise involved in POS direct debit.

The persepective of banks has been that POS direct debit will simply provide another alternative in payment systems — an alternative that will likely result in minimal competitive advantage and certain increases in operating costs. If banks truly controlled the payment system, they might very well decide to forego direct debit services. After all, the experience of many institutions offering Automated Teller Machine services has been that the expense is easier to identify than the return. Unquantifiable and intangible benefits must be cited by many institutions to justify offering ATM services.

ACCESS TO TRANSACTION ACCOUNTS

Fundamentally, the question in considering POS direct debit is one regarding the transaction account business.

An institution that wants to retain transaction accounts ultimately will be forced to provide access to that account via various convenient means, which include use of a small plastic card. Although this card may closely resemble a credit card or an ATM card, there frequently are reasons for it being a distinctly separate instrument, just as there also is a rationale for universal cards that may function as either debit or credit instruments — at the users option — and are usable in a variety of locations, including at cash machines and retail points of sale.

Taking the development of POS direct debit as a given focuses attention on the true issues: who will pay for this development, who will market the service and who will control it. In essence, three parties are involved: the consumer, the merchant and the banker. POS direct debit offers advantages to each and disadvantages to each without clear tilting of the balance in any particular direction. The slow emergence of POS direct debit, despite its anticipation for more than a decade, reflects this lack of advantage or incentive.

There are, however, at least two important factors at work today that may not tip the balance, but nonetheless could bring about significant advances in POS direct debit availability. Both of these factors leave the banking community in an ambiguous state, reacting and not leading.

The first of these factors is government initiative. For a variety of reasons, including cost considerations and control issues, government agencies from the federal level to the county courthouse are exploring the use of electronics for the disbursement of public funds. In particular, welfare benefit distribution through ATMs and POS terminals may bring about government funding of terminal deployment that neither banks nor retailers have been willing to fund. These terminals, much as federal and local highways, will be open to use by any citizen or legal private enterprise and will result in substantial growth of related businesses. In this case, however, the growth won't be of fast food stands and drive-through car washes, but of electronic funds transfer services.

The second factor is related, but quite different. It is the improved information technologies being put in use by retailers from the Fortune 500 level to the mom and pop store. The computerization of business has both made available and made a necessity of sophisticated marketing tools that include the ability to capture detailed information about customers. At no single point is that information more critical than at the point at which a transaction is concluded. A wise marketer wants to know a little bit about those potential customers who did not make a purchase, but he wants to know everything about those who did. They are his most likely source of the next sale.

THE MERCHANT'S POINT OF VIEW

To understand the merchant's point of view on direct debit at the point of sale, it is necessary to realize that collecting funds for a purchase is a relatively minor part of the process. While the ultimate goal of a sales process is to put money into the merchant's pocket, cash register, bank account, or whatever, the fact is that the sales process in itself is the natural focus of the merchant's effort. While merchants have proven willing to give up a percentage of their profit margin for the added business gained through acceptance of credit cards, it is not mere coincidence that the primary businesses expressing interest in direct debit at the point of sale are those that operate on extremely tight profit margins. Supermarkets, in particular, often are literally operating on profit margins of less than the 2% that credit card companies collect in the form of a discount for processing credit transactions. Supermarkets also are in the unique retail position of being the single largest outlet other than banks for obtaining cash, which is primarily obtained by presenting a paper check.

Analyzing the supermarkets' situation offers insight on the status of POS direct debit for more reasons than the fact that they are taking a lead in its development. Selling food is one of the most common and most competitive businesses anywhere. Consequently, it is a business in which any factor that may represent an advantage, no matter how narrow, will receive serious consideration. POS direct debit offers advantages to a food retailer, but not necessarily those that might be expected.

The major advantage of POS direct debit in a supermarket is increased speed of transaction completion at check-out. Studies conducted at Randall's Food Markets in Houston, Texas, which has been actively promoting POS direct debit services for several years, show that debit card transactions are completed as rapidly as cash transactions. Not only is that more than four times the speed of accepting a paper check, but — very importantly — debit card transactions are comparable in dollar value to check transactions — seven times the value of average cash transactions. Food retailers are critically aware that the consumer is never more impatient in a grocery store than when standing in the check-out line. Courtesy booths or check approval stands, along with check cashing cards, are standard features of supermarkets, all intended to hasten that final passage. Although sales of certain tabloid publications and other sundries may benefit from check-out delay, consumer attitudes toward the supermarket do not.

Secondly — and more importantly for some retailers — is the ability to capture instant, accurate information about consumers' buying habits. When combined with computerized inventory and ordering systems, retail management today has available unprecedented tools for decision-making and marketing. These tools particularly are important for retailers that are part of larger companies that engage in volume buying or have other centralized ordering/reporting functions. In supermarkets, the most common form of "captured information" is the check cashing card. Converting such card bases to debit card bases already is under way and is likely to accelerate. In other retail areas, one of the "hottest" merchandising concepts is development of frequent shopper programs. Clearly modeled after the airlines' nearly 10-year-old efforts, these programs often make use of a magnetic stripe card to convey information. The possibility of making such information cards also function as transaction cards offers opportunities for retailers and bankers alike.

A COMMON MISCONCEPTION

A common misconception is that POS direct debit's primary advantage is allowing the merchant to capture funds more quickly. The reality of how the banking system works, including the tremendous efficiency of today's check processing systems, means that "it just ain't so." The real value of the extra time the grocer holds those funds actually may be more than offset by the negative reaction of consumers who don't want to pay more quickly. In fact, one of the reasons some grocers are using the ACH for processing POS direct debit transactions is to ensure that a day or two of delay can be built into the system before funds are taken from the consumer's account. It is necessary to publicize that delay to promote POS debit as "just like a check."

A second misconception is that a business case for POS direct debit can be built on the prospect of consumer-paid transaction fees. Although transaction fees for "foreign" ATM usage are becoming common, there is no evidence that consumers see sufficient advantage in POS direct debit services to justify paying a fee. In fact, experience to date indicates that economic incentives may be needed to build usage. Consumers more readily use POS direct debit when it provides a discount or rebate on a purchase.

Finally, there is one important area in which the advantages of POS direct debit are not altogether clear — or at least are difficult to measure. Theoretically, POS direct debit provides greater control over fraud losses, particularly from bad checks. However, there are at least two fallacies to that theory. The first is that those criminals who attempt to use bad checks are likely to continue to do so rather than switch to the more easily controlled plastic cards. Therefore, it is likely that bad checks will be presented as long as checks are accepted. Second, many institutions — supermarkets, banks and other retailers — actually profit from bad checks through the fees that are assessed against those individuals who are caught. Only a very small percentage of bad checks are passed by individuals who then successfully drop out of sight. This final argument is one that most retailers and bankers are reluctant to advance and is a "profit" most would willingly forego.

Moreover, the debit card combined with a unique personal identification number (PIN) overall is one of the most secure forms of payment available to consumers. So long as the PIN is not actually inscribed or written on the card, it is secure even if lost, stolen or misplaced. While the merchant's fraud losses may not be significantly affected by acceptance of debit cards, the consumer's risk of being the victim of fraud is reduced.

PAYMENT AS AN INFORMATION OPPORTUNITY

Money is an information product as well as a means of conveying value during a transaction. An exchange of money is an exchange of information as well as an exchange of value. The most frequent occasion for this exchange is the retail point of sale (or point of purchase, depending on the perspective being adopted). The introduction of substitutes for money represents opportunities to introduce devices that both capture and convey more information than does printed paper.

The majority of all transactions today are conducted through an exchange of cash — currency and coins. However, there is a direct correlation between the size — dollar value — of a transaction and the likelihood that it will be completed through a non-cash alternative.

Paper payment, specifically checks, account for the bulk of consumer payments today, displacing cash much as coins once displaced barter. Now we are seeing the process of electronic payment alternatives displacing paper. As with many technology related phenomena, the biggest, wealthiest and most powerful were first able to use these alternatives, but the trend is for such capability to migrate downward in the market.

Although experience to date is limited, early indications are that POS direct debit transactions do indeed displace checks and, to a lesser extent, cash. Low-value cash transactions are likely to be displaced by inexpensive debit devices in situations requiring repetitive, minor payments such as public transit, public telephones and vending machines. These services all require handling of coins, which becomes expensive in relation to the value conveyed. Economies clearly are available when the transactions can be sold to the public in bulk and collected electronically as they are used. Magnetic stripe paper cards, as well as plastic, already are being used for such purposes.

The displacement of paper checks by POS direct debit is more problematic. It is most likely to occur in those situations when a debit device can more readily and rapidly convey necessary information than a paper device can. The supermarket check out line is one instance. The entering of a four-digit PIN clearly is faster than the process of verifying name, address, telephone number, place of employment, etc. as is often necessary in presenting a paper check. However, there is more than one direction in which the information can flow. Proprietary plastic cards can be invaluable to a merchant in providing information about who just made a purchase.

RETAILER VS. BANKER

Point-of-sale debit in the United States has had, and continues to have, its problems. A major factor in its relatively slow progress is cost, a factor that often pits retailer against banker in trying to decide who should pay and who really benefits most—and most immediately. This basic conflict is primary among the reasons that the banking community hasn't found a compelling need to develop a unified approach to direct debit. For several years, bankers said the unified solution was the Visa/MasterCard joint venture to create a national, on-line debit system called Entree. An anti-monopolistic lawsuit filed by a baker's dozen state attorneys general froze that effort in 1989.

Ironically, by the time the lawsuit was settled early in 1990, many bankers had come to believe that its filing may have been a favor to the financial industry. It provided an excuse for burying the expensive plans for a national online system to process and settle debit transactions, which would have paralleled existing, similar systems for credit card processing. Entree also would have duplicated some of the emerging functions of ATM networks, while cutting into the existing business of buying and selling transactions across the various regional networks.

Furthermore, such a debit processing system also would parallel the national automated clearinghouse network, primarily operated by the Federal Reserve, which currently offers national settlement services. But this debit processing system would be on a daily batch basis rather than in real-time, as individual transactions occur as an on-line system would support. If that were not enough reason to want to see Entree go away, bankers also were realizing that merchants were not enthusiastic about paying for a debit payment system and would not be likely to cooperate.

MASTERDEBIT AND VISADEBIT

In a way, bankers are having some revenge on merchants who sat on the sidelines while Entree was debated. With a national online system considered to be dangerously close to an illegal monopoly, the card associations' versions of offline debit cards were given new life. Since existing merchant agreements specified that accepting any card with a Visa/MasterCard logo meant accepting all such cards and paying discount fees for doing so, the card associations and banks turned to the alternative of placing those logos on debit cards, particularly ATM cards. To the merchant, the card is "just like a credit card," and the merchant generally pays the same rate for accepting it as is paid for accepting credit, although the debit card may displace a sale that would have occurred via cash or check and not have cost as much to accept.

While the card association-labeled debit cards do not address the needs of some of the merchants who have been most interested in debit, specifically supermarkets, gas stations and convenience stores, they provide revenue to banks and the card associations. They also expand the utility of ATM cards, particularly addressing the financial needs of middle-age consumers who may not be as interested in credit as they are in payment convenience.

In 1989, Visa launched an incentive program for banks designed to encourage greater issuance and use of the VisaDebit card. The plan gave cost rebates and marketing assistance to member financial institutions who put the Visa logo on their automated teller machine cards. The combined ATM card and Visa logo would make it possible for every such card to be used as debit at any location accepting Visa credit cards. The merchant would not be directly affected and perhaps would not even know it was a debit card, but would still pay a discount fee to the card association. The bank provides approval of the consumer's application for a card bearing both the Visa and bank logos, but Visa would separate the transaction on VisaNet from the usual credit transactions. Later the bank could post the debit to the consumers' bank account.

Visa's effort was followed by MasterCard. The MasterDebit card replaced the previously issued MasterCard II that had been issued and promoted in the same manner as the VisaDebit. National Bank of Detroit was scheduled to roll out the package to 12 of its banks in the greater Chicago area in 1990. In the summer of 1989, the $25-billion bank recalled all ATM cards and reissued a silver NBD Bancard with the MasterCard logo. It found cards were used an average of three times a month. Transaction totals averaged $45.

An added benefit to the user of the Visa/MasterCard debit program is the purchase protection afforded the consumer. Regulation E of the Federal Reserve System protects the consumer against lost or stolen cards, and regulates receipt formats, statement information content and the like. This makes the debit transaction an EFT transaction, the same as an ATM transaction. Product liability and purchase return policies are provided for under the auspice of federal regulation Z, which also applies to the merchant. This provides the transaction the legal protections afforded a credit transaction, literally, just like a credit card. The consumer gets the benefit of both protections.

As positive as these advantages are, there are also a series of negatives associated with this approach. Banks are not likely, for example, to issue one of these cards to every transaction account holder because of the potential of increased risk exposure. With the widely accepted association logo on the card, the advantage found in widespread acceptance can easily turn into widespread fraud. Current credit card authorization systems lack complete on-line authorization capability with its inherent total "zero floor limit" merchant coverage. In most instances, a purchase has to exceed a set dollar figure, which may vary from merchant to merchant, before authorization is required. Consequently, the risk exposure is tremendous due to almost unlimited "under floor limit" purchasing power.

This level of risk makes issuance of logo-bearing cards to the entire transaction account base unwise. While nearly any consumer with cash in hand can open a transaction account, credit is extended more cautiously. In fact, banks or regulators are likely to require a credit card type of underwriting before issuing any debit card. Unfortunately, this increases the costs of such a program to an almost unacceptable level. An overdraft line would also help limit the exposure, but that makes the entire relationship extremely similar to the existing credit card product, with the added feature of debit access. Furthermore, such a product may seem inherently logical, but runs head-on into the "turf wars" within banks that compartmentalize such functions internally. While credit and debit cards seem similar, their development and control tend to fall within separate departments within most institutions.

While Entree withered and card association debit cards were reborn, regional debit efforts based on existing ATM networks and ACH alternatives gained strength. These alternatives pose additional serious questions as to who will control the payment system at the point of sale, banks or merchants.

DEBATING OFF-LINE VS. ON-LINE

Off-line debit programs settled through the ACH have been cited by some merchants as a means to sidestep the obstacle of a banking community recalcitrant about introducing direct debit. Additionally, while it is still debated whether on-line or off-line is cheaper overall, it is acknowledged that on a transaction basis ACH often is the more economical. And it requires little cooperation from more than one bank. Many observers, therefore, have concluded that ACH-based programs may take a lead in the evolution of direct debit since it helps the retailer who may want debit to get around the banking community that may not.

So far, it hasn't happened. In fact, there seems to be a trend toward retailers offering both on-line and off-line programs for some very complex reasons. The on-line network operators are taking note. Some are reacting with more favorable pricing for on-line while at least one is developing a dual package to be sold by the network. And vendors in the midst of this dilemma are scrambling to offer it all, which includes coupling services and equipment with credit card programs.

What this means for the future of ACH-based debit isn't clear. What is clear is, thus far, point of sale programs cleared through the automated clearinghouse have hardly flourished. In fact, there are no concrete figures to determine how much, or little, its use is growing.

In 1987 the ACH industry handled nearly a billion transactions, according to the National Automated Clearing House Association. However, no one knows how much of that was point of sale. NACHA only recently has developed a method for identifying such transactions. Still there is little argument that POS' current role is probably very small. ACH's real bread-and-buttter business is still direct deposit, especially of government payments, newly initiated government pay programs such as Vendor Express, and growing corporate-to-corporate payments.

Crucial in the future of ACH-based POS, is the question of who really benefits from such programs. Except for the large banks that operate their own ACH divisions — such as Bank of America and Chase Manhattan Bank — few have found a clear business case for launching such programs. Indeed, few banks have found the business case for independently promoting direct debit at all.

Overall, growth has been slower than anticipated. Some observers say it is because consumers don't really want it. Others say it is because retailers and bankers have yet to come to terms on pricing, with both saying the other should shoulder transaction processing costs. Perhaps philosophy is the greatest divider between these two camps. Retailers look at the overall marketing value of POS while bankers tend to view it in terms of hard dollars-and-cents costs to implement and run it.

This last issue, perhaps more than any other, is why some industry experts expected many retailers to choose the ACH path, for essentially this means bypassing the banks in all but the end settlement. Changes in 1988 to the legislation that governs point-of-sale only served to strengthen this belief.

It was predicted that amendments to the Electronic Funds Transfer Act would give impetus to an explosion of POS debit programs settled through ACH. Generally, the amendments lift what had been one of the greatest potential costs of the ACH route, providing the consumer with a statement of all transactions conducted with the card. Retailers offering direct debit through proprietary cards no longer have to directly issue customer statements. A listing of the POS transactions on a bank statement is sufficient.

Immediately after the amendments were adopted, only one new retailer announced a decision to settle through the ACH. Ironically, the retailer, Wegmans Food Markets Incorporated in New York, also was negotiating agreements to offer on-line direct debit via several ATM networks, and may be signaling a trend in the grocery industry. But Wegmans isn't the first retailer to do so. At least two major oil company POS programs operate on-line, accepting bank debit cards, and off-line to accommodate proprietary debit cards. Additionally, at least one ATM network — Most in Virginia — is developing a program to sell to retailers that offers cheaper ACH settlement with more secure on-line authorization.

Such arrangements score no points for either method in this contest between the programs, a contest really centering around who — banks or retailers — will have control of payment systems through this newest evolution called direct debit. Many in the industry still maintain that ACH-based programs will flourish, and the reason it has not yet happened is because it takes at least two years to implement such a program. Meanwhile, the pros and cons, including the issue of which method costs the most, are still being debated within the industry.

To understand the dynamics of this puzzle and its effects on matters such as ATM volume, it is first necessary to look at why these industry leaders in POS chose their respective settlement routes. And it's equally important to examine how factors at work in the payment systems industry may affect the future of ACH-based POS programs.

WHY VONS CHOSE THE OFF-LINE PATH

One of the most successful ACH programs undertaken by an independent retailer was initiated in 1987 by Vons Grocery Company in California. Looking at how that program came about can give a basic comparison of off-line versus on-line.

The alluring factors to Vons of offering debit were the promise of increasing transaction size, the possibility that overall market share could increase and the likelihood overall volume would grow. Vons wanted a "universal program," that was, to be able to sell groceries to anybody that walked in the store. They did not want to be restricted to cards that belonged to a particular ATM network. There also was the opportunity of building a "leading edge" image, since few stores offered the option at the time.

Additionally, and perhaps more important to Vons, were customer convenience factors such as faster checkout and more payment options. Vons wanted fast response time, less than one second, both for management economy, especially with a $15 an hour union clerk behind the counter, and for customer service. Because ACH transactions are usually routed to a central computer in the store, response time is faster and the possibility of system failure is lower.

A low turndown rate that Vons would control also was priority. Just as the supermarket would be willing to accept a check without asking to see the cusomter's current account balance, it wanted to be able to accept an electronic payment without intervention from the bank. It was less interested in the bank's assurance that funds were available than in its own record of whether the individual was a good customer. The nature of the ACH allowed that option, giving the grocer control over how quickly the customer's account was debited.

Basically, the grocer wasn't interested in instant debit. Although a retailer gets same-day ledger credit for transactions that occur on-line before the day's close with actual credit the next day, the ACH provides actual credit two days after the transaction takes place. The cash management value of that delay for a $44 average (per transaction) was not important to Vons. In fact, the two-day float for the customer that occurs with off-line programs was seen as a way to better consumer relations. Marketing efforts could discount the perception that the money for the groceries would be zapped out of the consumer's account even before he got home. Additionally, Vons believed customers would buy more, and buy more often, if they had float.

Finally, with ACH debit the merchant can operate nationally through a single program. By comparison, there are about 165 local ATM networks in the country today, some offering debit cards. For an ATM debit card to be used nationally requires agreements, specifications, standards, contracts and prices for use within each of the regional systems. The ACH method allows the merchant to deal with a single bank, which handles all processing and settlement.

Another plus for retailers in an ACH system is that they can determine their own security levels, flagging accounts within the store's system as necessary and setting cashback and authorization levels independent of the rules of a local ATM network. The amount of money justifiably spent on security varies with the average transaction size, from the retailer's viewpoint. With an average grocery store transaction of $44, that might not be much. The risk generally is regarded as comparable to that involved in accepting a check.

And there were other points in favor of ACH programs for a merchant that are hard to put dollar amounts on. With the ACH, the merchant controls design of the system and can designate almost any card as the access card as long as certain rules are followed. ACH debit programs allow the retailers to issue plastic with the store's name, building store loyalty. Of great value also is the ability to get to know the customer, through tracking buying habits from data gleaned by providing the service.

COSTLY CONSIDERATIONS

While the ACH offers advantages to merchants who want to control this new payment system, the banking industry generally is still a bit divided on which option — on-line or off — is the more expensive. Industry estimates on ACH costs are widely varied and often obscure, in part because there aren't a lot of merchants offering ACH debit and in part because those who do are private companies who consider such information highly proprietary. A factor, too, is that cost can vary greatly from retailer to retailer since ACH expenses decrease as volume increases. Regardless, most agree that cost greatly depends on how automated the merchant already is.

Even proponents concede the ACH approach, overall, is probably more expensive that the on-line approach, because while transaction cost is cheaper — or at most comparable — to those of on-line transactions, the retailer must issue cards, sometimes invest in automation not already in place, and even more importantly, maintain the data base. For example, in California consumers change their bank account once every three years and they move once every four years.With an on-line debit program the merchant doesn't have to spend money to keep up with that.

James Hopes, the vice president of Chase Manhattan Bank in charge of its ACH activities, maintains that in most cases ACH is cheaper. Chase leads the nation in bank market share for ACH activities. In 1988, the bank handled 68.2 million transactions, 13% of the 529 million private sector ACH items originated by financial institutions, according to the *American Banker's* annual survey. Most of that volume is attributed to insurance premium payments but the bank has aggressive plans for its POS activities. By 1991, Chase anticipates handling 50 million transactions a year from POS/ACH programs.

Hopes bases his cost arguments on figures compiled by the Food Marketing Institute on the cost of processing checks and cash. He says those figures approximated cash handling costs at about 18 cents per transaction, with 50 cents marked for handling checks. Hopes estimates the cost of processing an ACH debit transaction is about 20 cents, taking into consideration the accounting and management aspects of the process.

The significant factor that could change that scenario, he says, is the absence of telecommunications networks, such as are available for retailers who deal with credit cards. That could boost the cost of an ACH item to about 32 cents. "The net effect (for ACH comparison)" he says, "cash is cheaper; if you have telecommunications in place it's close; and with no telecommunications in place it's twice as much."

The second significant factor is pricing by ATM networks, he adds. It's a difficult subject complicated by the myriad pricing alternatives that exist and the lack of understanding even within networks as to the differences between transactions conducted at an ATM machine for cash and transactions for purchases at retail locations. Hopes says depending on the bank's policy of what is a POS fee, the cost of handling an on-line debit transaction can cost the retailer about 35 cents per transaction, higher than through the ACH. An ACH merchant knows if he originates the transaction he pays. But in the on-line market, who pays often is unresolved. Because many networks have still not developed a system to differentiate between ATM transactions and POS ones, the consumer can be charged a "foreign ATM fee" for using his debit card at the point of sale.

"We're still in the embryonic stages for both systems," Hopes notes. But even if ACH and on-line were the same in price, he adds, the value of other factors such as control of the process, loyalty by the card holder, and access to a national card base are greater to the retailer than the price of running the program.

Others in the on-line industry are taking a hard business look at those philosophical values. "There's absolutely no question at this point that on-line is cheaper," says David O'Connor, president of the Most network in Virginia. But O'Connor believes the philosophical reasons for using ACH are strong, so strong that the Most network is developing a product for retailers that provides both options.

"Our intent is to be able to offer, through the banks, a service that encompasses a broad spectrum of needs for a wide range of retailers," he adds. Through cooperation with the Mid-Atlantic ACH and the Virginia ACH, Most has developed an ACH product for lower cost settlement and now is attempting to cost effectively integrate on-line authorization capabilities. It's all a matter of a "correlation problem" for banks' back rooms, he explains.

Vendors also are attempting to capitalize on new debit programs by offering such versatility. For example, Deluxe Data Systems offers a service called the Single Source Solution for a retailer. Dierbergs Markets in St. Louis is accepting Bankmate ATM network cards at the point of sale, but also is automating its check cashing system through Deluxe's service. However, that grocer, and any who employs Deluxe's particular services, will be able to also turn that check cashing automation into a proprietary debit card — if so desired.

BEST OF BOTH WORLDS

The type of debit offered usually has been an either/or situation for retailers, with grocers such as Lucky's in California opting to go on-line through the Interlink POS network, or Vons choosing the "electronic check" method. (Vons also accepts several bank debit cards in its ACH system by entering into separate agreements with each bank that wants to participate. The difference, however, is that Vons settles these transactions through the ACH — not on-line.)

In New York, Wegmans' situation may be unique, as is the grocer. On-line will be offered because the company already has ties to eight network endpoints (representing about 350 financial institutions) through its extensive in-store ATM program. In fact, Wegmans is quite a veteran in the automation arena, something it points to as a great contributor to its success. *Fortune* magazine has named the grocer the "Champ" among supermarkets. Wegmans has 53% of the market share in its hometown of Rochester; 15% in the rest of New York state. This compares to competitors' shares ranging from 10 to 25%. Wegmans has 76 ATMs in 40 stores and averages 9,400 transactions per month on each machine, according to a report in *EFT Today,* a magazine published by the Electronic Funds Transfer Association. That compares to an average 4,000 per month per machine in other supermarkets.

Wegmans chose to offer the ACH option for one familiar reason: to preserve the consumer's float. Although it regards the monetary value of float to a customer as only about a cent, there are customers who desire it from a convenience standpoint. "The guy who doesn't get paid until tomorrow but needs groceries today values that float at more than a penny," a spokesman said.

THE OIL COMPANIES' LEAD

Wegmans may be the first grocer to choose both systems at startup, but it isn't the first retailer. At least two major oil companies — Exxon and Mobil — offer on-line and off-line debit. For both companies, ACH debit is achieved via a single, dual purpose card that gives the holder the option of paying for his purchase by credit or punching in a PIN to pay by debit.

Because both companies were already automated with credit card systems, it was a relatively simple matter to piggyback the ACH debit cards. And both companies, like virtually every other retailer, say they like the loyalty they think proprietary debit can offer. "We've been in the proprietary credit card business since 1930. We understand the value of proprietary debit plastic," says Richard Phegley, Exxon's treasurer. And like Vons, both companies also wanted to have that universal sales ability.

Mobil has 20 agreements that hook its participating stations on-line to 17 card bases around the country. However, when the company decided to enter the debit card market, it had no assurances its existing 8 million credit card holders were "covered" from a debit standpoint though these network arrangements."To give them the flexibility to remain with their existing bank (and still be able to use debit at Mobil), we had to go the ACH route," notes Michael B. Park, Mobil's POS Debit Manager. Mobil Plus cards are now available in about 4,200 Mobil metro locations, with another 5,000 stations targeted to join the program by yearend. That will represents about 75% of total sales, Park says.

That ACH/add-on decision, however, struck fear in the hearts of many network operators. Mobil has traditionally been the major retail supporter — and promoter — of bank networks' fledgling debit payment programs. Park says, however, that Mobil never intended to pull its support from existing network agreements. In fact, he claims Mobil does not track the volume of ACH transactions separately from the on-line ones. "We don't have any intentions of comparing the two. They're two different products," he says.

Phegley acknowledges that Exxon does track ACH transactions separately from on-line, just as it tracks its proprietary credit separately from MasterCard and Visa. But he declined to disclose which yields greater transactions. "We just think there's a role for both, just as we accept other credit cards," he says.

FUTURE FACTORS

In light of the above points, it might be surmised that ACH debit is most attractive to automation-oriented retailers in markets where negotiating fees with network operators is still an awesome task. Those areas, however, may be diminishing in number since more networks are getting aggressive with their POS pricing. In Florida, for example, Honor used to charge the issuer 15 cents per transaction plus a 5 cent switch fee. Now only the switch fee is charged. Another recent program is that undertaken by the Pulse network in Texas through its Pulse Pay program. With Pulse Pay, there also is no interchange fee and switch fees are split by the card-issuer and the acquirer.

Across the board, POS transactions fees from networks are dropping, according to industry surveys. And they may become more uniform and even less costly around the nation as networks continue to explore the possibilities of merging to achieve economies of scale.

The most interesting development is that Visa actually is in competition with the Federal Reserve in ACH processing, with plans to extend its services nationwide.

Another potential cost-cutter for both on-line debit may be borne by technology. McDonnell Douglas Payment Systems and Digital Radio Networks Incorporated were the first to jointly market a radio-based telecommunications network for POS. The program is expected to increase speed — it will take 6 to 8 seconds to complete a transaction. Equally important, it is expected to lower costs because the merchant won't be required to make a phone call to enter transaction data to the network.

The Metroteller network in Buffalo also is testing another radio-based system with equipment provided by Bydatel Corporation. Although neither party says exactly how much might be saved, communication costs are the single largest expense of a POS network and represent about half of all expenses.

The valuable float feature of paper checks could also be affected by the Expedited Funds Availability Act that took effect in 1989. However, whether that effect will be negative or positive is still unknown and may be determined to an extent by consumer awareness. In general, Regulation CC requires banks to make funds available on deposited checks from the government or from electronic payments on the next day, local checks within three business days and non-local checks within seven business days. The unanswered question is whether consumers will perceive funds leaving their accounts more rapidly when checks are written as well as entering more rapidly when checks are deposited.

Because Reg CC is aimed at making funds available to consumers more quickly, it most likely would affect ACH credits, and probably not debits. Therefore, the customer using an ACH-based debit card could still retain the float that a check can provide. In fact, Bill Nelson, NACHA operations officer, adds optimistically that Reg CC could impact ACH debit programs favorably by encouraging banks to become more proactive in promoting — and presumably pricing — such programs to smaller retailers as a way to reduce the number of checks in the system.

PROPRIETARY PLASTIC

If all these events come to pass and affect ACH/POS as anticipated, its chief remaining strength would be the loyalty retailers feel proprietary plastic affords them. And some think that as debit card use and availability becomes more pervasive, this point will become less applicable.

"As POS in an on-line world grows, I think the window for ACH at the point of sale diminishes except for those retailers who want to keep loyalty through a proprietary card identity," says Honor network president Tom Bennion. "But that's the same argument they used to use in the early credit card days when nobody wanted to accept MasterCard or Visa."

In the meantime, many industry participants believe ACH will continue to grow, albeit at a slow pace, since it takes as long as two years just to establish such programs. NACHA anticipates a continuing "healthy chase" between on-line systems and the ACH-based ones.

Others expect more activity from retailers with established debit programs as they begin to investigate merging ACH and on-line programs, a move that several prominent retailers are reported to be studying. Either way, many agree debit at the point-of-sale is a given with the competition between on-line and off serving to bring down prices. Even small retailers may soon find the economies for offering debit. Whether that debit will be on-line or off — or the customer's choice of either — remains to be seen.

THE CACTUS SWITCH

One of the more successful ACH point-of-sale programs to date is one that encompasses a whole state and is a joint effort by 105 banks and thrifts institutions. Called the Cactus Switch, this Arizona POS program is distinctive both in how it operates and how it was implemented.

"When you talk about ACH-based programs, there are basically two flavors," says Paul Finch, president of the Arizona Automated Clearing House that operates the switch. Most ACH/POS programs in operation today operate on an off-line basis. The Cactus Switch does both. "Our flavor is modeled after Visa, MasterCard and American Express" systems, Finch explains. Authorization is done on-line to guarantee funds, but actual settlement is batched and processed through the ACH to hold down costs. The cost to the consumer's account-holding bank is about 5 1/2 cents per transaction.

The Cactus Switch serves more than 30 merchants. Those include seven major merchants: Dillards and Target department stores, Mobil and Exxon gas stations, Lucky's and Fry's supermarkets and Circle K convenience stores.

The Switch was initiated by two prominent Arizona banks, Valley National Bank and Interstate Bank of Arizona, which decided in 1985 to buck the on-line trend. They convinced their Arizona colleagues that ACH-based POS' future was bright enough in Arizona to build the switch. Years ago Arizona financial institutions set the stage for POS by introducing bank-issued check guarantee cards, the same card now used for debit transactions. That put them in wide use and made the transition from check to debit easier by using the same card consumers had grown accustomed to and simply taking away the check.

MARKETING MAKES A POS SUCCESS IN IOWA

Jerry L. Higgason, vice president-cashier, Farmers State Bank, Marion, Iowa, a member of the Shazam network, says that banks like his have been working hard to perfect POS locally and would be foolish to let it get away. "What are we going to do? Work with it until it's breakeven then tell major merchants, 'Now, you can have it and make profit.'" Nonetheless, Higgason says bank management continues to be skeptical that consumers will use POS.

"They still don't believe consumers want to lose the float they get with checks," he says. "That's old news. Today what consumers want is convenience, and they will use the best and the fastest method to get it."

And on whether banks can make a profit, Higgason says his bank's experience is a case study example that shows you can.Farmers State has three merchant locations and two are making money, he says. One site, a 73,000 square feet mega-grocery facility, is netting $300 or more income each month after factoring in the cost of equipment, terminal fees, and processing costs.

What is breakeven transaction volume? Higgason says it's 6,500 a month at his most successful POS location, which has seen volume grow from 1,000 the first month of installation to 5,048 in the first year, 7,884 in the second year, end up to 9,718 in May, 1987. The key was merchant promotion, Higgason admits. "The store manager was sold on electronics. He put up banners, made announcements over the speaker systems, and gave incentives to employees who encourage customers to use POS."

Success breeds success, Higgason asserts. "As customers stand in line, they see the person in front of them using a debit card and checking out quicker and it prompts them to use it too. "

An experiment last summer in Dayton, Ohio, among "Money Station" card issuer banks and merchants discovered that in addition to merchant/bank cooperation on advertising, the key to getting customers to use the cards was to get merchant employees to understand them, use them, and to tell customers to use the card, says Bill Petrarca, senior vice president-EFT strategies, National City Bank, Cleveland, Ohio.

Indeed, retailer experience across the board has shown that consumers are willing to try out POS. But getting consumers to try POS involves a number of crucial "ifs." They will use the systems if they see benefits (i.e., Lucky Stores' "Easy Checkout" campaign promoting shorter, faster grocery lines) and if they are given initial incentives (i.e., Mobil's money-off campaign).

Ronald Nuti, corporate store systems manager, Lucky Stores, Incorporated, Dublin, California, adds that consumers will be more likely to give POS a try if they are given account security via self-activated terminals or secret PIN numbers and if they are reassured that embarrassing situations, like an NSF message at the checkout counter, can be eliminated via balance-inquiry terminals at store entrances.

Technology issues aside, it appears the most important commitment that must be made on POS is to marketing the systems to both consumers and to merchants.

Mobil's POS Debit Manager, Park, says that his company gets very good cooperation with some bank partners, but suggests that because banks still don't recognize a sufficient revenue stream they are very reluctant to make a commitment to marketing. "Some partners do a very good job of marketing, but there are others who do a mediocre job. They're not very good or consistent in their marketing efforts." Park says that some banks argue that the networks should worry about marketing.

Actually, Park concurs with this view, suggesting that if more banks pooled their resources at the network level, they could maximize their marketing dollars. "I'm dumbfounded that the networks spend big money on marketing ATMs, while for the most part ignoring POS capability that can add both value and flexibility to the card." Much more needs to be done in marketing to consumers and adding value to debit cards, Park asserts.

WILD CARD FACTORS AT WORK

There are wild card factors at work in POS direct debit, one of which is government involvement, particularly through the emergence of electronic systems for distributing various welfare benefits. With involvement by agencies from the federal to county courthouse level, a clear possibility is developing that, at least in some cases, government may be the entity that issues cards and pays for the installation of terminals — or terminal enhancement — to allow recipients access to their benefits at retailers' check-out lines or financial institutions'

ATMs. This is occurring because electronic distribution is expected to reduce fraud and provide better recordkeeping, while providing recipients, who frequently do not otherwise have financial accounts, an intangible benefit of a less conspicuous means of obtaining aid than receiving food stamp booklets or a check that must be cashed. Ultimately, the electronic systems are expected to be less expensive than paper.

Yet another possible wild card in direct debit is the development of merchant information systems that readily could include electronic funds transfer options. These systems are currently evolving as means of rapid and secure communications between manufacturers and wholesalers, with a link to the retail level available in some cases. Although this is now occurring at the level of large-scale business to business communications, the migration path is downward. It does not require a great leap of logic to see that these systems have the potential for automating a variety of high volume merchants who would then have available — and be familiar with — the technology for accepting electronic payments directly from their customers.

Furthermore, these computerized ordering and inventory systems are being linked to marketing systems that capture information about individual purchases. While the inventory and ordering portions of these systems fully provide a cost justification for their development, the marketing information that they provide creates opportunities for enhancing profits. Among the items of marketing information being captured is detail about the individual making the purchase. In some cases, retailers are issuing proprietary cards as a vehicle for that information capture. Most such cards clearly have the potential to be tied to POS direct debit systems, whether ACH-based or on-line.

BANKERS' PERSPECTIVES ON POS DEBIT

Banks have a profitable business in credit cards and direct debit could threaten that business. Rita Champ of the California-based Star network argues — based on research her organization has completed — that such fears are unfounded. Star, which has more food store POS terminals than anyone in the country, has 8,000 debit-accepting terminals and is second only to California's Interlink in debit terminals of all types. "I don't believe the typical credit card user will be the typical debit card user," she argues, adding that point-of-sale provides a niche service banks and merchants can tap without the fear it will replace something else.

In the Star network study, 78% of those who had used point of sale debit viewed that payment option as an alternative to cash or checks. Only 7% saw a debit card as an alternative to credit cards. Backing that up was a question to non point-of-sale debit users on why they didn't use the payment system. Of that non-user group, about 7% cited credit cards as the preferred other means. "Don't go out, Mr. Banker, with the idea credit card customers are going to give up their credit card and take debit," Champ warns.

Such information may give credence to the assumption that a reduction in checks will reduce operating costs for banks, but Don Maurer, senior vice president of CoreStates Financial Corporation has a different perspective. He says just because a half million checks are taken out of the bank processing system because of electronic ACH transactions doesn't necessarily correlate to less expense for a bank. A half million checks are not a significant percentage of those processed. Check processing volume is so large that a greater percentage of checks must be taken out of the system for economies of scale to be affected.

If there is work to be done to sell bankers on debit, it might be in the areas of objective and fair assessment of what it costs an institution to deliver the service. Also working against debit are banks' efforts to make the debit activity profitable. "We had some banks out there who were going to charge customers for POS transactions in the same fashion as the ATM world simply because their systems haven't been modified to differentiate between the two types of transactions," says George R. Hood, director of electronic banking services at Wegman's Food Markets, one of the most progressive food retailers endorsing on-line debit activity.

When Randall's Food Markets Incorporated of Houston, Texas, launched a POS debit program through the Texas network Pulse, it quickly learned many bankers were not recognizing POS transactions though the network carried no interchange fee. When supermarket customers — who had been told using a debit card carried no additional charge — found charges of as much as $1 or $2 on their statements, the outcry resulted in Randall's posting at each checkout stand a list of financial institutions charging for debit, an action that quickly resulted in a withdrawal of those fees by most of the banks who had treated the transactions as foreign ATM withdrawals.

THE CONSUMER PERSPECTIVE

The consumer holds one of the keys to success of POS direct debit. Consumers will use the service if, and only if, significant investment is made in education. Otherwise, the level of awareness is too low for significant response. The alternatives work well enough to limit demand for this new service. Once the consumer is aware of the service, increased usage follows. With ATM card penetration in the United States at 59.6% of all households as of 1989 (Source: Payment Systems, Inc.), only one household in ten that has an ATM card is aware it can be used directly to make purchases in many locations.

Awareness can be changed by marketing and very well may be in the near future because ATM cards are the most obvious and popular POS direct debit vehicle for many debit programs. Thus, it seems reasonable to conclude that a substantial number of the 88% of households that indicate that they do not have a POS direct debit card may indeed have an ATM card that functions as a POS debit card, but are not now aware of that fact. Many of these households simply are not yet aware such services exist.

Once consumers are made aware of the service — such as has occurred in California — convenience, widespread acceptance and availability convince them to become frequent users. The initial use, however, is crucial to the success of the service. A survey conducted in 1989 by the Star network in California indicated that 82% of consumers decided which payment method to use before they left home. A surprising 48% of first time users tried the service in response to some sort of emergency, such as being short of cash or having no checkbook. In other words, first use of a debit card was accidental rather than deliberate, but led to subsequent usage.

Star also found that 51% of its POS direct debit users surveyed first learned about the service from a retailer. Only 22% learned about it from their financial institution. Marketing not only brings about first usage, but encourages repeat usage. Convenience is the single most important factor once the service is tried. However, some sort of incentive may be necessary to get consumers to try the service for the first time.

Adoption of debit service is not dependent on the operational characteristics of the service. The consumer is not concerned whether the process is on-line real time or ACH based. They do not seem to discriminate between those services that require a PIN number like an ATM over those that require a signature, such as the Visa and MasterCard debit programs. Finally, it seems that there is no particular age factor relative to use of debit POS. Although younger consumers tend to be the first users of many such alternative payment services, debit users mirror the age range of the general population.

Additionally, consumers do not seem to have an aversion to paying a fee to use the service. In California for example, users of the Arco Paypoint system have been charged 10 cents per debit transaction at its 1,700 gasoline stations since the inception of the system. For much of 1988 and 1989, Arco processed 20% of all debit POS transactions in the United States, which equates to around 2 million transaction per month. Although not all of that volume can be attributed to their gas stations, a substantial amount of revenue is being generated.

According to recently published figures, Interlink, Star and Vons generate an average 6.5 million monthly transactions, which is 47% of all U.S. debit POS transaction volume through their combined 26,456 terminals. Although this volume is roughly only 11% of the ATM traffic across the same networks, it demonstrates rather dramatically that consumers will use the service if it is available and promoted.

CONSUMERS' PERSPECTIVE ON POS DEBIT PRICING

When National Bank of Detroit debit card holders use their MasterCard-marked ATM/debit card to make a purchase of a pair of slacks or any other product, they are charged a user fee of 20 cents. It's the same fee they incur to use other banks' automated teller machines. (If certain account balances are maintained, the fee may be waived.) Another approach is to charge an annual fee for the card, as is done with credit cards. First Bank System Incorporated of Minneapolis, which is placing the Visa mark on its ATM cards, offers the card free for the first year, but plans an annual fee of $12, which probably will be billed as $1 a month. Consumers accustomed to free ATM cards may complain initially, but if the method is convenient, history says they'll pay. Merchants may be more concerned that consumers will blame them for per transaction charges, rather than the bank.

California-based efforts in POS direct debit provide a large-scale test of consumer resistance to per transaction pricing for debit and the results affirm that consumers will pay. In addition to ARCO's PayPoint system, in 1987 First Interstate Bank of California examined its pricing structure and decided debit transactions represented a fee opportunity. The bank initiated a flat charge of 10 cents per transaction, regardless of the cardholder's balance or account type. Although some California merchants were vocally opposed to the decision, fearing that First Interstate's action would subvert their efforts to promote usage of debit cards and encourage other banks to impose such fees, very little consumer resistance appeared.

First Interstate says the imposition of the transaction fee may have caused a flattening of the growth curve for POS debit during 1988, but that a slowdown in merchant marketing probably was a more important cause. As marketing efforts have resumed, so has growth in debit usage. Even with the flattening, debit usage through California's Interlink network grew about 25% from 1987 to 1988. From 1986 to 1987, usage grew by 63%, although from a much smaller base. The last quarter of 1986 saw approximately 5.5 million transactions, volume that was being equalled each month by the last quarter of 1988.

Interestingly, First Interstate notes that many consumers appear to have recognized that the 10-cent per transaction fee the bank charges for using a debit card can be cheaper than using ATMs where a foreign transaction fee is imposed. California merchants will provide from $20 to $200 cash back at the point of sale, in some instances not even requiring a purchase to do so. First Interstate says research within its customer base has shown that heavy ATM users typically conducted eight separate transactions per month prior to the advent of POS debit services. That frequency among heavy users has slipped to seven times per month, which appears to be directly correlated to POS usage of the ATM card. With lines forming at many of its ATMs, the bank is quite willing to offload volume to merchants.

THE MERCHANT PERSPECTIVE

Without extensive involvement of merchants, POS direct debit has no chance of developing, much less succeeding. In fact, merchants have provided the spark for most programs to date. However, each type of merchant has a special set of needs defined by their particular business plan parameters. Motivations vary for being involved in POS direct debit.

A number of factors are encouraging supermarkets to develop POS direct debit capabilities. The emerging field of customer marketing information provides one motivator. Several chains now are better able to segment their market based upon discrete information gathered by monitoring purchase behavior of customers. The items purchased and frequency of visits are compared and contrasted to determine patterns of purchase behavior. By doing this, the participating supermarkets can more easily target promotional campaigns specifically to likely product buyers. Other benefits include programs like frequent shopper clubs, which reward consumers for loyalty by giving discounts based on accumulated purchase volume. Additionally, check losses prevented by the installation of check cashing systems more than pay for POS direct debit capabilities. Once the systems are in place, the POS direct debit function is an add-on benefit.

Convenience stores exist because they are exactly that, convenient. They are able to charge higher prices for their goods because a consumer can zip in, get what is needed, and zip out, without having to wait in a long line. Generally speaking, they do not accept any payment medium other than cash, with the exception of those convenience stores that also sell fuel. These accept both proprietary credit cards and bank cards. Few would accept a check under any circumstances.

As convenience stores expand in terms of geographic penetration and annual sales, they are constantly in search of products that meet the needs of their consumer base. Many seek to expand or change their clientele and upgrade their image. Any product they offer must be convenient, obviously, but must also be competitive, timely, fit the needs of their customers and of increasing importance recently, must be fashionable. A product or service must also be fast and provide a high profit margin.

POS direct debit fits all of these criteria but the last. As is the case with other merchant business case developments, POS direct debit can not support itself as a free standing product. When developed in conjunction with credit card authorization and draft capture capabilities, it becomes an attractive ancillary benefit. It provides the consumer with the ability to spend more money than is available in cash, thus increasing impulse buying.

Gasoline retailers were the first merchant type to develop widespread POS direct debit capabilities. The infrastructure developed to accept proprietary credit cards and bank cards, with POS direct debit as an add-on feature. Those dealerships that provide convenience stores along with their gas stations recognize the benefits of promoting impulse buying and do what they can to encourage it. The average POS direct debit ticket is larger than a cash purchase, much as credit card purchases tend to have a higher average value.

Specialty stores have little or no compulsion to develop POS direct debit capabilities, but at the same time have absolutely no reason to turn down the capability when processors offer it in combination with credit card authorization programs. This is more common if draft capture capabilities are inherent in the credit card system, as upgraded terminals with appropriate memory capabilities are available readily. The PIN pad and printer option must be priced attractively by the service provider and well-supported by services such as being able to replace terminals quickly when they break. The best services are those that support the widest variety of options, including check verification and guarantee services.

Department stores must be segmented into traditional department stores and discount department stores for purposes of looking at POS direct debit business case development. Neither segment represents a real opportunity for growth relative to POS direct debit, but for different reasons. Traditional department stores generally accept most forms of payment, including checks, cash, bank cards, Discover, Amex and the like. However, they do not generate any noteworthy volume of checks during a given day. There is simply no volume-related issue to solve as with supermarkets and no necessity to develop the capability. Almost 61% of purchases made at traditional department stores are made with the store's proprietary credit card. Also, given the fact that each ECR in a given store must be retrofitted for PIN pads, and all of the clerk staff must be trained to handle the transaction, little opportunity can be foreseen.

Discount department stores, on the other hand, generate substantially more check volume than a traditional store. They generally use third-party check approval services, passing the associated risk of check-related losses to service providers such as Telecredit. Conversion to on-line capabilities is also cost prohibitive. KMart, for example, has approximately 2,000 stores. Given an average of 10 check out lanes per store, the installation of a $1,000 POS direct debit terminal with PIN pad and printer for each would require a $20 million investment chainwide. Add in the cost of support hardware, software, telecommunications and marketing, and it is easy to see why the discount stores have not as yet jumped on the bandwagon.

The typical hotel chain accepts bank cards or travel and entertainment credit cards such as American Express almost exclusively. What few checks they do accept are generally well-secured by multiple identifications and often cashed solely as a convenience to a guest who is paying by other means. The hotels are more than likely, however, to have an infrastructure developed that can be modified to accept and process debit cards. Only a PIN pad upgrade may be required. The problem is consumer acceptance. With the exception of traveling families on vacation that may have a penchant for using cash and might use debit as a replacement, there appears to be very little demand for POS direct debit within this industry. Education of both consumers and hotel industry executives of the benefits associated with POS direct debit could start the process of development.

Restaurants can be divided into several categories; the traditional "fine" restaurant; the family "sit-down" restaurant; and fast food restaurants. Each of these have differing considerations and interests when it comes to POS direct debit. The traditional "fine restaurant" generally accepts cash, all bank credit cards and T&E cards. They rarely accept checks. Their credit authorization terminal capabilities are easily expanded to include POS direct debit. They have a consumer base that is largely accustomed to paying with cash. These consumers would be the most likely target for conversion, but the restaurants have little or no motivation to attempt to have their customers do so. Having the infrastructure available makes no difference. In addition, they still have to figure out how to effectively handle gratuities.

The family "sit-down" restaurant chains, historically a cash-only type of establishment, now recognize the drawing power of accepting bank credit and T&E cards. These chains are looking for ways to attract a clientele that does not usually carry a great deal of cash, but is reluctant to regularly charge family meals on a credit card. These consumers historically stop at fast food restaurants because of the lower prices. However, fast food prices are rising steadily and now are approaching those at family restaurants. POS direct debit represents an opportunity to attract these families away from the fast food chains.

Fast food restaurants also recognize the narrowing of the gap between family restaurant pricing and theirs. They are experimenting with credit cards as well as debit, in order to capture any sort of market share from non-cash customers. There are a number of pilot trials taking place in this area, which would permit rapid approval of a transaction with minimal reason for consumers to fear rejection of their transactions. Scrip terminals, which issue a pre-paid coupon or chit, are one solution to this problem, allowing consumers to preauthorize the transaction before entering the food ordering line. This also permits limited cash back on the transaction as well. Once again, the infrastructure must be developed before widespread acceptance can be expected, and the credit function will more than likely provide the impetus to develop the infrastructure. If current credit acceptance tests are successful, debit may piggyback with little added expenditure.

THE SYSTEM PROVIDERS

POS direct debit also has the undivided support of the vendors and suppliers of the infrastructure of the service. It represents their livelihood. In fact, these vendors hold some of the responsibility for many of the early false starts in debit POS. They have heralded its arrival for years, and created the impression of tremendous activity where there was little or none.

There are 30,400 supermarkets in the United States, with an average of seven checkout lanes per store. This represents a potential of 212,800 terminal locations in supermarkets alone. Obviously the immediate market potential is really for add-on devices for the store ECR systems, which still represents a possible PIN and and card reading device. *POS News* reports 15,856 terminals installed as of June 1989 or a penetration of 7.5%. Vendors of this equipment have a great future ahead of them.

Convenience stores also represent a lucrative target with over 50,000 locations. With only 2,343 terminals installed, there is still 95% of the market available. In addition, there are over 100,000 gas stations in the United States and 17,830 terminals installed, representing a market penetration of around 15%, better than the other markets but with plenty of room for growth. All told, these merchants represent the best targets for POS debit, due to their popularity as indicated by consumer research, and the fact that they, for the most part, do not currently have credit authorization terminals installed.

There are 63,000 pharmacies that would represent a solid market were it not for the fact that over 40,000 of them already have on-line links to processing companies by which they initiate insurance claims and process forms. It is an extremely simple matter to upgrade this installed base to include both debit and credit functionality. In fact, National

Data Corporation, which provides processing to 28,500 pharmacies, recently hired a senior staff member whose specific duty is to upgrade every existing NDC-supported terminal to accept debit cards.

Existing credit card authorization terminal locations must also be taken into account when discussing POS direct debit. Given that MasterCard and Visa report having 2.7 million merchant locations in the U.S. and the associations have been pushing for on-line authorization for some time now by offering merchants favorable rates for doing so, one must presume that a large percentage of these locations have an authorization terminal at their location. As these convert to electronic draft capture (EDC) capabilities, the number available for POS direct debit programs will expand as well. This bodes well for continual expansion of the service. In particular, terminals with electronic draft capture capabilities contain almost all of the necessary capabilities to support debit POS. Only a PIN pad is additionally required, and for the most part, the EDC terminals are already prewired to support such a pad as a plug-in module. Currently, about 500,000 EDC terminals are installed, representing spectacular potential. This is roughly nine times the number of on-line debit POS terminals that were installed at year end 1989.

THE FUTURE DIRECTION OF POS DIRECT DEBIT

As it stands today, POS direct debit is an evolving, dynamic service that is developing on a wide variety of fronts. It is driven by the needs and recognition of opportunities by the players involved in the process. There are almost 50,000 debit terminals installed at the point of sale across the country today, the majority of which are found in grocery stores, gas stations, convenience stores and specialty stores. The supermarket segment represents the largest source of growth, having installed more than 13,000 new terminals during 1988-1989 for a total of about 15,800 devices available nationwide. Most of these devices are linked to regional ATM networks, although ACH POS devices represent a growing segment. POS direct debit transaction volume has soared during the same period, from 3 million transactions a month to more than 13 million transactions a month authorized by these networks.

This growth will continue well into the forseeable future. Each of the authorization and settlement alternatives explored in this discussion will remain as viable parts of the POS direct debit system as it evolves. There is no compelling argument for any of them to be overcome by the others, and each has economically strong contingents supporting them. There will be be continued development of ACH capabilities among several on-line segments — most notably the supermarket industry — as pricing policies for continued membership in regional and national ATM networks are being hashed out among the players. These merchants perceive the need for some type of economic clout to defend themselves against bank controlled regional networks and even the Visa/MasterCard networks.

The ACH alternative provides such protection, allowing providers the alternative of pulling the on-line plug and continuing to offer POS direct debit to their consumers. This would require a different activation device, probably the store-issued card. The regional networks will continue to develop terminal capabilities through their member banks, who will continue developing them for their merchant clients. MasterCard and Visa also will continue to develop their proprietary debit card offerings, now that Entree has been given last rites. The third party networks also will push POS direct debit further into their client bases as EDC terminals will be upgraded to accept these transactions. This service represents an incremental revenue stream from an existing infrastructure, requiring some additional investment to develop the capabilities, which can be recaptured through enhanced service fees.

The remaining delivery mechanisms also will gain from widespread development of POS direct debit as more consumers will be exposed to electronic alternatives. Familiarity with a technology has been seen to lessen the fear of other, similar types of technologies, and the industry can expect the same experience here. Only the ATM networks may see some level of negative impact, presuming use of the cash back feature at the point of sale becomes widespread. Consumers will not have to stop as frequently at an ATM for cash, but can simply get the amount needed as a byproduct of a purchase transaction. This also may lead to retailers having to supply more cash, but since supermarkets are net providers of cash to the banking industry now, significant impacts are not forseen.

POS direct debit is in a confused state of development, but is emerging as an important part of the payment system with the potential to offset many paper checks.

CHAPTER

7

Automated Clearinghouse Services: A Backbone Service

ACH POISED FOR GROWTH

Transaction volume through Automated Clearing House networks has grown considerably due to regulatory changes, corporate sector demands for more versatile transmission formats, and the emergence of new, low-cost technological capabilities. With steady annual increases in the number of credit and debit transactions generated, the ACH is America's largest single electronic payments network. The system today handles about 2% of all transaction volume, but is positioned to play an increasingly important role in the nation's payments system.

As automation proceeds in piecemeal fashion, there is a need for an entity such as the ACH system, which can accommodate both automated and non-automated transaction processing. However, the non-automated portions are holding the system back from its potential to offer great efficiencies to financial institution transaction processing, but are necessary to provide a bridge for institutions in transition.

From the point of view of the public, this role raises the possibility that at some point taxpayers may be asked to subsidize the provision of services for non-automated institutions. This likelihood is more than conjecture given that Visa USA literally has gone into competition with the Federal Reserve system in processing of electronic transactions. With Federal Reserve pricing based on cost, Visa's efforts may skim off the volume of inexpensive, fully electronic processing that helps hold down overall processing costs for the Fed. There is nothing wrong with Visa's strategy, which is to become the dominant, full-service provider of transaction services worldwide. The public policy questions may come to resemble those that brought about the disastrous efforts to preserve the savings and loan industry. When competition makes obsolete an industry or a large segment of an industry, to what degree is it in the public interest to preserve that industry? Perhaps a bit of education as to what the ACH is, what it does and how it is changing will help prevent such mistakes.

THE NATIONAL AUTOMATED CLEARING HOUSE ASSOCIATION (NACHA)

Membership in the National Automated Clearing House Association (NACHA) is comprised of 42 regional Automated Clearing Houses which provide ACH services on a not-for-profit basis to more than 40,000 institutions. There are over 17,500 Depository Financial Institution (DFI) members of the regional clearinghouses. The ACH system was established in 1973, when the growth in check volumes threatened to overwhelm the paper-based clearinghouse system. Although it was seen by some as essential infrastructure for the checkless, cashless society, it was primarily designed to handle low-dollar, repetitive payments on a batch basis. With few exceptions, it is operated by the Federal Reserve Board.

Banks have utilized the Automated Clearing House (ACH) network since the early 1970s to transmit various types of payments among ACH member institutions. Recurring, fixed payments like Social Security benefits, insurance premiums and mortgage payments have historically been among the largest contributors to ACH transaction volume. In 1976, government retirement benefits, processed as credits in the ACH system, accounted for 89% of total volume. As the system has matured, private sector debits, (such as consumer auto loan or insurance payments) and credits (like direct deposit of payroll or dividend checks) claim larger and larger shares of the yearly transaction totals. These types of preauthorized payments of deposits (PPDs) have, in recent years, surpassed government sector credits to become a majority of what the Automated Clearing Houses process.

In 1986, twelve years after the ACH system was inaugurated, check volume was maintaining a 4 to 5% annual growth rate, while ACH transaction volumes increased 27% from the previous year, to over 734 million. The one-billion transaction mark was passed in 1989 and growth continues to soar. Recent campaigns to promote direct deposit of payroll have further contributed to growth, but some of the greatest immediate potential lies in the corporate sector. This growth comes as an adjunct to general automation of corporate data systems.

However, perceived lack of security for ACH transactions, as well as limitations on the type of data that can be included, initially tended to prejudice corporate adoption of the network for sending sensitive intercorporate payments and data. As a consequence, large corporations like General Motors in the late 1980s created other ways to electronically transmit this information. These corporate efforts, which have emerged as complements to Electronic Data Interchange (EDI), have forced changes in the ACH system.

Spurred by the prospect of a viable corporate sponsored alternative to the ACH payments system, NACHA encourages the creation of several new format types for corporate electronic messages. These formats allow remittance data to be formatted to the specifications designated by the American National Standards Institute (ANSI) X12 committee. The resulted was the addition of the Corporate Trade Payment (CTP), Corporate Trade Exchange (CTX) and, Cash Concentration or Disbursement with Addenda (CCD+) formats to those the ACH system can process. These formats allow the transmission of more extensive—and pertinent—corporate information, such as not only the amount of a payment and the name of its recipient, but also the invoice number that triggered the payment.

Other new services were introduced at the same time as corporate payment formats were being created. For example, international direct deposit of Social Security benefits became an option in 1988. Expatriate recipients residing in the United Kingdom were the first to be offered the service with expansion following to Canada and West Germany. There also have been increases in the more traditional sources of transaction volume, such as direct deposit of U.S. Treasury checks in this country and payments to government vendors via the ACH. Use of the ACH for direct debit at the point of sale has grown as well, although is yet relatively minor.

The continued growth of ACH processing volumes depends on continued low cost in using this medium. Much of this efficiency occurs because of the off-line batch processing employed by the ACH. However, changes are needed to retain that efficiency. Transactions are settled in two daily cycles, which were developed to assure delivery of ACH items to all receiving points, including large numbers of non-electronic ACH receiving points. NACHA recognizes that current processing schedules reflect methodologies designed to accommodate computer systems of a decade ago, including the assumptions that several hours are required to process a batch of payments and that delivery of items is made by the same couriers that deliver checks for the paper processing system. New processing schedules are being considered that would improve the quality and reliability of the ACH network without increasing transaction costs.

FACILITATING MIGRATION TO ELECTRONIC PROCESSING

The Federal Reserve and the U.S. Treasury have been active proponents of electronic payments and have done more than simply issue policy statements to encourage the financial industry's migration to full electronic processing.

The direct deposit of Social Security checks, initiated during the 1970s, was responsible for providing sufficient transaction volume to see the ACH network through the early years. These payments were once the largest component of ACH volume and, in every year since 1973, there has been continuous growth in the numbers of consumers who participate in the Social Security Administration's direct deposit program. Today, approximately 55% of all Social Security recipients receive their monthly benefits in the form of an automatic electronic deposit made directly to their account at one of the ACH network's 17,000 plus depository financial institutions.

The Armed Forces have taken to direct deposit in a big way also, with the Sure-Pay program representing tangible evidence of their commitment. All branches of the military have shown high rates of usage for direct deposit of payroll. Prior to 1986, about 70% of the army's active soldiers and over 90% of air force personnel used the payment option. In the aftermath of the Grenada invasion in 1987, in which there were problems distributing paychecks to soldiers not enrolled in the direct deposit program, this method of payment was made mandatory for all new recruits.

Another of the developments in EFT/EDI that bodes well for increasing ACH transaction volumes is an effort by the Treasury Department to gradually convert its paper based corporate payments from check to ACH format. A program launched in 1987 called Vendor Express has the potential to give corporate electronic payments the same kind of boost that initiation of direct deposit of Social Security benefits gave to retail electronic payments in the 1970s. The government began using the Fed Wire funds transfer network to pay invoices for amounts greater than $25,000 in the early 1980s. It now uses the ACH for these, as well as for payments involving smaller amounts.

Vendor Express is intended to eventually automate all government payments to suppliers of goods and services. The program began with a volume of about 45,000 payments per month, with volume projected to grow tenfold to about 4.1 million payments per month within two years. By 1989, actual volume was reported at 311,000 for the first quarter, but growing by more than 10% per quarter. By the end of the first quarter of 1990, volume had reached a half-million payments per quarter, still short of projections, but representing a 40% annual growth rate. Proponents of Vendor Express expect that as many as 77 million payments (with remittance data) can be made through the ACH each year without significantly disrupting current processing capabilities.

The Treasury programs' use of the Automated Clearing House system encouraged the development of enhanced ACH standards incorporating greater ability to provide information along with payment. These standards, including CTX and CCD+, do not, however, have the capability or flexibility of general EDI standards in supporting information communications. Many observers noted that the development of the enhanced national funds transfer standards clearly was in reaction to the private initiatives by GM and a few other corporate players, whose efforts were resulting in varying requirements in specific areas such as encryption and authentication security measures.

The primary motivation for the Treasury was the prospect of a substantial reduction in processing costs associated with automated clearinghouse transactions. These costs are expected to decrease from the 26 cents currently required to process a check down to just 3 cents per item, or an incremental savings of 23 cents per check. If and when all 77 million paper checks written to corporations each year are converted to the ACH-based Vendor Express system, estimates by Treasury's Financial Management Services project an ultimate savings of $18 million a year in processing costs.

The ACH system was designed to move money quickly and cost-effectively. However, as the American corporate community discovered, it failed to meet the security standards and data transmission requirements of large corporations like General Motors. In response to this deficiency, the American National Standards Institute developed ANSI X12 as an electronic communications format to be the standard language of corporate EDI. Designed for the data interchange needs of big business rather than the electronic funds transfer needs of financial institutions, this protocol facilitates transmission of encrypted payment and remittance data.

GM initiated EDI as a way to reduce the costs associated with its paper based invoicing and remittance procedures. With 20,000 suppliers to pay, GM has a substantial quantity of paper and cost associated with each payment. In order to eliminate most of this cost, and the error factor inherent in manual data entry, the giant automaker opted to bypass the ACH network and initiate an almost totally electronic remittance procedure.

GM's alternative payment system began with a nucleus of eight banks that agreed to electronically pay willing suppliers in a manner consistent with the requirements of the automaker. Prominent among the eight financial institutions was First National Bank of Chicago, which developed the banking software used by most of the banks involved in the system. The other institutions involved were Citibank, Chase Manhattan and Chemical Bank in New York, Pittsburgh National Bank, California's Bank of America, and in Detroit, the National Bank of Detroit and Manufacturers' National.

Essentially, these banks agreed to employ the ANSI X12 format to encrypt and authenticate all messages, as well as to permit the inclusion of remittance data. They established a PC based interchange system that was capable of transmitting both payments and data between their institutions. The procedures begin with the telephone transmission of encrypted data that has been formatted to ANSI standards and is programmed for authentification. This transmission is received by a personal computer located at one of the eight GM affiliated institutions at least two days before the date of payment. The receiving institution authenticates and acknowledges receipt of the transmission. Afterwards, the bank's host processor checks and validates ABA numbers and account numbers and then sends a second acknowledgement to GM, which confirms that the contents are in order.

Payments are then separated into three electronic "stacks": one for the on-us items, where a supplier's account is at the same institution; one for suppliers whose payments are to be deposited in one of the other seven banks in the GM system; and one for suppliers whose banks are not in the network. Suppliers without a banking relationship with one of the GM banks receive their payments through the Automated Clearing House system. Although GM has noted as "positive" the ACH adoption of similar ANSI X12 style formats, there is no sign that the automaker will abandon its new payments system.

EDI MOVES CORPORATE PAYMENTS TO ELECTRONICS

The example of General Motors, even though it is one of the world's largest industrial companies, might be regarded as an anomaly except that a wide variety of prognosticators see corporate communications migrating toward electronics, specifically through formalized EDI systems. EDI Resources Incorporated estimates 1989 EDI revenues were $345.9 million, of which $157.5 million was derived from software, $136 million from hardware, $43.1 million from transactions and $9.3 million from consulting services. The estimate includes non-financial and financial EDI. *Cashflow* magazine estimates that within 10 years 50% of all business transactions will be handled electronically.

International Resource Development, Incorporated (IRD) predicts that growth in EDI will accelerate from a current rate of approximately 35% per year to 50% annually for both services and software by the mid-1990s. IRD estimates that more than 20,000 companies in 50 different industries have implemented various EDI applications.

EDI is a means of facilitating and expediting accurate information transactions. These information transactions typically result in payment transactions, but are not in themselves payment transactions or electronic funds transfers. However, EFT can be a component of EDI with completion of the payment transaction through the ACH system. The similarity and relationship is obvious, although not always well understood. As business is driven by needs to manage growing volumes at faster rates with high levels of accuracy, just as in financial transactions, computerization (and automation of business functions generally) plays an increasing role. EDI and EFT are close cousins whose development appear to be synergetic.

U.S. corporations, banks and individuals spend $20 billion each year to operate payment systems, estimates *Cashflow* magazine. The cost to process one paper purchase order has tripled during the last 10 years, from $50 to $150, it says.

GM's Robert H. Harvey, director of worldwide banking and U.S. cash management, addressed the National Corporate Cash Management Association conference in Atlanta in late 1987 about the firm's EDI program. *Funds Transfer Report* quoted him as saying that evaluation of EDI economics must consider "the total administration efforts for a paper payments system, which includes check remittance, information preparation, efforts to handle lost or stolen checks, account reconciliation, paper storage and retention."

Harvey noted that concerns about loss of float due to electronic payment may be neutralized by adjusting nominal paper check paper terms to reflect real effective payment terms. A GM study found real float present in the check based system between GM and its suppliers to be 3.6 days. The EDI system provided suppliers with good funds in three days, which Harvey said improved their position by .6 of a day.

Conversion to EDI from all paper based systems can reduce a company's combined inventory and days sales outstandings by at least five days, says Paul Mayland, VP and Director of Corporate Payment Services at Manufacturers Hanover Trust. MHT finds that in a paper environment, 17days are consumed before an invoice is generated, Mayland told *Funds Transfer Report*. The steps include generating a request for a quote, mailing it to the prospective vendor, receiving the request and checking the price and the inventory status, preparing and mailing the response, preparing and mailing the order, receiving and processing the order, generating and mailing the shipping notice, shipment, and receiving and logging the goods.

Mayland notes that transmitting a business document electronically costs between 50 cents and $1.50, while mailing a paper equivalent costs $3 to 10. He estimates a minimum transaction volume of 30 to 40 items per day or 10,000 annually is necessary to justify a business converting to EDI.

Bernard J. LaLonde, Ph.D., Mason Professor of Transportation and Logistics at Ohio State University, surveyed 100 distribution executives in 1986 who projected EDI transactions to go from 7 to 23% of customer transactions between 1986 and 1990. Vendor transactions were seen going from 3.5% to 15% by 1990. EDI/vendor transactions were projected to increase tenfold by the end of the 90s and

EDI/customer transactions to increase to 50% of all customer transactions. While bar coding of inbound shipments was expected to increase from 8% in 1986 to 39% in 1990, and 62% by 2000, the number of warehouses was projected to drop 25% between 1986 and 1990. By 2000, almost 40% of the inventory volume moving through the distribution channels will be driven by some type of "just in-time" system, the professor told *Stores* magazine in 1987. The forecasts appear to have been on target so far. Economists credit such systems with having reduced inventories to a degree that in 1990, when recession was widely expected, the usual ballooning of inventories that signals the onset of recession simply did not occur.

EDI FORMALIZES BUSINESS COMMUNICATIONS

EDI is a general term encompassing a variety of standards and means of exchanging formalized business communications. It is more specific and defined than electronic mail — the exchange of paperless messages by computerized telecommunications. With EDI, national and international standards organizations (the American National Standards Institute, ANSI, and the International Standards Organization, ISO) are engaged in an ongoing process of establishing specific computer formats that are intended to provide consistent cross-industry means of defining all elements in any business document. These elements include the contents of invoices, purchase orders, requests for quotations, shipping forms and other business communications. EDI standards are the province of ANSI's X12 committee.

Formalization of data interchange is a means of coping with a bewildering variety of computer operating systems, languages and communication standards. In essence, EDI provides a universal communications tool. The potential volume of information transactions that may be communicated electronically is staggering, rivaling and probably exceeding current paper based mail volume and incorporating at least a portion of current voice telecommunications.

Besides the early applications of EDI in manufacturing, interesting possibilities within retailing exist when EDI is regarded as a communications link for firms that have already installed or implemented comprehensive, computerized inventory management systems. Through use of UPC (Universal Price Code) scanning or SKU inventory control numbering systems at the point of sale, a retailer can capture sales information, update inventory and initiate ordering in a single operation. The supplier, in effect, becomes the store's warehouse. By use of bar code scanning, retailers foresee being able to label each shipping carton, thereby having a packing slip for each carton rather than each shipment and improving inventory control and tracking.

Retailers active in this area include K-G Retail, Carlisle's, Designs, D.H. Holmes, Service Merchandise, Mervyn's, Bullock's, Dayton's and Carter Hawley Hale corporate. *Stores* magazine noted in a recent article that "it is not necessarily the sophistication or size of the retailer that determines whether it enters into this kind of arrangement, it's how it defines the partnership with the vendor."

Companies in the chemical, automotive, transportation, manufacturing and medical supplies industries are credited with being particularly instrumental in EDI growth.

PIONEERS IN EDI

Two American companies are frequently cited as pioneers in implementation of EDI, both vehicle manufacturers and consequently firms that rely on an extensive network of vendors. General Motors acquired Ross Perot's Texas computer company, Electronic Data Systems, in the process of implementing EDI and has become a major competitor in providing EDI services. GM began researching EDI in 1984 and initiated its program in 1986. By yearend 1987, about 1,600 of the automaker's vendors were using EDI. The firm, which incorporates trade payments within its EDI system, says $2.5 billion in disbursements were made through it in the first 10 months of 1987. GM's stated goal was to have 20,000 vendors on-line by 1990.

Navistar, the reorganized International Harvester Company, credits implementation of EDI with producing major cost reductions that assisted the company in emerging from bankruptcy. In the first 18 months of use, truck inventories were cut by a third or $167 million. Ben Milbrandt, EDI manager for the firm, told *The Wall Street Journal* inventories have been cut to a 6-day supply from 33 days during the seven years the EDI system has been used and premium payments for rapid shipment of freight have fallen more than 90% to less than $500,000 a year.

A number of major corporations that have substantial subsidiaries or divisions engaged in telecommunications or data processing are competitors in providing EDI services. However, this arena also is providing opportunities for smaller competitors able to address particular needs such as software development.

GEISCO, the General Electric telecommunications and data processing subsidiary; McDonnell Douglas' Tymenet; Telenet Communications Corporation of Reston, Virginia; Western Union Corporation's EasyLink; Control Data, Minneapolis' Redinet network in a joint agreement with Spectrum Concepts Incorporated of New York; GM's EDS; IBM's Information Network and CompuServe are among the largest competitors. On the sidelines, primarily because of regulatory restrictions, are the Regional Bell Operating Companies, although most are engaged in at least exploratory efforts.

Additionally, a few smaller companies appear poised to play major roles, including Harbinger Computer Services of Atlanta, which is providing EDI services to Georgia Power, Westinghouse, Pacific Power & Light, Southern California Edison and Compaq Computer Corporation, and Sterling Software of Columbus, Ohio, which was an early service provider through its Ordernet Services Division and the first to actively seek interconnection with other EDI networks. Tandem Computers Incorporated, Cupertino, California, has announced a joint marketing agreement with TransSettlements Incorporated, Atlanta, for a product called TranSlate that runs on Tandem NonStop hardware.

BANKS INVOLVED IN EDI

American Banker's third annual survey on cash management trends, released in the fall of 1987, found 26% of the nation's 100 largest cash management banks had already made a "significant investment" toward research and developing EDI capabilities. Another 30% planned to make such investments in 1988. However, 49% of the top 100 banks rated customer interest in the technology as moderate and another 47% reported it as weak. None rated it strong.

By 1989, a survey conducted by TransData Corporation for the *American Banker* found 87% of respondents representing 381 banks with $75 million or more in deposits expected EDI to be the banking technology most likely to be widely used within five years. The increased optimism about EDI growth reflects the extent to which such applications have proven beneficial. NACHA estimates that there are potentially 10 billion corporate-to-corporate payments alone that may be converted from checks to EDI payments.

First Chicago Corporation began an internal EDI pilot program in November 1985 and by 1988 had processed 4,700 transactions between the purchasing department and more than 30 suppliers, said Raymond Farrell, vice president for the purchasing division. An annual savings of $500,000 was realized from the shift to EDI, he estimated. Projections were that 50 vendors would be in the program by the end of 1988 and cost reductions would reach $2 million annually.

By 1990, many banks had entered alliances with value-added communication networks to provide EDI services to corporate customers. Sears Communication Company connected with eight banks (Bank of America, CoreStates, Continental Bank, National Bank of Detroit, Harris Bank, The Northern Trust, First Wachovia and Mellon); General Electric Information Services (GEIS) and First Interstate Bank and Seattle-First National Bank; Harbinger and Citizens and Southern, Marine Midland and First Bank Systems; and IBM and First Chicago.

For those banks not wanting or not able to develop in-house services, a variety of correspondent bank services are available. The accounting firm of Coopers & Lybrand conducted a survey of major cash management banks that found expenditures for developing software and external services ranged from a quarter- to half-million dollars.

ADDITIONAL FACTORS PROMOTING ACH GROWTH

Electronic payment is becoming an integral part of EDI implementations, NACHA said in its 1990 EDI Payments Progress Report. Not only are financial institutions working with companies to design EDI systems and develop a wide array of services, but companies themselves are electing to incorporate "dollars with the data" both for convenience and to minimize potential liability. The Uniform Commercial Code, which governs all commercial transactions, suggests that a company may assume additional liability if it separates payments and remittance information.

New EDI payment applications include state tax payments, commercial loan payments, child support payments from the employer to the state, electronic dealer drafting payments and international EDI payments.

There are 14 states currently implementing corporate payment of taxes electronically with a number of additional states studying the issue. As many as 31 states are expected to have approved such legislation by early 1991, NACHA estimates. In the first seven states to implement such programs, a quarter of a million electronic tax payment transactions totaling nearly $23 billion will be made annually. Incorporating such large volumes of payments in everyday operations is expected to play a major role in educating corporations and financial institutions in the operation of EDI payment systems and thereby encourage further usage.

Corporations benefit by increased certainty of timely payment, although NACHA has recognized the need for standard means of providing legal proof of payment. State regulations vary widely and efforts are under way to develop uniform regulations. Organizations including the Federation of Tax Administrators and Committee on State Taxation are working with NACHA to develop such rules.

A nationwide program began in November 1990 that mandates child support payments be withheld from an absent parent's wages or income along with income tax and Social Security deductions. With a series of such federal regulations going into effect, states will be required by 1994 to implement electronic wage withholdings with all child support orders issued. Employers will be responsible for the withholding and will use the ACH to make deposits to the state. The potential volume of payments between employers and the states could reach 9 million per month, with $30 billion in funds collected.

IMPACT OF EDI ON THE ACH

The initiatives taken in the EFT/EDI field by corporations like General Motors have had an impact on the way that the ACH does business. New formats, intended to accommodate the stated needs of potential corporate users, have been authorized by NACHA and adopted by the membership. By being flexible enough to address these issues, the ACH networks seem to have guaranteed themselves a larger role in the funds transfer and data interchange requirements of this country's corporate accounting and cash management departments.

The federal government, motivated by the prospect of substantial savings, will continue to generate increasingly greater levels of ACH transactions. Its commitment to consumer and corporate direct deposit is genuine and total. Every tax return, armed forces payroll check, corporate supplier remittance, and retirement benefit payment potentially will be converted to an ACH credit.

Consumer usage of the ACH will expand also, but not because consumers directly will demand such services. The ACH provides a vehicle that corporations will use to develop services for the general public, particularly in bill payment. Consumers, like corporations or government, today have a variety of on-line and off-line payment alternatives capable of accessing transaction accounts. Generally speaking though, the bill-paying public is not concerned about the mechanics of a funds transfer. With the likelihood that more retailers will begin to offer proprietary debit cards, there also is the likelihood that more point of sale transactions will flow through the ACH, a fact of which the average member of the consuming public will be blissfully unaware. However, whether corporation, government, or consumer, the most significant concerns of any payor are convenience and efficiency.

Despite efforts to rationalize the means by which funds and information are exchanged, players in the EFT/EDI arena are likely to continue to implement non-conforming new systems and applications in pursuit of competitive advantages. In this constantly changing and competitive environment, the automated clearinghouses are adjusting their rules and operations procedures to assure that they will remain the nation's largest electronic payments network. While important but unresolved questions exist about the mechanics of integrating the disparate requirements of financial institutions, consumers, corporations, and retailers, the ACH of today stands ready to capture ever greater shares of their financially related transactions.

The culmination of ACH development will be the implementation of an all-electronic ACH. NACHA has asked the Federal Reserve to implement such a system by July 1991, but no commitment to a specific date has yet been made. A low-cost software package that runs on ordinary personal computers has been introduced by the Fed for financial institutions as a step toward making electronic access available to even the smallest institution. With such cost obstacles falling for financial institutions, there is little excuse remaining for the Federal Reserve not to require this logical next step in the evolution of the backbone of the nation's electronic payment system.

CHAPTER

8

Telephone Based Services: The Next Growth Area

AUTOMATED VOICE RESPONSE BANKING

Voice response technology allows a customer to use a telephone to get information directly from a bank's database without human intervention. While just a few years ago, many bankers argued that they could not see ever replacing personal contact with machines, changing public attitudes and dramatic decreases in the cost of providing such services have created one of the fastest growing areas of automation within financial services. Current growth is primarily in information services, but transaction capabilities often can be added readily if a financial institution's internal automation system is structured with such possibilities in mind.

The cost of providing voice response has plunged in the last half of the 1980s from the low to mid six-figure range to a $20,000 to $30,000 range, well within the reach of most institutions. At such price levels, replacing even a single staff position can offset the investment and provide the ability to offer 24-hour service. With personnel costs soaring and skilled help more valuable, institutions that once said "never," now have systems that answer incoming calls automatically and instruct callers to "just press one..."

For example, *Voice Processing Magazine* reported in 1990 on the installation of a voice response system at the Bank of Newport in California. Before automation, the bank needed 13 operators to handle daily calls, most of which were routine inquiries. Now the bank needs only two part-time employees to provide special customer assistance. The system, which is called MagicVoice, paid for itself in nine months and nearly 75% of customers use it to perform banking chores.

Banks that have analyzed their incoming call volumes have been among the first to apply automation, not only answering and directing calls, but also providing access to basic account information. Studies in some institutions have found as much as 90% of the calls received regarding transaction accounts are requests for current balance information. The voice response system that can handle that routine task also can handle a variety of other routine information tasks and provide marketing features as well. One of the most fully integrated automated systems in the country is operating in Detroit.

THE NBD TELEPHONE BANKING CENTER

In 1987, a task force at the National Bank of Detroit studied how to move time consuming — and therefore costly — routine transactions out of branches while simultaneously attracting more of the consumers that generate that very type of business. NBD calculated that at the rate its routine transaction business was growing, with the resulting increased volume in account inquiries and transfers, it could not afford to continue to add staff and build additional facilities. Further, the bank had a significant investment in an already highly successful ATM network. Charles Raphael, vice president of EFT services for the bank, says the conclusion of the study was to develop telephone services as a complement to branch and ATM services, even to the extent of using the ATM personal identification number (PIN) as part of the access requirements. The larger strategy is to build service delivery around the ATM card, not only increasing usage of ATMs, but also building card use at the point of sale.

The result was the NBD Telephone Banking Center, an unusually well integrated, in-house automation system. It built upon several existing elements of automation, as well as paralleling non-automated or partially automated systems that included an existing telephone bill payment program. With the new system, callers conduct business by entering the last 12 digits of a personal account number and the four digit PIN for an ATM card on a touchtone phone pad. A customer then can perform a variety of functions, guided through the process by a recorded human voice. Using it, customers can check their balances, transfer funds, pay loans, find out about the last five checks that have cleared and/or the last five deposits, inquire about checks by number, and obtain information about interest rates.

For customers who don't want to deal with machines, the center has human representatives. All customer service representatives came from the NBD branch system. And even though they have an average of 10 years branch experience, they received special training to prepare them for their new positions serving customers by phone. Telephone Banking Center customer representatives can do all of the things the voice response system can do, plus they open accounts, take loan applications, provide information about credit cards, ATM locations, branch hours, etc.; and they sell, cross sell and often handle product promotions without additional staff. The service is staffed seven days a week, including limited hours on Saturday and Sunday.

Access to all services is through one "gateway" phone system. That is, customers only have to call one phone number to reach the automated service or a service representative. During the first three months of service, 53% of the calls went to the voice response service.

NBD views its Telephone Banking Center as a way of differentiating itself from competitors. It looks at the telephone customer service system as a "total delivery strategy to duplicate the functions of a branch." Customers who have telephones can do all their banking via phone if they choose. Routine transactions can be handled quickly by way of the voice response system. Customer representatives handle the services that require a more personal touch as well as the routine.

There are some tradeoffs to using the automated system versus a conventional branch, which mainly represent sensible combinations of automated and non-automated service strengths. For example, when a customer uses the telephone service to open an account, the representative sends out by mail a kit containing all the forms along with explanations of how to complete the forms and where to sign them. The customer must return the forms along with his or her deposit before the account opening process can be completed. It is less immediate than going into a branch and opening an account, where the process is completed on the spot. On the other hand, by visiting a branch to open an account immediately, the customer is giving up the time and place convenience that the Telephone Banking Center provides.

But the parallel systems are not isolated. The telephone customer representatives can interact with the branch. Continuing with the same example, if a customer needs to open an account right away, the customer service representative can tell the customer where the nearest branch office is, take the information necessary to open the account over the telephone, contact the branch, and have everything ready for the customer by the time he or she gets to the branch with the initial deposit.

There is currently no charge for NBD Telephone Banking Center services and no plans to charge for them per se. But part of the overall strategy of the voice response aspect of the system is to enhance the value of the bank's ATM card. The voice response system is available only to those customers who have ATM cards, which carry the 12-digit Personal Account Number (PAN) that the customer must key in to gain access to the system. The PAN "front-ends" the system to the customer's entire account relationship. Once in, the customer can move from one account to another by keying a single digit as instructed by the system rather than having to key in all of the digits of each account he or she wants to inquire about. The voice response system also parallels the bank's ATM system in that both require the same personal identification number.

Even though the NBD Telephone Banking Center does not directly generate any fee revenue, the bank believes that it is more cost effective than face-to-face contact. The system has more technology than a typical branch had prior to the introduction of the system. Customer representatives work from screens. The core of the system is an in-house central information file that contains customers names, addresses and a listing of all the account relationships they have with the bank. It serves as a bridge to all the bank's on-line application systems, and when the customer representative logs on in the morning he or she is automatically logged on to all the application systems. Shifting from the central information file to the appropriate application requires pressing just one button. The bank expects to export such features to the branch system.

NBD finds that customer service representatives in the telephone banking center take less time than branch personnel to perform the same functions (e.g., account openings, loan applications, etc.). Certainly much of this is due to technology. Unlike branch personnel, telephone banking representatives have all the benefits of a particular product listed for them on a screen that they can read from; there is no digging through desk drawers to locate visual aids nor time spent in presenting them. But a considerable part of the difference can also be attributed to the difference in working environments. Telephone representatives can stay focused on what they are doing until the transaction is complete. There are none of the interruptions, like phone calls and questions from other employees, that branch personnel must contend with. And there are no private offices, which in the branch are conducive to spending more time with customers in a sort of business hospitality. With calls automatically routed to the next available person, telephone representatives are trained to get on the phone, get the job done, and get off and on to the next call.

There also are legitimate concerns about such efficiency. A major one is the potential loss of cross-sell opportunities when a customer bypasses personnel for the computer. Raphael says National Bank of Detroit decided the savings with the voice response system and the enhanced ability of the customer service representatives to do more selling and less routine work, offset the potential loss of opportunity. However, NBD also places all telephone transaction data on another system that helps it keep track of schedules. For example, if a loan application is mailed out for a signature and is not returned by a designated time, the customer is called to check on the application. "We found through our research that we could dramatically increase sales if we just followed up," Raphael adds. "Plus, we felt that customers using the voice response system wanted to get in and out quickly and weren't in the frame of mind to be sold something."

In the first three months of operation, NBD found the Telephone Banking Center brought in the business normally produced in the same span of time by a new branch and found overall the phone center six to seven times as productive as the conventional branch. The center far exceeded NBD's projections in new balances, loans and overall customer usage. The bank is hailing it as a complete success, both in offloading routine transactions at the branches and in attracting new customers by differentiating NBD in the market.

GROWTH IN VOICE RESPONSE INSTALLATIONS

Today, most of the nation's largest banks use voice response for many banking inquiries and transactions. And that trend is quickly spreading to even the smallest competitors. Financial institutions find automated voice response systems provide both a customer service and cost benefits. A somewhat unexpected finding has been that some customers prefer the anonymity of dealing with a machine, avoiding potential embarassment about situations such as a low account balance or overdraft.

Many institutions first explored telephone automation to provide service to commercial customers, for whom daily balance inquiries are routine. Automating balance inquiries for business customers expanded naturally to retail customers. Business customers, particularly in the West Coast market, were beginning to use such automation themselves and quickly found it not only acceptable, but essential. At the same time, the general public was becoming accustomed to answering machines and other automated voices on the telephone, which created tolerance if not preference.

According to research by the Bank Administration Institute, growth in voice response system installations in the late 1980s almost doubled that of 10 years earlier. That finding is supported by the experiences of vendors in the voice response industry.

Periphonics, the oldest provider of such systems, reported a steady 30% growth curve through the decade of the 1980s. A young competitor in Arizona, Syntellect, saw a similar increase in 1988 as the five-year-old company brought to market products targeted at community banks and other small financial institutions, according to Executive Vice President Bill Sparks. Frost & Sullivan, a New York-based research firm, estimated in 1988 that voice systems were a $300 million industry that could grow by an average 60% a year into the1990s. A study by the firm forecasts $3.2 billion in sales by 1992.

One reason for the tremendous sales increases is that use has become common in a far broader market than just the financial services industry. Systems now are being installed by retailers, insurance firms, catalog mailers, and brokerage houses, to name only a few. Part of this interest is being generated by lower prices made possible through the advent of newer systems, many based on low-priced personal computers. For example, a basic PC-based system that accommodates four phone lines can be installed for about $25,000 — a third of the cost of a similar system in the mid-80s. Technology improvements also have played a part in expanding capabilities and even making the computerized voice sound warmer, more human.

Renewed interest within the financial services industry comes in part because the seemingly more glamorous technologies that once eclipsed interest in the telephone — ATMs and home banking by computer — no longer cast such shadows. Home banking has experienced myriad problems and many programs have been abandoned within the last five years. Conversely, ATMs have been so successful as a delivery mechanism, that they have helped encourage the use of other automated systems.

In fact, research shows that those most likely to use the telephone to do their banking from home are the same consumers who avidly use ATMs. And those consumers groups — primarily the Baby Boomers — are becoming the majority of the wealthier consumers as that population group enters midlife. For example, although 50% of the overall consumer market for telephone banking services is adverse to the idea of banking by phone, 42% of them are over the age of 55 and 49% earn less than $25,000 per year, according to studies by PSI, the financial services research company. Conversely, 31% of those who use phone banking earn more than $50,000 annually and 33% of them are between the ages of 35 and 44.

If customers will use automated systems regularly, substantial savings can be gleaned from reductions in personnel — or at least by staving off the need to hire new staff as business grows — from the reduction in facilities needed to streamline back office operations through less time-consuming, more efficient operation. Syntellect's Sparks estimates that users can displace $20,000 annually in labor costs alone with just one or two phone lines. Periphonics estimates 50 to 70% of all calls taken by bank customer service representatives are routine enough to be cost-effectively automated. There also can be dramatic savings in phone line connections, as the average voice response call takes about half the time to complete as that to a live operator.

With cost savings paying for the installation of most current voice response systems, few institutions have charged fees for usage, particularly for balance inquiry. However, in a few instances, a charge per inquiry is levied.

Institutions that have policies of making all services fee based argue that such strategies in the long run are the most fair to all customers. While logical, the problem is that the industry traditionally has used certain services as loss leaders, most notoriously "free checking." A change in attitudes may be forced by the commodity nature of financial services, which pushes pricing toward a per-use fee basis. However, when the marketing leads potentially generated by inquiry services are considered, the possible fee income probably will be forgotten.

OPPORTUNITIES FOR FEE INCOME

Bill payment by telephone has the potential to be a fee generator. However, the potential is defined by competing payment alternatives and does not become viable until the cost of delivering such an electronically generated payment is significantly less for the institution offering the service than the cost of conventional methods. Failing to understand that simple bit of basic business sense has caused a number of institutions to struggle with telephone bill payment, finally writing it off as not viable. Often the assumption has been that such considerations were of little importance because consumers would be willing to pay for convenience, which is not an altogether unreasonable assumption. But the service must in fact be convenient to the consumer, which often has not been the case for two primary reasons.

First, the process of entering numbers on a touch-tone pad becomes increasingly difficult at an exponential rate as the number of digits entered increase. In other words, it is easier by a quantum factor to select 1 or 2 — yes or no — from a voice menu and press the appropriate response than it is to key in an account number and dollar amount without being able to see the number displayed as it is entered. While telephone users routinely enter seven digits (or 11 when calling long distance), they have been trained by years of experience as to the sequence of three digits, then four, and have committed to memory frequently called numbers. Account numbers do not fall into that familiar pattern and dollar amounts for payments inevitably will vary.

Second, because even with a "pay anyone" bill payment service, which tends to be the exception, the consumer still is very likely to also continue to use paper checks. Consequently, to maintain a current balance record while making telephone bill payments still requires the entry of notations in a check register, along with records of

ATM withdrawals and possible point of sale debit purchases. Even if the consumer were not to write any checks, most current systems provide no printed record except a notation of the debit on a monthly checking account statement. If a creditor says payment has not been received, there is no cancelled check available to refute the claim.

Interestingly, institutions that have offered telephone bill payment services find that there is a loyal core of customers who do in fact find such services convenient, despite those limitations. They typically represent about two percent of the total market, although in a very few instances institutions claim more substantial percentages of transaction accountholders as users of their bill payment services. Those users have proven willing to pay monthly fees generally ranging from $3 to $5 for a certain number of transactions. Other services charge purely on a per transaction basis, basing that price on the obvious comparison of the cost to the consumer of writing a check and mailing payment, which is the predominant means of paying bills from home. Postage stamp-priced services therefore charge 25 to 50¢ per item.

The problem with this approach has been that it ignores that first dictum of business common sense — know what it costs to deliver your product. Without an automated, electronic — and therefore less expensive — means of making the payments, the financial institution has not created a fee opportunity, but produced a cost center. The financial institution now incurs the cost of cutting and mailing the check in addition to supporting the telephone service that customers use.

Programs introduced in the 1970s yielded these tough lessons before usage sharply declined at about 1980. Not just coincidentally, that decline occurred as credit unions and thrifts, which had been major proponents of such systems, gained regulatory approval for offering conventional transaction products, particularly checking accounts. Without the need to promote automated payment methods as an alternative to paper checks and having learned the expense involved in supporting such programs, many institutions dropped marketing, sometimes closing operations altogether.

All such programs suffered from the back office costs of supporting them. Despite the image of automation, most services simply collected information so that bank employees could make payments on the customer's behalf, using paper checks. Usually a vendor or merchant would be paid with one check and list of payees, compiled by the bank. Not only was that an exception process for the merchant, but among the many drawbacks, if just one payee account at the bank turned out to have insufficient funds, the whole process often would have to be replicated. The problem was compounded in that few institutions charged for the service. Most learned that they should have.

FULTON FEDERAL SAVINGS & LOAN

Perhaps the best example of these problems is provided in a short history of the telephone bill payment experience of Atlanta's Fulton Federal Savings & Loan. In mid-1988 the thrift announced that it was dropping its long running bill payment program, which often had been cited as a success because of the relatively high numbers of its accountholders who used it. After spending an undisclosed but presumably hefty sum in updating its telephone automation program, the S&L decided that the program was costing too much to run.

The program was begun in the pre-NOW account era of the 1970s to help the thrift get around regulations that kept it from offering checking accounts. As with many such non-banks, there was a recognition that transaction services were critical to obtaining sufficient low-cost consumer deposits to be profitable. Electronic delivery appeared to be a means of getting around the problem. Its early successes in building consumer usage contributed toward convincing regulators that forbidding certain institutions from offering paper checks as transaction services was pointless. Clearly technology could be used to get around the regulations. Once the battle was won, however, the institutions that had invested time and money in developing and marketing services such as telephone bill payment simply continued offering them, rather than reconsidering how they fit into delivery systems that were quickly being revised to mimic the older structures of conventional banks.

With the benefit of hindsight, Fulton Federal concluded telephone bill payment should have been positioned as a product, not a service. Recognizing that some customers desired the convenience of the service and would pay to receive it, the thrift concluded that it should have become fee based with minimum balance requirements similar to checking account price structures. Furthermore, instead of continuing to offer to "pay anyone," which had been necessary in a substitue for checking, the institution advised the industry that it would recommend limiting the number of vendors, particularly promoting those payments the thrift could execute through the ACH.

HOLLYWOOD FEDERAL SAVINGS BANK

In contrast is Hollywood Federal Savings Bank in Florida. At about the same time Fulton announced its 1988 decision, Hollywood said it would expand its InTouch bill paying system into a PC-based home banking program as a statement of its commitment to electronic delivery systems and a reflection of the success it had in telephone bill payment. Out of a potential user base of 60,000 account holders, 35,000 customers were using the telephone program. "It is a service to our customers, but it is a money-maker for us. We started out that way," a Hollywood representative told *Payment Systems Newsletter*.

For more than a decade, the name Hollywood Federal (formerly as an S&L) had been synonymous with successful telephone bill payment and its percentage of usage among its customers unmatched. Originally named Bill-O-Matic, Hollywood Federal's program started out on a strictly manual basis, begun to meet the need to provide transaction services. All calls were operator assisted, and initially the operators would take the calls, write down the information and write the checks all at once.

Automation of Bill-O-Matic began almost immediately. The institution was one of the leaders in the movement to adopt new rules for automated transactions sent through the National Automated Clearinghouse Association system. A new format was adopted as a result called the Customer Initiated Entry format or CIE, which allowed a financial institution greater ability to use the customer's keystrokes in initiating an automated transaction, reducing the amount of data entry for the financial institution. From the beginning, the institution attempted to reduce overhead by automating as many transactions as possible.

But it kept one feature of the service that others in the industry questioned and that Fulton Federal later was to cite as one of its mistakes. Hollywood Federal's InTouch allows customers to pay anyone. Not only is there no institution-specified payee list, but customers do not even have to give advance notice when they want to pay a new vendor. Hollywood Federal has remained true to its objective of offering a telephone service as flexible as a check.

If there is a key to the InTouch program's success, however, it undoubtedly is marketing. The association not only promotes the service to all eligible customers opening accounts, but all new transaction account holders automatically get a personal identification number (PIN). "We want to make it as easy as possible for the customer to use the service. We tell them about it at sign-up and they can use it from then on even if they don't want to use it right away," said Hollywood Federal Vice President and Director of Marketing E. Allen Tubbs. To remind customers of the availability of the service, the association employs such marketing techniques as statement stuffers, occasional media advertising, in-lobby videos and periodically highlighting the service in its customer newsletter.

Customers pay 23¢ per item for touch tone telephone-initiated transactions and preauthorized payments (standing orders to pay) and 38¢ for transactions initiated via operator-assisted calls. In 1988, InTouch Banking processed about 150,000 payments per month from approximately 25,000 users, suggesting that the average user paid six bills per month by phone, which would represent about half the bills paid from an average U.S. household each month. About 40% of the InTouch transactions were customer-entered through the telephone, 22% were preauthorized and 38% came from operator assisted calls. A bit of multiplication suggests fee income from the service was running at approximately $43,000 per month at that time. But more interestingly, it also suggests that even though customers have been able to enter their own data at Hollywood Federal for about 10 years, about half of the service users prefer to deal with a person.

Bill-O-Matic was renamed InTouch Banking in the mid-80s as part of a major change in Hollywood Federal's marketing approach. Until that time, as the association added features to the telephone-based service, each was considered to be a separate product. For example, Bill-O-Matic was seen as being different from Telefund, Hollywood Federal's telephone transfer service. The association was focused on selling the deposit account, a natural inclination for a thrift whose initial (pre-NOW account) purpose in offering telephone banking was to attract customers' transaction funds. As NOW accounts, then Money Market Deposit Accounts and SuperNOWs were added, telephone access to each was marketed separately. Rather than continue such a cumbersome approach, telephone access was recognized as a delivery system and all remote electronic banking services were combined for marketing purposes under the InTouch moniker.

InTouch, then, is more than just telephone bill payment. In fact, a quarter of all Hollywood Federal customers use InTouch for account information services only, for which they pay no fees. The services include balance inquiry, check status inquiry, interim statement ordering, and rate information. In addition, users can obtain information on the last payment to a particular merchant and the last transfer of funds to another account by phone. Telemarketing and expanded messaging applications are being added. Hollywood Federal's strategic direction is toward a total bank-by-phone concept.

MARKETING VIA TELEPHONE AUTOMATION

Despite the apparent success of telephone bill payment at a relatively small thrift in Florida, few larger financial institutions have had comparable experiences, undoubtedly reflecting at least in part that few other institutions have placed such a marketing focus on that particular delivery system. However, when the focus is on marketing of financial services in general, telephone automation once again makes sense.

One means of adding marketing to telephone automation is to add "commercials" to a voice response system. For example, a customer using the system to get a checking account balance may hear a brief message about a new type of account while the system is retrieving the information requested, much as a similar message may appear on an ATM screen while the user is waiting for a transaction to process. But vendors warn banks not to clutter the systems. Many have made the commercials optional, asking the customer to press a specific button to hear a particular message.

Other banks take a somewhat different approach, providing teaser information, but limiting the marketing information a customer may receive over the phone. First Wachovia in North Carolina does not give out rate or loan information/payoffs through the system so that the bank won't miss a sales opportunity, says Gaylon Howe, vice president and manager of Wachovia's electronic banking services.

Changes in telephone services available nationally also are expanding the options that may be combined with internal automation. Most financial institutions are familiar with the use of incoming 800-number services as a means of collecting sales leads and providing expanded geographic access for customers. A few have made use of 900-number services, for which there is a per-call charge billed through the local telephone company, to promote high margin products such as secured credit cards. The secured card is specifically aimed at individuals who can not qualify for a conventional credit cards due to no credit history, bankruptcy or other credit report peccadillos, but have cash available. In return for a cash deposit, a card is issued bearing a credit line in the amount of the deposit. The cardholder is extended only as much credit as the institution already holds in cash.

While the 900-number is associated with the sometimes sleazy images of services that target consumers banks do not usually cultivate, it may be used as one means to charge for information that currently is provided through other marketing materials. For example, commodity financial products such as certificates of deposit may be marketed nationally with at least part of the expense covered by making rate shoppers pay for their inquiry. Such uses of 900-numbers also allow databases of marketing prospects to be developed while the prospects pay for their own data entry!

Various telecommunications service providers also offer the capability to link internal information systems with incoming calls, such as American Express has done with Automatic Number Identification. Using advanced data communications capabilities, information about a particular caller may be brought to the customer service representative's screen as the call is answered. One now apocryphal lesson from the American Express experience was that callers found it somewhat disconcerting to be greeted by name. It is better to have the information available and use it to speed the service process.

NOT JUST FOR BILLS ANYMORE

Potential uses of the telephone in banking are not limited to consumer information and transactions. Commercial banks also have adopted the system to automate some routine commercial cash management functions. And some banks are using automated phone systems to expedite credit authorizations for retailers.

Some of the more unusual uses of phone technology center around the use of *speech* recognition — where the system can "recognize" key words or phrases, eliminating the need to type a response on the touchtone pad — and *speaker* recognition, whereby the system is programmed to recognize the specific *voice* of an individual.

Experimental use of the latter is occurring at a prominent West Coast bank. The bank is using speaker recognition technology as a security measure for transferring sensitive documents via fax machines. To use the system, an authorized bank officer telephones a remote fax location. Authorization is verified by the officer speaking a designated word or phrase over the phone. (Often with speaker recognition, the speaker simply says his own name since research shows he probably will say it more distinctly than he will any other word.) The system is "trained" to recognize his particular speech pattern and tone. Once authorization is verified, the officer is allowed to use the system to transmit confidential data.

The bank already has achieved reduced security costs in password maintenance alone, further enhanced by increased security. Although this application is still in its infancy, progress continues in developing larger vocabularies for such systems, greater speaker independence and systems are being developed to recognize a more fluent rate of speech. Currently, with either speech or speaker recognition, the speaker is require to speak very slowly and distinctly.

Because it takes more time, and therefore more patience on behalf of the user, such technologies may never gain widespread use in traditional banking applications, except in areas where touchtone phones are not available. In fact, use of these systems are more prominent in Europe, where touchtone phones are often scarce. But even in the U.S. a surprising percentage of the population — estimated to be as much as 25% — still has rotary dial phones, not "readable" by most computer systems, thereby creating a need for speaker recognition.

For example, Hollywood Federal uses an InterVoice voice response system with VoiceDial for speech activation. Located in southern Florida, Hollywood Federal implemented the system a number of years ago to ensure its cornerstone electronic banking program was accessible to its entire customer base — even those without touchtone service or equipment and particularly those unable to easily manipulate it. While the proportion of bill payers using the speech activation system is insignificant, the program has developed a small following among car phone users.

Speech recognition is time consuming: access digits must be spoken in isolation (not fluidly as one would do in conversational speech) and the caller cannot interrupt the computer prompt. Also, consumers tend to make more mistakes with speech recognition systems, yielding a 75% accuracy rate, compared to 95% with touchtone pads.

The next generation of speech activation technology is just on the horizon, particularly offering larger vocabularies and the ability to recognize continuous speech. AT&T claims it will have a system with a vocabulary of 1,000 words, with 95% accuracy by 1991. InterVoice has also upgraded its systems to handle continuous speech and alpha recognition, although its first installation is still pending. The systems will have niche applications, such as for disabled customers, although some institutions are exploring using speech activation exclusively to simplify access.

OUTBOUND TELEPHONE AUTOMATION

Banks should be, and many of the larger ones already are, looking outward when considering the myriad uses for telephone systems. The number of vendors offering such systems has grown within the last few years, although perhaps not as quickly as those who offer inbound, PC-based systems.

An example of perhaps the most successful outbound system is one offered by Washington state-based Digital Systems, Incorporated. The company made quick and significant inroads into the financial industry beginning in 1987 through its VoiceLink Intelligent Dialing System. By November of that year, just over a year after the system's debut, eight major financial institutions — among them Chase Manhattan, NCNB and American Express — had bought the system to automate collections. Since that time the system has made steady progress in industry, according to Michael Darland, president of the company.

Such systems expedite mass calling by eliminating calls that aren't likely to be answered by a human. For example, with VoiceLink a live operator only completes connections with live customers, since the system recognizes busy signals, no answers, answering machines, and can differentiate between a computer voice and a real voice before connecting the call to the collector. Voicelink also allows for quick account review and update, since it can interface with multiple host computers and perform multiple functions simultaneously, and it can dispense update in graphic form.

Since the customer's complete file appears on a screen before the collector, two important parts of productivity are achieved: the collector spends all his time answering calls, not trying to place them; and when he does reach a customer, he has the complete account history to refer to and update. A Barclay representative told *Payment Systems Newsletter* in 1988 that his bank increased average contacts per collector per hour from five to 28 on the bank's 30- and 60-day overdue accounts. Also, while the system cost the bank close to a quarter million dollars, payback was achieved within six months based on increased productivity.

Such systems are revolutionizing the financial industry for collections. Recently Digital helped take that a step further through a program written specifically for FM Services, a Phoenix, Arizona-based collections agency. FM President John Fogleman explains that his new skip-tracing program is helping his company make great strides in resurrecting "dead" accounts for client banks.

The new system takes information, such as the name, address, and up to four phone numbers — from a "skip" file and loads it onto the computer. That program is then merged with another data base that looks at similar names and addresses in a given geographic area. The program tries to match similar data to that of the skip file. For example, it can list up to 10 surnames the same as the customer's, and 10 addresses near to the customer's last known address and in turn match that with the surnames. The process helps the collector find possible relatives. The information goes to a half screen — the top half includes all information from the account and the bottom half lists likely calls. VoiceLink can then efficiently auto-dial the likely candidates for inquiries, skipping over the no answers, answering machines and busy signals.

Fogleman says he is still tabulating actual collections made through the system but that its success rate in helping reopen accounts has been "absolutely phenomenal." Currently he is planning an interface with another database system that will match account information with that from voter registration bureaus, county tax administration offices, trade information from credit bureaus and utility connects/disconnect records.

But outbound systems aren't limited to collections alone. They also can be used cost-effectively in telemarketing, which can use automatic dialing to reach prospects and connect them with a live operator, an approach generally found more acceptable than prerecorded messages.

DISPLAY PHONE BASED SERVICES

The next development for in-home use of electronic banking will come from a variety of devices that combine a display screen with a conventional telephone. The screen lets the user see the bills and transactions as they are carried out. At least three organizations have announced products for this market.

Citicorp is the most prominent innovator in this area. Its well-known research and development subsidiary TTI is in a joint venture with consumer electronics giant Phillips International, one of the manufacturers of the French Minitel terminal. The Enhanced Telephone (E.T.) has a fairly sizable monitor, a hidden, compact keyboard and is leased for $9.95 per month, including the banking service, with a $49.95 sign-up fee. The telephone features include speed dialing, on-hook dialing and a personal directory, similar to what many advanced consumer telephones offer.

E.T. allows typical telephone banking functions, including bill payment, as well as the ability to open new accounts, send electronic mail and stop payments. Citibank expects to add brokerage information and trading capabilities in the future. The device is currently offered only as a pilot program in two New York City branches.

AT&T is also experimenting with a display telephone. The unnamed device has a streamlined appearance, includes an LCD touchscreen and was designed to support advanced telephone features similar to those of E.T. AT&T is seeking various service providers as potential partners, including local telephone companies and banks.

Bank of America also is testing a new telephone device that uses a television screen as a monitor. The bank currently uses a similar AT&T-made device in Home Banker, its home banking program. The new device essentially adds a telephone handset.

A number of other consumer electronics manufacturers are certain to introduce such products during the next few years as the market for new and replacement equipment in the home continues to grow. The addition of a screen directly addresses the consumer problems of needing simplified menu access and the ability to see the data being entered.

For financial institutions, however, no matter how sophisticated the device in the consumer's home, internal banking automation systems must be fully integrated and designed to take advantage of the opportunity.

CHAPTER

9

Home Banking: What Works and What Doesn't

NOT A PRODUCT, BUT A DELIVERY SYSTEM

The term "home banking" carries a negative connotation within the banking industry. This is largely due to the low consumer usage and perceived failures of services that were introduced during the 1980s that were delivered either via home computers or telecommunication devices attached to home television sets. The technology was not truly adequate for the task, often because the true task involved was not understood. The device in the home was only one part of the needed technology. As the 1990s begin, a number of bankers once again are enthralled with home banking as the epitome of electronic banking. Many believe that the growing sales of computers and other electronic devices for the home at last are providing an avenue for the success of home banking as a revenue-generating, financial services product.

This round of enthusiasm is likely to conclude with another spate of deep disappointment because too many advocates of home banking are operating from a seriously flawed assumption. The fundamental failure is to assume that home banking is a new financial service product that can be marketed and priced as a standalone entity. This misperception contributed to significant, wasted expenditures on hardware and software to support home banking on a standalone basis during the 1980s. Although the current approaches are more rational, they suffer from the typical financial institution approach to electronic banking on a piecemeal basis rather than as an integrated whole.

Specifically, more than a dozen financial institutions are providing transactional services to some extent through Prodigy, the IBM-Sears joint venture in computer based videotex that first offered nationwide service late in 1990. As an interactive, electronic information service that is used through a personal computer, Prodigy is exploring new territory. Most observers of the evolution of telecommunications believe services similar in nature to Prodigy eventually will play a role in home communications. Whether Prodigy will survive to be one of the service providers is very much an unanswered question. At their most optimistic, Prodigy's developers expect it to be used in only a minority of households at any point in the short-term future.

For financial institutions, there is no concern that interactive computer services will soon constitute a significant portion of financial service usage and consequently systems are not being developed to handle them as a primary avenue for consumer transaction business. A few institutions, notably Citibank and Bank of America, have supported computer based home banking services on a standalone basis with separate processing facilities and staff. Most banks that have attempted to do so have closed those operations as expensive failures. At this point, the service usage volume for banks offering service through Prodigy is modest and can be handled by the financial institutions on an exception basis. The rationale for the extra expense is that this is a period for evaluating what specific services are desired and how they are used.

Only four of Prodigy's financial institutions — Wells Fargo Bank, Manufacturers Hanover Trust Company, First Interstate Bank of Denver and Chevy Chase Federal Savings Bank — are offering service nationwide. Of the other institutions offering service on a regional basis, most are using the services of Manufacturers Hanover for processing. In fact, most could not handle such processing themselves without substantial investment, which points out exactly the problem. Home banking still is being developed by banks as a new product with its own infrastructure rather than approached as an extension of existing services.

More correctly, the concern in developing home banking services should have been and continues to be to examine the ways in which electronics can be used to provide efficient delivery of financial services to wherever the consumer may be, but particularly to the consumer at home. This shift in perspective places the emphasis correctly on consumer needs in financial services and business opportunities in meeting those needs. The immediate conclusion is that many of the early efforts in home banking were overly enamored of the technology involved and particularly fascinated by the potential of the home computer. This infatuation caused an overly enthusiastic estimation of market potential, which was aggravated by an essential lack of understanding of why consumers were buying home computers, how the machines were being used and how difficult it would be to securely use such devices as remote banking terminals.

The infrastructure for home banking as a service was far less well-developed in the early 1980s than many envisioned it to be. The investments required to develop computer and telecommunications systems were wasted if the resulting systems were not integrated with existing operations. Financial institutions that regarded home banking as a discrete, revenue-producing product for the mass market failed to appreciate that consumers saw little value being added to the transaction services they already obtained at a minimal price.

For most banks, the fundamental problem continues to be a lack of complete automation of the process of conducting any financial transaction, even that of providing or verifying an account balance, which limits the usefulness of electronic delivery of any such effort to consumers, merchants and to banks. So long as the automation of a particular institution is only partial, its ability to efficiently offer electronic delivery services will be compromised, making them either too expensive to offer or too difficult to conveniently use — or both. Nonetheless, there are services that can and should be automated both for efficient service delivery, and to remain competitive in a marketplace in which banking increasingly is one of many information businesses that have been transformed by the advent and implementation of computer and telecommunication technologies.

To focus on home banking as a product is a self-defeating strategy that is all too typical of the organizational structures of financial institutions that result in elements of electronic delivery such as automated teller machines and automated clearinghouse transactions regarded as separate concerns, managed in separate divisions and overseen by managers who may report to different executives. An institution with a vision of an integrated payment system recognizes that there is more importance in the common elements than in the superficial differences — including even the obvious difference that one is an on-line transaction process and the other is an off-line process. In each case the common element is that a transaction is automated. Which method is used — on whose'"turf" the transaction belongs — is both an economic and strategic question that may vary depending on the precise application.

Determining an appropriate strategy first requires identifying financial services and products that may be automated, given current technology, and the degree to which consumers want those services separate from services and products that are not or can not be automated. That is almost the diametric opposite of a product strategy that begins with the question of how to market something such as home banking.

The first step is to identify the needs. That process should suggest sensible hybrids of automated and non-automated services, recognizing that most financial institutions are in a position of partial automation and unable to simply design the ideal electronic delivery system from scratch, even if such a system were available.

SELECTING SERVICES FOR ELECTRONIC DELIVERY TO THE HOME

Home banking can be defined as an automated service used in the home that addresses a financial service need, even something as seemingly simple as the ability to obtain a current account balance.

The most basic of financial services is providing or verifying an account balance. A banking relationship begins with the ability to fulfill that need. No bill-paying service can be considered a true automated extension of financial services to the home without being able to provide a current account balance from which the bills are to be paid.

Certainly it has been demonstrated that consumers will use various check-writing software packages for personal computers or telephone based services that generate an account debit to make a payment. But such services are at best contributing elements in an integrated payment system that extends the full concept of financial service automation to the consumer at home. If those services cannot provide a current balance, the consumer will have to obtain access to it elsewhere, whether from personal records or by contacting the financial institution. Each of those additional steps reduces the efficiency of the service to the consumer and misses an opportunity for adding convenience.

It has become routine for financial institutions to maintain information such as account balances in a computer database. Information can be extracted from such a database essentially in two ways: (1) either by real-time access in which a query is made directly to the computer and a current status report is delivered or (2) through a batch mode in which a status report is provided on a periodic basis, which could mean a daily printing of a hard-copy report, or an electronic transmission or downloading of information at a certain interval to a computer or computer terminal.

Once retrieved, the information may be printed, displayed on a video screen, translated to audio information via voice synthesis or digitized voice, or stored on digital recording media, including magnetic tapes and disks and optical media. Each of these introduces possible delivery system strategies incorporating some or all as delivery methods, any of which may serve the consumer at home.

How such alternatives should be used in a home banking strategy are likely to be determined at least in part by the capabilities of the computer system that already is in place. The industry has seen competing trends in the design of computer systems for financial institutions. Strategies of centralizing or decentralizing data alternately gained or lost favor, as new systems have been introduced which offered greater functionality and flexibility with one approach or the other. The improving capabilities of telecommunications links in such systems have been a factor affecting such designs, allowing greater ease of access to data, wherever it is located.

The basic trend through either approach, however, has been to make information readily, conveniently and directly accessible to those who should have access to it. The evolution has seen data access move away from being the exclusive province of the data processing department to direct access by tellers and platform officers and, finally, directly to the end users, the customers — whether they are merchants or consumers.

Access to information concerning an account balance becomes critical when it is a transaction that will result in a transfer of control of funds.

The more current the information, the less risk involved in the transfer. Given that all banking is a matter of evaluating risks, systems that reduce risk are of interest to financial institutions, merchants and consumers, although perhaps for different reasons at different times.

The instantaneous access to such information that electronic delivery systems provide allows reasonable certainty that the information is the most accurate available. Consequently, specific financial services have arisen that take advantage of that capability. A standalone machine that dispenses cash after electronic verification that funds are available (the Automated Teller Machine or ATM) is a familiar example. The related retail point of sale acceptance of ATM debit cards as a payment method is another. Similarly, the authorization of a credit card transaction verifies credit availability.

Obtaining a current balance or verifying that a particular balance is available is the first step in most transactions, whether at the teller window, at the retailer's point of sale or in writing a check for bill payment from home. For the consumer at home, the application is somewhat different than in a situation where cash is dispensed or the availability of funds is guaranteed, although the electronic availability of the information raises several possibilities. Until recently, a consumer's choices were to refer to the most recent bank statement and a checkbook register or, if the service were offered, to telephone a bank representative who would check a ledger or call up the account from the computer database.

By extending electronic access to account balance information directly to the consumer at home, the first step in home banking has been automated, and attention can focus on suitable devices for providing that access, as well as additional services that may flow from access to that critical piece of information.

SELECTING DEVICES FOR ELECTRONIC DELIVERY TO THE HOME

Even worse than addressing home banking as a product is to regard it solely as something delivered through a personal computer. Approaching home banking from the perspective that a personal computer is the answer for all home banking ignores what the question should be. Account balance information certainly can be provided in a form that would allow access to it by personal computer. But the limited market penetration of such devices and the bewildering variety of telecommunication software possibilities makes such access by itself impractical. The power of even the simplest of computers is often not used and may not be necessary for such a task.

A variety of custom designed, inexpensive computerized devices could be devised to obtain and even retain an account balance(among other things). Besides the concept of a telephone with a small screen and some form of keyboard, such as the French Minitel terminal or the Citibank-developed Enhanced Telephone, one can envision devices such as an electronic checkbook, which could be plugged into a telephone jack for downloading of a current account statement and uploading of new transactions.

However, each of these devices — no matter how clever or sophisticated — faces the problem of market penetration. Until the device is widely distributed or otherwise available on a universal basis, current methods of providing service also will be maintained. Even if the device is so inexpensive that it literally can be given away or sold for a very modest price, it represents additional expense in providing a basic service that can be obtained by the consumer at little or no cost today. Only competitive necessity — meaning other institutions have adopted the delivery device and are successful in marketing it — can justify that additional expense for most financial institutions.

In implementing electronic delivery of financial services to the home, first consideration should be given to mimicking current methods of obtaining information to as great an extent as possible, specifically by taking advantage of trends in the automation of basic bank operations.

For example, automation of current systems can provide convenient, easy-to-use electronic access to account balance information by a device that is in virtually every home with a bank account — the telephone. Digital technology allows electronically stored information to be presented comprehensibly in a spoken fashion. But customer interaction is still necessary. To automate the process, technology still requires the caller to provide information in a form comprehensible to a computer, which means digitally, whether via touchtones or data transmission.

However, even with the simplest digital service — touchtones — becoming nearly universally available, approximately one-fifth of the market still lacks either access to such service or to a touchtone telephone. Furthermore, nearly half the market indicates no current interest in using such a service even if it is available.

If the industry should choose to force the issue because of rising labor costs in handling such inquiries, behavior might change dramatically if a fee were imposed for obtaining information from a human representative. Those who choose to deal with customer service representatives would pay for the privilege. A similar example exists in telephone directory assistance, in which consumers are charged a fee or given a limited number of free inquires for directory assistance. In the United States, however, telephone companies have been restricted by regulations from offering a fully electronic alternative to directory assistance such as exists in France or such as is more readily feasible for a financial institution providing account balance information.

Ultimately, the answer lies in reducing the need for the consumer to have any special hardware or particular knowledge of how to use the electronic service. Perhaps within this decade, speech recognition will have reached a stage of development that the service user will need only to speak directly to the computer to obtain the response a human representative might have given, but such systems are not yet commercially viable even though becoming technically possible.

With rising labor costs and declining automation costs bringing automated call directing technology into virtually every large institution, providing a link between such a system and a computer that can provide account balance information is becoming routine. For a financial institution to invest in internal telephone automation and not explore automation of at least that aspect of customer service is foolish, even if it is expected that only a small portion of the customer base will use the service. The operating costs are so low after the initial technology investment that even minimal labor savings can offset the expense. Additionally, there clearly is a subset of the consumer market that is ready and willing to use such a service and is appreciative of the convenience.

Consequently, telephone access to account balance information by automated voice is quickly becoming a competitive necessity as have previous innovations in electronic delivery.

Meanwhile, other technological possibilities exist that could automate the intermediate steps and allow for competitive advantage, even in this most basic of services, via electronic delivery. For example, several electronics manufacturers offer credit card-size devices that generate a sequence of touchtone sounds when activated. Equipped with a calculator-like screen that could display a series of user selectable, programmed functions, such a device could activate a computerized account information service even if the caller was not at a touchtone telephone. This could minimize, if not eliminate, the need for the user to punch in a lengthy series of numbers to obtain basic information. Creative minds will focus on such alternatives if the dictum is to remember the customer's needs.

The first piece of information that any electronic delivery system must be able to provide or verify is the account balance. Experience at the teller cage, at the ATM and through automated telephone inquiry systems all suggest this is the most frequently requested item of information. It may even be provided without request, either automatically printed on an ATM transaction statement or recited automatically upon connection with an automated telephone information service. With the primacy of the account balance established, attention can turn to the other services that follow.

BEYOND THE BALANCE, OTHER SERVICES FOLLOW

The next step is to provide a link between multiple accounts. Nearly every central information file (CIF) software package offered to the financial industry today does this. However, this seemingly simple and obvious step can become extremely difficult in institutions where credit card accounts or personal credit line or other lending products may be managed on separate computer systems from checking account information. Furthermore, the question must be addressed as to which additional accounts to include, and what information to provide. For example, a current balance on a 30-year mortgage may be of little immediate use, but the due date of the next payment, date and amount of the last payment received, current escrow balance or interest paid in the calendar year may be very useful.

Adding to the complexity is the frequent necessity of merging incompatible systems resulting from the mergers of institutions. This emphasizes the importance of the first step mentioned earlier. A complete inventory and analysis of existing system capabilities and weaknesses is critical in setting a strategy for electronic delivery systems.

The good news is that from a consumer's perspective, obtaining balance or other information electronically on another account should require no different device or usage procedure than obtaining the first balance. If customers can learn to use an automated system to obtain a current checking account balance, other information services easily can follow. Providing the linkages is a process internal to the financial institution, which again should seek to make the process as simple and easy-to-use as possible. If the internal linkages are competent, it should not be necessary for the user to enter additional account numbers, for example, unless perhaps there are duplicate accounts held.

Additionally, once the customer has mastered basic operation of the system, a new realm of possiblities is opened for marketing applications. Just as sophisticated CIF systems should integrate product information to alert customer service representatives to additional marketing opportunities, a customer operated system should provide information about other products and services that are available, as well as current rates and fees, locations of ATMs and hours of operation and locations of brick and mortar branches. All of this should be available, but not intrusive to the process of conducting the basic transactions involved.

This is one of the first points at which analysis of electronic delivery should consider a hybrid with non-electronic access. Perhaps the simplest example is to respond to an information inquiry by generating a follow-up mailing piece. The first access by the customer should have provided sufficient information so that a current mailing address could be linked to the system. The mailing could include a toll-free number for direct connection to a customer service representative at the customer's initiative. Although the customer might be asked to request such follow-up, the inquiry itself might be considered evidence by the institution that the individual was shopping for a financial service or product and is likely to be a qualified prospect.

Another example of combining electronic and non-electronic delivery may lie in the very process of a caller contacting an automated system. Among the first choices will be an opportunity for the caller to enter a code, which might be based on a checking account number, an ATM card number, a credit card number or some proprietary access code to identify the legitimacy of access to specific information. Any caller who attempted to do so and encountered difficulty should be immediately switched to a live operator who could determine whether the individual simply erred in entering a number or was perhaps unfamiliar with the system and needed assistance, which might include assistance in opening an account or obtaining a particular product.

The process of obtaining verifiable, legitimate access may itself be automated in a number of ways, whether the access device is a telephone, computer or proprietary device. Again, other existing services and products might play a role, particularly credit cards or ATM cards. For some years, electronic service product developers have considered the possibility of providing the in-home consumer with a device that might mimic the merchant's point of sale terminal. That device could be a magnetic stripe reader for various cards, a light pen that could read bar codes or the kind of tone generator described earlier. In addition to verifying or obtaining account balance information, such tools clearly could take part in providing additional transactional services.

Enhancements to the basic telephone services generally provided to business and consumers also suggest innovative ways of simplifying legitimate access. Specifically, Automatic Number Identification (ANI) can be combined with existing information databases to allow the answering party, which in this case would be the financial institution, to recognize a high likelihood of who the caller is. Applications of artificial intelligence or expert systems further can streamline the process to bring appropriate information on-line as the call is received, whether as an assistance to a live operator or as a direct, automated service to the caller.

After multiple account information availablity, the first transactional service is to transfer funds between accounts. This may include the ability to make a payment on a credit card from a checking account, or payment on any other loan product held with the primary financial institution. Opening new accounts or purchasing a product such as a CD also may be offered, encouraging the customer to concentrate business with the institution.

However, account transfers immediately introduce a new level of complexity to the activity from a consumer's point of view and for the financial institution. Specifically, a transfer requires the customer to select an account, indicate a direction for the transfer, enter an amount and note the date the transfer is to occur, if not immediately. The financial institution must have a system in place capable of recognizing, capturing and completing the transaction, including providing appropriate documentation both internally and to the customer.

The telephone still provides the consumer an adequate means of performing the task by allowing selections from a voice menu and entry of figures through the touchtone pad. However, with intra-account transfers, a display screen of any kind becomes an advantage, reducing the amount of time required to select from menu items compared to listening to voice menus. It also allows the user to actually see the figures that have been entered for the transfer. Furthermore, a printer of some type allows the consumer hard copy evidence of the transaction. But even without reaching that level of complexity, once again the market has been reduced, narrowed to those individuals who own or will purchase appropriate equipment—telephone or computer based—or to those to whom it is worthwhile providing such equipment, even if it is simply the hand-held, calculator type device that emits touchtones.

TECHNOLOGY AND AUTOMATION AREN'T ALWAYS THE BEST APPROACH

Approaching the problem of increasing complexity in transactions from a functional basis, a financial institution will recognize that there are several fundamental activities that frequently occur in transfers between accounts. An analysis of this activity may suggest marketing opportunities, as well as the kinds of products that should be offered. The access that should be provided may vary depending on the target markets and product mix.

One common transfer activity is to move funds from a non-interest or low interest account to a higher interest account. In addition to providing customers with convenient means of doing so, an institution might consider offering an account that did so automatically, perhaps on a daily sweep basis. Such a service would also have fee potential. This is potentially an entirely internal automation step.

Alternatively, the customer might be encouraged to establish an automatic transfer at a regular interval, perhaps coincident with deposit of a paycheck, which may involve an automated exchange of information with a third party. Encouraging direct deposit of that paycheck allows an even better opportunity to automatically split the deposit between non-interest and interest bearing accounts and may reduce or eliminate transactions.

In each case, electronic delivery strategies incorporating conventional products and delivery systems may reduce burdens such as the need of customers to frequently check a balance or to make transfers.

The second likely activity in intra-account transfers would be moving funds from an interest-bearing account to a transaction account (the reverse of the first activity mentioned above). Although an automatic transfer would be among the options, in this case it may be more appropriate to suggest a tiered account that automatically would pay interest on balances above a certain amount, which also would encourage account consolidation. Alternatively, automatic overdraft protection could be offered at minimal risk by asking the customer to authorize a transfer between accounts if a transaction exceeded the balance in one account while another contained funds. If the activity suggested that the accountholder relied on the interest-bearing account for income and made the transfers at regular intervals, the accountholder may be a candidate for a bill paying service, particularly a service that would provide a direct debit just prior to a due date.

Testing the potential for such bil paying services could begin by encouraging preauthorized payment for the third kind of account transfer, payment of a credit card minimum or full balance. Various linkages may be made between transaction and credit card accounts, including using the line of credit associated with the card as an overdraft line for the checking account. Maintaining a certain average transaction account balance might also qualify the holder for a lower credit card interest rate.

But the best immediate application is to offer the customer the assurance that the credit card account would never be subject to a late payment fee as long as the linked account held adequate funds.

INCORPORATING CREDIT CARDS IN ELECTRONIC DELIVERY STRATEGY

Another potential consequence of linking credit card and transaction accounts would be to encourage use of credit cards at the retail point of sale as an alternative to checks. In effect, a credit card could indirectly access the transaction account much as a debit card does directly. It could also have the indirect effect of encouraging the cardholder to maintain a credit card account with the same institution providing his transaction account.

Encouraging continued use of the credit card as part of an electronic delivery strategy most directly offers the possibility for a card-issuing financial institution to retain interest earnings from the rollover of outstandings — balances due. Also, the credit card already has widespread consumer acceptance and merchants would not be encouraged to believe they are being shortchanged. This could happen when there is better understanding of the pricing structures for off-line processed, card association-labeled debit cards that substitute for cash or check payments, yet can carry the same cost to the merchant as honoring a credit card.

The multiple results of such a strategy are to reduce paper processing costs by substituting credit card draft capture (which already may be done electronically) for collection, sorting and crediting of checks. The financial institution would still realize credit card discount income from merchants. This income may simply substitute for check deposit charges, but also may provide an offset to potential discount income reduction from growing consumer use of point of sale debit instruments. The net result may be that substituting one payment media for another is a zero sum game for the banking industry, but individual financial institutions know well that profits are to be had in market dysfunctions while the impact of change is sorted out.

This discussion of additional and indirect impacts of linking account information is intended to emphasize that electronic delivery simply cannot be considered as a separate area in banking. It is inherent to banking today and is affecting the entire structure of financial services. To attempt to consider it in isolation or as something simply linked to particular technological devices, such as personal computers or telephones, is to miss the entire nature of change in financial services delivery.

It also must be recognized that some of these suggestions may run into obstacles from current regulations, but that should not be allowed to restrict an effort to devise the best overall strategy. Regulations frequently fail to consider the ongoing impact of technological change and need constant review to keep in step with such change.

THIRD-PARTY TRANSFERS: FINAL STEP FOR HOME BANKING

Continuing the process of identifying the individual steps in the information/action matrix of delivering financial services directly to the consumer at home leads to the final, critical and most perplexing area: third-party transfers — the process of paying someone other than the financial institution.

Each household in the United States makes an average of ten to a dozen payments each month by mail from home, primarily by check, according to studies conducted over the past decade by the Bank Administration Institute, the American Bankers Association and private research organizations such as PSI. For 94 million households nationally, that represents approximately 14.3 billion payments annually, of which more than 10 billion are by check. This behavior has not changed significantly even in the face of other changes in payment behavior, such as increased use of credit cards for point of sale purchases and purchases made by telephone.

Bill payment from home is and has been primarily a matter of writing checks. There are significant advantages to consumers in using checks for bill payment, but there also are potential advantages to electronic payment methods. Telephone bill payment and computer based payment services have not been able to exploit those advantages. It might even be argued that they have not even offered the very advantages often cited, particularly greater convenience, ease of use, accuracy and reliability. Potentially, electronic delivery of financial services can be more advantageous to a consumer than using checks on each of those points, but clearly that has not yet occurred.

In their current forms such services have such low usage as to make detailed statistical profiles meaningless. But rather than dismissing such services, analysis should address reasons for the low market penetration, once again approaching the subject from the perspective of consumer need. Once consumer needs are clearly understood, the development of services that meet those needs will follow, and the business needs of financial institutions can be met as well.

In contrasting paper checks to current telephone and computer based electronic financial services for payments from the home, this analysis will examine four points — convenience, ease of use, accuracy and reliability. It also will consider how such services might work ideally. The analysis focuses on the consumer, but it cannot ignore the positions of financial institutions and merchants.

Both convenience and ease of use are relative, which immediately suggests that there will be segments of the market that will find a particular delivery system more convenient or easy to use than another. While checks clearly dominate, accounting for more than 80% of payment volume from the home, some households today would argue that telephone bill payment or computer-based home banking already are more convenient than checks.

First, these would be households that have such service available. Second, they would be households that possessed the necessary equipment. Third, they have learned how to use the systems and are familiar with their operation. Fourth, they almost certainly continue to use paper checks for at least some of their bill payments.

Convenience and ease of use also must be considered from the point of view of financial institutions and the merchants that are to receive electronic payments from homes. Even though the services may be advantageous to a segment of consumers, there are virtually no financial institutions or merchants to whom that is equally true, once again reflecting the lack of full automation of such functions. To both financial institutions and merchants, electronic bill payment services have required the development of systems parallel to existing systems without any significant gain in efficiency or competitive advantage.

The answer must lie in developing electronic delivery systems that contribute to the absolute efficiency of existing systems and offer potential competitive advantage. As transaction processing is increasingly automated, that is not a particularly farfetched concept. Specifically, as checks are truncated and settlement is conducted electronically, as image processing and character recognition become more sophisticated and prevalent and as electronic data interchange services include integration of payment information, there are opportunities for fully automating the process of accepting, processing and remitting an electronic payment made from home.

This is not simply a matter between consumers and financial institutions. Much as with point of sale debit programs that rely on merchant willingness to accept such forms of payment, three parties are involved in electronic bill payment programs and the reluctance of any one to participate severely limits the possibility of successful implementation. Merchants must be full participants in any such programs.

The great myth of telephone bill payment services from a banking perspective has been to consider them to be an electronic service. Even when portions of the process are automated, most services still rely on the cutting and mailing of a paper check to complete the transaction. The check writing process simply was shifted from the consumer to the financial institution or service bureau. The consumer, of course, did recognize some gain in convenience, but the financial institution paid the price. Such non-automated telephone bill payment services have been closed by a number of financial institutions in recent years despite sometimes fierce customer loyalty to the systems. Computer based payment services, both the on-line and off-line varieties, basically pose the same problems.

To merchants, such payments have been at least as much of an inconvenience as they are to the financial institution because the financial institution submitting payment on behalf of the consumer usually does so in the form of a single check and a list of individuals to whom the payments are to be credited. The check and list constitutes an exception process for the merchant, who often has a highly automated system in place for processing consumer check payments sent by mail, which are accompanied by the merchant's own payment stub or coupon. Without the returned remittance information for reference, the list of individual accounts and amounts to be credited often requires a manual search of billing records, further adding to the merchant's expense and inconvenience.

There are several answers to these problems and some are evident if the full range of consumer payment methods is considered. For example, consider preauthorized payments, which have been utilized for many years by insurance companies as an arrangement between the company and the consumer to guarantee payment. The use of preauthorization points toward at least one of the ways in which electronic payments can be integrated in overall financial institution and merchant procedures without causing disruptions or exceptions. Such integration puts convenience and ease of use back in the process from the merchant and bank perspectives. At that point, the reliability and accuracy factors take effect and the advantages become greater for all parties involved.

Preauthorized payments sometimes have been overlooked as an element in an electronic banking strategy, yet including them may make more sense for many consumers, financial institutions and merchants than do the device-oriented systems alone. Preauthorized programs are likely to continue as standalone programs, but also should be linked to electronic payment services. There are potential benefits in both directions and such links become easier as the preauthorized payment increasingly becomes an electronic entry through the automated clearinghouse system.

In fact, a form of preauthorization does exist in most on-line electronic payment services in the ability to schedule a payment. However, that is an arrangement between the consumer and the financial institution. The merchant is merely recipient of the payment, not a party in a specific agreement as to how or when to be paid. The other primary difference — and an advantage to the consumer in using the electronic payment service — is the ability to conveniently reschedule the payment, retaining control up until the actual payment date. With many standalone preauthorized services, the consumer has no ability to reschedule or delay payment, often only being able to stop such a payment through written notice. Such payment scheduling particularly has been one of the strong features of computer based home bill payment services.

The preauthorized payment concept primarily has been used for insurance premium payments, mortgages and some loan payments, all of which tend to be fixed amounts. Such programs potentially could be expanded not only to other fixed amount payments, but also to variable amount payments in areas in which consumers typically do not challenge the payment amount and also are unlikely to withhold payment. Utility payments offer the best examples of such possibilities. Gas, water, cable television, electric and even basic telephone service utilities are possible candidates — all of which can and do enforce payment by denying service. With both electric and telephone service virtually universal in U.S. households, those two utilities alone account for more than 1 billion payments per year, most of which are made by sending a check in the mail.

One of the major reasons that preauthorized programs have not been successful in such instances has been the consumer's desire to retain control over the timing of the payment. With many households relying on the arrival of a paycheck to make bill payments, the dollar amount of a particular variable bill may determine whether it is paid immediately or deferred. Combining a form of the preauthorized process with an electronic delivery system could allow the consumer to retain that critical element of control over the timing of payment, yet add the convenience and reassurance that payment would be made automatically unless action to the contrary were necessary. The strategy becomes more convenient, easier to use, more accurate and reliable when it also incorporates direct deposit of the paycheck and an automatic overdraft line of credit, each of which helps assure funds will be available.

Interestingly, with bank-issued credit cards also reaching nearly universal status in U.S. households, banks are in a position to immediately test the market for electronic bill payment by encouraging bank card holders to pay at least a minimum balance through a deduction from a checking account, which could be preauthorized as a standing payment or paid only upon confirmation from the consumer. With consumers who have checking accounts with the same institution as their credit card, linking account information electronically and authorizing such a payment should be relatively simple. It also would be a way of introducing such a service with minimal risk because customers would not expose themselves to the possibility of an undesired payment being made. At worst, an interloper would be able to pay the victim's credit card bill.

Any—or none— of the devices discussed earlier could be used for this service. The simplest form of offering this program would be to ask the customer for a voided check to allow a preauthorized debit of a designated account for a minimum, fixed amount or full balance payment each month. The electronic banking would occur internally to the bank or in an electronic exchange via the ACH system with the bank holding the transaction account. The process would be convenient to the consumer and to the financial institutions involved. Accuracy and reliability should be improved because there would be little or no data entry from paper to introduce the possibility of error and only a failure of the financial institution's computer system — which presumably is multiply redundant — should cause the potential of non-payment. Ease of use hardly could be greater. The consumer need only sign an agreement one time.

A similar strategy might be devised by a utility company or perhaps by the marketing side of an electronic banking department, which could propose the service to the utility. A financial institution might consider sweetening the offer to consumers with some sort of credit line on the transaction account that would prevent an accidental overdraft and, not incidentally, potentially earn as much income for the institution on an ongoing basis as is derived from late payment fees and overdraft charges.

As an alternative or perhaps parallel program to reach those customers who are unwilling to surrender as much control as is entailed in signing a preauthorization agreement, the same essential system might be put in place with the customer's assent required for each payment, perhaps delivered as simply as by pressing a single button on a touchtone telephone to indicate, "yes, make the payment."

Before such a customer controlled service would be efficient for the financial institution, however, there needs to be greater ability to exchange information electronically with the utility involved. Again, the capability clearly is available in the automated accounting and billing systems used by today's large businesses. With utilities particularly active in the area of electronic data interchange, which is discussed in more detail in the next chapter, introducing the concept of an electronic exchange of data would not be alien. To the utility, the incentive is the possibility of greater accuracy in forecasting cash flow as well as greater flexibility in billing cycles.

Combining familiar service concepts such as preauthorization with electronic delivery is one of the intermediate steps toward full automation, which ultimately also involves electronic delivery of billing information by the merchant as well. Exchanging such information electronically with a financial institution would be the first step toward making such information available directly to the consumer. Combined with the introduction of new telecommunications channels, such as data channels that can use existing telephone wiring without disrupting voice communication, such services eventually can arrive in the ultimately convenient fashion—delivered directly to the consumer at home. Potentially, that will mean the availability of electronic billing services, eliminating the need for delivery of paper notification of a current amount due.

The financial industry and merchants and service providers in general are only at the threshold of being able to provide such services in a fashion that is of benefit to both consumers and themselves. The current stage is focused on telephone automation, particularly in providing one-way delivery of information services. Transaction services by telephone using voice as well as touch tones are very close, as are transaction services delivered via telephone lines to specialized devices such as are suggested by the current generation of enhanced telephones.

THE TRUE MARKETS FOR COMPUTER BASED FINANCIAL SERVICE DELIVERY

The home computer even in its simplest forms basically is more of a device than is necessary for mass market home delivery of financial services, even though it can be used for that purpose. For the sophisticated financial service user, meaning the more affluent investor and the small businessperson, the home computer is an invaluable adjunct to the office machine because it can be used for many of the same analytical purposes, particularly in financial management. For these individuals, a simplified version of corporate cash management services is needed and should be part of any financial institution's current electronic delivery strategy, if it intends to serve those markets.

The importance of efforts such as the IBM-Sears joint venture, Prodigy, is often magnified by the same kind of misguided enthusiasm that led the financial industry into its early mistakes in tying home banking to particular devices rather than approaching it as an extension of existing services. While Prodigy represents an enormous effort, a tremendous investment in research and a demonstration of faith in the evolution of telecommunication services, it is only marginally different from the mid-1980s newspaper-led efforts to preempt the market for interactive electronic services. Two critical differences in its strategy from that of the first generation of videotex are to target current owners of personal computers, who already have the needed equipment, and to exploit the potential of the media as a direct response marketing tool for advertisers, which is Prodigy's primary hope for developing an income stream.

Not surprisingly to those who have studied consumer interest in technologically advanced services such as on-line information and transaction systems, the users are significantly above average in affluence and education. Unfortunately, it does not follow that therefore all of those who are above average in income or education will be interested in such a service. Other factors are involved and at least one of the significant factors is the presence of children in the household. Research further suggests that parental concerns about providing children with access to such service, which is perceived as being part of the future, are more pivotal than actual demand from children. Even with the enormous effort and investment in launching the service, it has not yet demonstrated that it has found a sustainable audience.

Ironically, one of the best hopes for Prodigy specifically, is that it will succeed in persuading its users to avail themselves of financial services through the system. The affluent demographics of its early users provide an attractive potential nationwide target market for financial institutions, which could yield an immediate revenue stream for the service while generating marketing leads for financial institutions that advertised on the service. The value of those leads ultimately will be weighed and measured against other marketing tools. In the long-run, Prodigy must not only demonstrate to consumers that it offers an easy to use and convenient means of conducting financial business from the home, but also that it represents something other than additional expense to both financial institutions and merchants who participate.

While the main focus here is to discuss financial services from the home, it is useful to note what factors are driving the development of new interactive media such as computer-based information and transaction services. Excitement over presentation formats and interactive capabilities sometimes obscures the fact that such services are primarily communication media. Their success depends on providing a useful means for individuals to communicate, whether about their love life, fascination with celebrities, interest in gaining specialized knowledge or to check a bank account balance. Such services are developing, but in a mass market environment that also includes very sophisticated entertainment devices, which also may be communications devices. Whether video games or videocassette recorders are considered, visual presentation is rapidly improving while controls become both more sophisticated and easier to use.

For the mass market, an interactive, computer-based information and transaction service should have the ease of use of a television remote control and graphic presentation that not only exceeds the color and motion of video games, but incorporates full motion video and broadcast television-quality graphics. To users of personal computers, the current state of the art involves using a mouse, pull-down menus and windows. The leading edge is much flashier. It is called multi-media and incorporates electronic imaging — still and full motion digital video — as well as digital sound. The direction of personal computers already is set and includes the capabilities of a variety of devices currently used for home entertainment.

The link in this scenario that is least complete, although perfectly obvious, is the telecommunications connection that can support such devices. Theoretical standards exist for delivering voice, data and video on a single channel, but the greatest practical obstacle is that today's physical links to households are not adequate to support the band width necessary for delivering the needed data. Either the mass market will have to be rewired, hybrid systems must be used or a technical breakthrough in data compression must occur. The latter is perhaps most practical, but is a technological development that has not yet occurred.

For financial institutions who face the business necessities of evaluating delivery of financial services into the home, the future is very enticing but very definitely the future. The biggest task right now lies in the institutions' own back shops, in automation of basic bank operations. This includes the electronic linking of existing product information and delivery systems efficiently and securely. Home banking — or in-home delivery of financial services — is part of an evolution in information access and availability that is one of the consequences of the automation of the entire financial services industry through electronic delivery systems. It is not a discrete product.

CHAPTER

10

Government's Role in Electronic Delivery

While the U.S. Treasury and the Federal Reserve Bank have encouraged the financial industry's usage of the automated clearinghouse system, most such usage does not directly affect consumers. Recent government initiatives in finding cost-effective means of accurately distributing various forms of public assistance benefits are changing that situation.

These initiatives are leading to the development of potentially important alternative, electronic-based financial service delivery systems. They are specifically geared to serve segments of the consumer population that otherwise are the least likely to be technology innovators, either because of age or inability to afford the necessary devices or services. The best known of these efforts is the more than decade-old direct deposit of Social Security benefits, now used by approximately half of all recipients, and most new recipients, who receive payment by check only if a special request is made.

The concept of electronically distributing government payments came directly as a result of the U.S. Treasury's Financial Management Services (FMS) studies of the soaring volume and associated costs of writing, mailing and processing checks. In 1975, the year direct deposit of Social Security was initiated, more than 700 million federal checks were issued, FMS estimates. Volume had increased approximately 40% in less than five years. By 1988, with electronic payment volume steadily increasing and overall volume at an all-time high, check issuance declined to 462.3 million items with 290.4 million additional payments made electronically. With an estimated cost of four cents for each electronic payment and per check costs ranging from 30 to 50 cents each, the potential dollar savings is tremendous.

The FMS has been leading the government's conversion from agency paper-shuffling to modern collection and payment systems since the Reform '88 program that began in 1983. That program was implemented with a goal of making the government run like a Fortune 500 company by 1988. And while Uncle Sam as a whole may not be on target, FMS has had some successes.

A first priority was to develop a comprehensive cash management system that emphasized the time value of the federal government's $2 trillion in annual cash flow. Since 1983, such efforts have saved an estimated $4.3 billion, principally through programs that include the Treasury Lockbox Network, currently collecting and processing $25 billion annually, and the Credit Card Collection Network that allows agencies to accept credit card payments from the public. In its first year of operation, 30 agencies participated in the credit card program and total collections were $70 million. Another FMS-initiated program is Vendor Express, which allows agencies to make electronic payments through the automated clearinghouse to private firms doing business with the government, as discussed in Chapter 7.

THE ELECTRONIC BENEFIT TRANSFER CONCEPT (EBT)

Systems for distributing government benefits electronically to individuals fall under the general umbrella of a concept called electronic benefit transfers (EBT). They are making use of existing automated teller machine (ATM) networks and point of sale (POS) direct debit systems, as well as the automated clearinghouse (ACH) and other components of the electronic infrastructure for payment transactions. Projects are occurring at federal, state and county levels of government.

No single means of handling EBT transactions has emerged, but the tests under way are intended to identify the best approaches for the agencies and governments involved. While this alternative delivery system development is not driven by consumers, it is significant in its likely impact through education. It is familiarizing a large segment of the population with electronic means of obtaining financial services, in this case, government-provided financial assistance. It also is providing electronic delivery system experience to merchants who otherwise might have little incentive to explore the concept.

In the most familiar form of these government-driven electronic delivery systems—direct deposit—the recipient simply receives a credit to an existing financial account. The government generates batch files of transactions that are routed to the appropriate institutions via the automated clearinghouse system. While this approach has been successful with Social Security, where the vast majority of recipients already maintain relationships with conventional financial institutions, most other entitlement programs deal with segments of the population least likely to have accounts with conventional financial institutions. Consequently, these benefit recipients have no means of receiving a direct deposit via the ACH system or any other electronic payment system. FMS estimates that 8 million recipients of federal benefits and 20 million recipients of state-provided benefits do not have bank accounts.

Consequently, some of the approaches being tested include the creation of special financial accounts at participating financial institutions from which funds can only be drawn by use of a plastic card that functions in certain ATMs or at point of sale terminals offered by certain retailers, particularly grocers. In other instances, storefront check-cashing operations are the intermediary and recipients obtain cash upon presentation of a card or other special identification.

EBT has been well received by recipients and disbursement agencies where it has been tried. However, there have only been a handful of trials to date, which have raised major questions about costs. Because of differences in attributing possible equipment and software costs, the cost per case is not clearly more or less than with existing systems, although the cost of a single electronic payment is less than the cost of writing a check. Additionally, it is not clear the extent to which merchants and financial institutions will participate without incentives or subsidies, and whether regulatory obstacles can be overcome. Other areas of concern have been raised by the federal government's Office of Technology Assessment (OTA).

Congress in 1989 received a report from the OTA, called "Electronic Delivery of Public Assistance Benefits." This document concluded that bankers, retailers and government officials must address concerns about computer security and personal privacy if electronic benefits transfer is to win acceptance. The document also recommended that program personnel be actively involved in the design and implementation of any EBT system to ensure that policy considerations as well as technology drive the process.

THE EVOLUTION OF EBT

New York City, which alone handles a greater volume of public benefits distribution than many states, was the first government entity to institute a replacement of paper distribution with electronics. In 1981 the city first issued plastic cards as a replacement for paper authorization forms that recipients used at check cashing outlets to obtain benefits. The cards in essence are for identification. The electronic delivery is between the city and the distribution points. Participating outlets have merchant-operated terminals that allow confirmation of eligibility and the amount of benefit available when a recipient presents an identification card and requests funds. The system operates in a batch fashion, with merchant accounts credited electronically overnight for the amount of disbursements, plus fees for providing the service. The city estimates that it has saved $9 million annually in administrative costs and that recipients have saved $9 million in check cashing fees, says FMS.

The New York City program, however, represents partial automation of distribution because it still requires the check casher as middleman to dispense cash and verify eligibility. The next step is to allow the recipient to use the card directly at the point of sale for purchases, which was not tested until 1984.

In 1982, two counties in California were the site of a demonstration program to study the possibility of distributing food stamp benefits by direct deposit to checking accounts. Although the program had minimal participation, it was considered a technical success in that direct deposits were made successfully to recipients' accounts and that doing so was less expensive than issuing checks. However, it highlighted two critical problems. The first was that a large number of the potential users did not have checking accounts and opening such an account was more expensive in service charges than what was typically spent on check cashing fees. The second problem was that many of the recipients could not responsibly manage a checking account and incurred substantial overdraft charges. That experience led to efforts to create special accounts that would only be used to disburse benefit funds.

The first fully automated system was devised in 1984 for distributing food stamps in Reading, Pennsylvania. Benefits were distributed to 3,400 low-income families via plastic cards, which recipients used to make purchases electronically 25,000 times each month during the 15-month test. The cards were presented at the point of sale for payment and were processed through special debit terminals installed at 125 food stores. Accounts were maintained on a central computer file run by the USDA. The response was overwhelmingly positive from all participants — the food retailers, benefit recipients and financial institutions. The program has continued since, operated by the state. However, the cost of the operation was more than expected.

In 1986, ABT Associates, an independent consulting firm hired by the USDA's Food and Nutrition Service to assess the financial results, found that the electronic system exceeded the cost of a paper based system nine-to-one, largely because of the expense of the special terminals and supporting telecommunications. ABT Associates concluded that the operational cost of administering the program might be lowered substantially by piggybacking it on an existing electronic funds transfer system. The original equipment was leased for a short term and used only for the project. However, the operational aspects of the system ran smoothly.

While the Reading test answered positively the question of whether electronic distribution of benefits would be accepted by users, merchants and financial institutions, it focused attention on whether such programs could be cost-effective. A second test begun in Ramsey County (St. Paul), Minnesota, in July 1987 directly addressed cost reduction. TransFirst Corporation, a Dallas-based transaction processing company, operated the program for Ramsey County. At a cost of $300,000, nearly all underwritten by TransFirst, the company provided network and processing services. The pilot used an existing ATM network to distribute benefits to recipients under the Aid to Families With Dependent Children (AFDC) program and to those who receive refugee assistance funds. Ironically, it was initiated by the state after local banks informed the county that they would no longer cash benefit checks for non-depositors. Not only was acceptance again overwhelmingly positive — 88% of recipients surveyed said they preferred it to receiving checks — but Ramsey County documented reduced costs compared to previous paper check expense.

Three similar concepts were tested in the program:

- A Point of Sale card usable in selected groceries and pharmacies;
- Access via specific dedicated ATMs and Instant Cash network ATMs; and
- Unrestricted ATM/POS access.

The Ramsey County program was deemed cost-effective enough to be expanded to include 13,000 households within the county in 1988 and helped Minnesota win more than $385,000 in grants to add to the program for 1989. The preferred means of benefit delivery was determined to be use of a card at the point of sale.

While the test demonstrated the merits of using existing EFT systems, implementation of the next phase provided an even stronger object lesson in the pitfalls of installing new systems. As more grocers became involved in the installation of in-store debit terminals, some balked. While the program worked well as a test, grocers feared that plans to place EBT terminals in only selected check-out lanes would result in federal regulators ruling such special treatment of benefit recipients to be discriminatory. The USDA, in turn, balked at the expense of equipping all participating merchants' check-out lanes with the terminals, but noted that third party service providers could install terminals if they were able to link to the system holding the data base for the electronic food stamp program. A 1991 start-up depends on resolution of the conflict.

The problem in Minnesota illustrated that while EBT technology for the delivery of food stamps is readily available, terminal technology that is adequate for distributing welfare benefits may not be appropriate for use as a direct debit system by the general public, which would reduce the possible efficiencies of using existing terminals. However, government planners have a mandate to use existing and available technology, which would seem likely to steer them toward systems that could piggyback on existing networks or services.

A variety of companies are prepared to offer EBT technology, including TransFirst, SmartCard International, GM's Electronic Data Systems division, First Data Resources, National Data Corporation, American Transtech, MTech, and others in the transaction processing arena.

Federal regulations also may still be a significant barrier to implementation. For example, administrators must determine what to do about benefits left over in accounts. How long should they be kept, when do they revert? Other questions point to the need for maintaining a dual system in the event that merchants refuse to purchase the on-line terminals or chip card terminals needed to participate in the program. Some of these questions may be addressed by the results of USDA trial programs.

BEYOND ELECTRONIC FOOD STAMPS

Other pilot programs are being conducted in Maryland, Iowa, New Mexico and Washington state. Federal benefit programs involved include Supplemental Security Income (SSI), Black Lung, Social Security, Veterans Compensation and Pension, Civil Service Retirement and Railroad Retirement. State-administered programs include not only the Aid to Families with Dependent Children (AFDC) and Food Stamp programs, but also Child Support and Unemployment Insurance. The goal of FMS is to eventually bring all such efforts together through a single plastic card, recognizing that many recipients in one program also receive benefits from another.

In addition to the USDA's activity, FMS is testing the disbursement of supplemental Social Security benefits through the use of debit cards. SecureCard, the name of a pilot program in Maryland, involves approximately 1,000 recipients in the city of Baltimore. Participants are issued an automated teller machine (ATM) card that will function through the MOST network, which serves that area. In addition, a number of grocery and convenience stores participate via POS terminals.

The supplemental Social Security benefit program has the lowest direct deposit rate, 14%, of any such government program, according to Social Security officials. It costs the government about 40 cents to process each payment by check. While the test will cost about twice that, long term savings could be substantially lowered, especially if the system successfully can be piggybacked on an existing network, and perhaps run in conjunction with other social benefits participants receive.

The test particularly is intended to reach benefit recipients who do not have bank accounts. The national SSI program currently serves 4.5 million aged, blind or disabled persons, disbursing a total of $14 billion annually in payments that average $185. Recipients in the Baltimore test are able to withdraw their funds immediately or in partial amounts, although change and odd amounts will be available only through retailer POS terminals.

The Treasury anticipates reduced administrative costs as well as savings from not printing and mailing checks. It has stated that its intentions are to tie into existing ATM and POS networks to minimize costs for itself, the networks and banks that participate. Dallas-based TransFirst Corporation is serving as the technical liaison and will provide the connection between the government and the ATMs and POS terminals. First National Bank of Maryland is the participating financial institution.

At least 12 ATMs will be used for the test and special POS terminals will be installed at nine sites. First National will distribute the ATM cards necessary for the program. FMS will use the automated clearinghouse to send SSI payments to special accounts set up at the bank. The bank will keep the payments but send information about them to TransFirst, which will enter the information into a data base. When a recipient uses an ATM or POS terminal to access funds, TransFirst will electronically access the SSI account at First National to debit the account. Participants will not have to maintain a traditional bank account. A benefit for the bank is that it will maintain a large amount of cash each month without having to pay interest.

In Tacoma, Washington, unemployment insurance payments are distributed via ATMs and POS terminals in a state-run program operated by TransFirst Corporation. The unusual feature of the Washington test is that recipients use an automated telephone system to call in their weekly eligibility reports. After verification of eligibility, payment is made through the recipient's choice of the ATM/POS terminal network, ordinary paper check or direct deposit to a bank account.

ISSUES IN EBT TESTS

The various tests of EBT are intended to address several issues, including who will pay the direct and indirect costs of EBT, whether participation should be mandatory or voluntary, whether the accounts used should be government owned or the recipients' personal accounts and the degree to which the frequency of withdrawals from ATMs or at POS terminals should be limited.

The first issue is highlighted by the example from Minnesota, in which grocers and the government are balking at the prospect of outfitting all possible check-out lanes with EBT terminals. A partial compromise is offered by the USDA in saying that any terminal may be used so long as it can communicate with the EBT system, but no offer has been made to cover any software or telecommunications costs that may be incurred as a result. Financial institutions generally have supported the concept of using existing networks as a means of distributing benefits, but have asked that usual interchange fees be covered.

The second issue, voluntary versus mandatory participation, is likely to eventually be resolved in favor of mandatory participation, although consumer organizations and current regulations favor retaining access to paper checks. So long as participating is an option, paper systems will have to be maintained in parallel with electronic delivery, significantly reducing the potential cost savings that are part of the rationale for EBT. Furthermore, the tests are demonstrating that one of the advantages of the electronic systems is that they reduce fraud. If paper based systems are more easily defrauded, fraudulent-minded recipients will continue to use them if given the option, again reducing the potential cost savings. However, as long as the programs are unproven and remain in testing phases, it is unlikely that participation will be mandatory.

The third issue is not likely to be answered by a single approach. Where recipients commonly have existing accounts with financial institutions, it is far more efficient for disbursement to be made by an electronic deposit to that account. However, a major reason for the move to EBT is to address concerns about charges to low-income persons for financial accounts and check cashing services. FMS studies find that fees of 5% or more are common for check-cashing, meaning the recipient of a $500 benefit check may pay $25 to cash it. Also, while the banking industry has established a wide variety of so-called "lifeline" accounts for the poor and elderly, many of the potential benefit recipients are not fiscally responsible and can not manage even such low-cost accounts without incurring overdraft charges.

Those factors suggest the government and recipients are better served by accounts that the government holds with access provided through on-line systems that verify available balances. Once again, however, current regulations in some instances require that if transfers are made electronically, they must be made to an account in the name of the recipient. The American Bankers Association notes that the issue of account ownership may be critical if there is a question about losses from an account.

The fourth issue concerns whether recipients will use EBT accounts for frequent, small withdrawals. Since each withdrawal has a cost associated with it, potentially including a fee paid to the owner of the terminal by the operators of the benefit program, the question is whether to restrict the frequency of withdrawals to hold down costs. The likely compromise is to offer one or more withdrawals at no charge with fees for additional access. Withdrawals for purchase amounts only at the point of sale probably would not have a fee.

FUTURE EBT PROJECTS

In addition to the various tests described, the USDA's Food and Nutrition Service is exploring off-line smart card technology that would use a calculator-size card with a built-in memory chip that would contain information about eligibility for benefits. The project is in a study phase, but an actual test will be conducted if an acceptable proposal is made. The concept is to provide a card that could be presented at a point of sale or, possibly, an ATM, to make purchases or obtain cash without need for verification from a remote database.

As conclusions are reached about the most effective structure for EBT, it appears likely it will first be implemented in 15 cities that have been identified as having the highest rates of theft of government checks. The cities, which are not presented in any particular order, are: Los Angeles, San Diego, Houston, New Orleans, Birmingham, Atlanta, Miami, Chicago, Detroit, Cleveland, Jersey City, Washington, D.C., Philadelphia, New York and Boston. In several of those cities, armed guards currently accompany postal carriers on days that benefit checks are delivered, representing one of the direct expenses of the paper-check system that could be eliminated by electronic delivery.

The various government agencies participating in EBT are pursuing a five-year, three-stage strategy, directed by the FMS. The first part of the strategy focuses on costs, educating all participants in the paper check benefit delivery process as to actual costs of the current system and costs of electronic systems. Secondly, target markets for EBT are being identified and advertising campaigns developed. Finally, the last stage calls for development of standards and protocols for issuing cards, training, marketing, customer service, privacy and security considerations and account specifications. That point optimistically is expected to be reached in 1995.

The Treasury regards EBT as the next phase in the federal government's efforts to reduce paper handling with all its associated costs. It is seen as a means of reducing operations expense, cutting fraud and waste and providing more timely service to beneficiaries. That commitment to electronic payments undoubtedly is stronger than what can be found anywhere else within the financial industry or the corporate world generally. Even if institutions currently have no interest in abandoning existing systems, the pressure to accommodate the federal government is likely to be irresistible.

CHAPTER

11

A Vision of an Integrated Payment System

PAYMENTS AS ELECTRONIC INFORMATION

A series of sometimes contradictory trends are in place in the nation's payment system. On the one hand the system is being fragmented, with control of parts of it in more hands than has been the case since the rise of national monetary systems. On the other hand, it is being unified by being universally reduced to the exchange of electronic information.

These contradictory trends are nevertheless taking us toward an integrated, information based payment system that relies on ready access to accurate and reliable records of financial activity, as opposed to a system oriented toward physical representations of wealth. The implications include the likelihood that banking as we know it increasingly will become a business built around providing electronic access to information, entailing an ever changing record of credits and debits and a service that permits the transfer of such information to an endless variety of potential recipients of such information through a wide variety of channels.

Technological developments underlie this change, enabling a series of economic decisions to participate by the government, financial institutions,merchants and, ultimately, consumers. The decisions fundamentally are whether and when to substitute electronic payment methods for conventional paper based methods. Those economic decisions are furtherdriven by the needs for the payment system to respond more rapidly, with greater accuracy and with greater capacity in the handling of routine transaction activity. The government has made policy decisions that push its many agencies and departments away from paper and toward electronic methods, primarily as a result of numerous studies that again and again demonstrate the cost-effectiveness of the change. Financial institutions and merchants, which lack any similar policy mandate and respond to competitive pressures, are moving toward electronic automation on a piecemeal basis, led by the strongest and most innovative among them. For both, the reaction of consumers is a great unknown, and anticipating how readily consumers will accept such payment methods is critical.

The rate of change in the consumer market is accelerated by demographic changes that are providing an unusually large and influential generation that creates change by its very existence. When a majority of the population falls in a single age group, the interests, attitudes and needs of that generation tend to dominate. The Baby Boom generation is not only more familiar with electronic payment methods than older members of the population, but also is more driven by needs for convenience and control over personal affairs, which reflects a greater level of financial sophistication than consumers previously have demonstrated.

Over the next decade, consumers will use a wide variety of devices and services for payments, some of which may not now be imaginable. However, it is relatively safe to say that new devices and services arise from existing trends. Electronic delivery itself is the paradigm, not some individual transaction device or new electronic means of access to information. A vision of an integrated payment system requires the ability to look beyond individual products or services to recognize the myriad opportunities in an evolution from a paper based to an electronic business.

CASH IS NOT OBSOLETE

This trend toward electronic delivery, however, does not make cash obsolete. One of the negative implications of payment automation is the possibility that much routine consumer transaction activity will be more easily recorded and monitored in the process of verifying availability of funds or credit. Much of electronic automation of payment requires an identifying mechanism, whether a signature, card number, voice characteristics or personal identification number, etc., that must be verified against a database. Many transactions are too minor or too personal to justify the recording or even transmitting of information about them. In most instances such information-gathering will be resisted by continued use of cash, the anonymity of which is not easily replaced electronically.

However, there are many instances in which an electronic equivalent of cash is potentially useful, particularly in small-dollar transactions such as at vending machines. Such cash equivalents appear most likely to be based on plastic cards, perhaps protected by biometric means of identification and resembling today's credit cards. Various prototype smart cards, plastic cards with microchips embedded in them, could be used for such purposes. An inexpensive form of the smart card could act as such a prepaid card by retaining a current balance that could be debited by a card reader device.

The precursors of such methods of payment appear in the form of disposable, prepaid transit fare cards, which use a magnetic stripe to retain data. Similar devices potentially may be applied in other instances in which large numbers of low-value transactions occur. Financial institutions generally may resist such developments because they perceive better business opportunities in continued expansion of existing credit and debit card systems. However, financial institutions also may be in the best position to exploit such demand if it should arise. Existing devices, including ATMs and point of sale debit terminals, might be used to "recharge" prepaid cards for a fee, creating a new line of business.

Change in anonymous means of payment, whether in the so-called "underground economy" or in the purely convenience-driven world of small dollar value exchanges, is likely to be more remote than change in methods of payment when information is exchanged in addition to value. The fact is that coins and currency provide a highly efficient, although less secure, method of making such payments than pre-paid cards because they do not require that the recipient have any equipment or device to record value from such cards.

The best applications for such devices appear to be locations where an electronic value reader can be incorporated efficiently as a substitute for coin and currency collection machinery, such as in transit systems, metered parking, public telephone services, vending machines and any other business in which large volumes of payments currently are collected in small denominations of coins and currency. Coin-operated vending machines could become obsolete. While vending machine inventory still would have to be physically replenished, funds could be collected remotely and usage monitored. The vendor would be alerted that a particular location's stock was depleted. The expense of collecting, recording and safeguarding that cash makes electronic payment alternatives highly attractive in those situations.

PAPER CHECKS: TARGET OF CHANGE

The primary immediate target of change through electronic payment automation will be the paper check. The processing and handling of paper has been automated extensively and paper is unlikely to disappear even from fully electronic systems, but much of the function it provided is more efficiently provided electronically. The paper check is not only a means of exchanging value, but information as well. There is much more information activity in presenting a check than is involved in presenting cash. Much of the information exchanged is intended to guarantee that funds are in fact available. Secondly, information is being noted for recordkeeping purposes. Each element of information may literally be stripped away and handled separately in an electronic system, yet efficient operations will find advantages in securing links between the information elements.

Consider the amount of routine information that is carried by an ordinary consumer's check written at the point of sale. First, the check carries pre-printed, magnetically readable information as to the financial institution that holds the account that has the funds that will be used to make the purchase. Generally, the kind of account is immaterial to the recipient of the check, but the MICR line determines the routing for that check as it flows through the processing system. Whether the account pays interest to the account holder or not, whether the account is backed by a line of credit or if in fact the check is a draft on a line of credit does not matter. The only concern of the recipient is that the check is in a standard format so that it will be honored in expeditious fashion by the recipient's financial institution for the amount for which it is written. That information about the account may be represented by a unique number in a variety of formats—embossed on a card, encoded on a magnetic stripe, entered by the consumer and so on.

Since the concern is securely obtaining the value the check represented, the merchant accepting the check may have its own information file electronically accessible to identify individuals who previously have presented invalid checks or may contract with a third-party firm to obtain a guarantee that the check is valid or at least that the writer does not have a history of writing bad checks. Furthermore, the recipient's procedures may require other forms of identification, pre-approval, or that the check be written on specific — usually local — institutions before it is accepted.

Each of these steps to verify the validity of the check represent additional expense to the recipient, whether in direct expenditure, foregone sales or increased personnel time at the point of sale. These are indirect expenses of the checking system that cause merchants to be more amenable to the prospect of alternative forms of payment, even when there is explicit pricing associated with such payment. Consequently the merchant is willing to pay to accept various cards, whether credit or debit, that may require an online authorization to similarly verify that funds indeed are available. In some instances the process of electronically transferring funds begins at the instant of inquiry. With offline systems, much as with a check, the recipient of the payment assumes more risk, although that also can be reduced just as with a check system by verification systems that assure the holder is legitimate and has no history of fraud.

Second, the check is pre-printed with the name of the institution and the name of the accountholder as well as an address, telephone number, driver's license number or other identifying information such as the accountholder may wish. While such information may not be required for processing, it provides additional security to the writer and recipient, allowing additional means of verifying that the instrument is not being forged. Although many financial institutions will provide new account owners with an initial supply of such checks at no charge, generally the consumer pays for pre-printed checks. Income from such check orders, although considered realtively minor, increasingly is being siphoned off from banks to third-party check printers (and yet another bank source of income from checking is under seige). This information has the potential to be marketing information, advertising the institution offering the payment method on one hand and providing the recipient with information about the customer on the other hand. The address and other incidental information that the check provides ordinarily are of use only if collection efforts are required. If an address is desired for marketing purposes, the merchant is not likely to obtain it from a check.

Traditionally, the merchant collected addresses for marketing purposes by various devices such as contests that require written entry, from proprietary credit cards, by requiring pre-approved check cashing cards or indirectly by obtaining addresses from third parties such as mailing list services. Automation of payment systems introduces the possibility that the merchant can not only track and control inventory through monitoring of the point of sale, but also allows the capture of direct marketing information. Some financial institutions have begun or are exploring programs that in essence sell the merchant's own information back to him by reporting aggregated items such as sales by the zip code of buyers. However, by issuing a proprietary card, whether credit or debit, the merchant has the capability of developing an automated system that captures detailed purchase information by individual customers, allowing highly sophisticated target marketing.

Electronic payment methods introduce a new level of marketing information tools as compared to checks in particular, also providing greater levels of security, greater ease of use and less possibility of error being introduced during processing of information entered manually on the check.

The check also carries a pre-printed number that designates it as one in a sequence. That seemingly minor detail enables both the writer and the recipient to distinguish a particular check from others that may carry similar or even identical information and assists the writer and processor in accounting for checks written and processed. Without sequential numbers, balancing a check book register against a bank statement would be considerably more difficult, although not impossible.

As additional means of access to the account are used, whether through ATM withdrawals, preauthorized payments or debit card transactions, the sequential number on the check no longer identifies and orders every transaction on the account, but remains critical as a means of tracking actual check writing. Similar unique transaction numbers are assigned to electronic transactions, but rarely are they used by the consumer in as direct a fashion as the check number is used. Their existence, however, allows the potential of a computerized information system to link the other information elements to allow a valid and accurate response to a consumer's inquiry such as, "How much did I pay for milk on Tuesday at Ralph's Grocery?"

Finally, there is the information manually entered on the check to record the date of the transaction, the name of the payee, the amount of the transaction — noted numerically and written out — and the signature of the writer of the check. A notation line also may be used to record other incidental information. Most of this information is entered for the benefit of the customer's recordkeeping. Beyond the pre-printed information, the merchant and processing bank need only have the amount of the transaction and verification that the customer approves of the transaction, approval which alternatively could be provided by a signature alone or by an electronic signature, such as entry of a personal identification number.

Not only does manual entry introduce error potential, both in errors made at the point of sale and in transcribing the information in processing, but this manual entry of data takes time that a busy merchant would rather have spent in ringing up the next sale. Electronic cash registers at the point of sale have the capability to print out a very detailed record of the sale on a receipt that the consumer may retain. If a plastic card is used for payment, that is all the information — with the obvious exception of the signature, physical or electronic — that may be necessary.

While applications of technology have allowed the introduction of enormous efficiencies in check processing, partial automation wastes potential opportunities. Partial automation of the payment system is inevitable, but the constant direction for financial institutions must be to ensure that partial solutions contribute to the goal of a fully automated, integrated system. Consider, for example, one of the next proposed steps in automating check handling, which is to potentially eliminate the flow of paper past the point at which the check is first presented.

TRUNCATION IS NOT AS EFFICIENT AS ELIMINATION

The truncation of checks at the bank of first deposit has become relatively common, representing about 8% of total check volume, the Federal Reserve estimates. Checks that are written on such accounts where the consumer has agreed to forego return of canceled items carry a specific designation in the MICR line. At first examination, truncation of checks at the point of sale seems logical as an extension of the process of automation, but it doesn't add great efficiency compared to eliminating the check altogether.

Truncation of checks at the point of sale reduces paper handling for the bank and allows the merchant and financial institutions to process payments electronically, but its first disadvantage is to the consumer. Not returning the check eliminates the recordkeeping aspect the check offered, unless an image of the check is captured and returned with the statement.

American Express has made an advantage of a similar procedure, capturing an image of its credit card slips as a first step in processing and returning images of the charge slips with monthly statements. Financial institutions are investigating automation equipment that would do the same for checks and inevitably some will pursue such a course, further prolonging the demise of the paper that could be eliminated now.

If such systems are implemented at the point of sale, replicating the current system of returning the check by returning its image, the merchant is required to either acquire or be provided with a device that captures the image of the check. The development of such a device is feasible, but immediately raises a host of questions ranging from who will pay for it to whether the image file it creates will be compatible with existing standards and formats for information exchange. As with most partial automation schemes, such a system must be able to demonstrate that it will pay for itself directly in some fashion, because it is not going to substitute for other payment methods that will still have to be supported.

Alternatively, the truncation process simply could involve electronic capture of the check's MICR information (bank identification and routing data) and electronic processing of that information along with the dollar value of the transaction. Such a system would accomplish at least one of the merchant's objectives, more rapid receipt of funds. However, such a scenario essentially describes the situation that would exist with a merchant-issued, ACH-based debit card, yet still would require handling of the paper check.

Any such scenario of partial automation returns to the question of what to do with the check. The preferred solutions eliminate the paper altogether. The means of replacing it at the point of sale are already in consumers' hands, wallets and pocketbooks in the form of plastic cards, whether debit or credit.

However, the process is not simply a matter of reducing or eliminating use of paper checks at the point of sale, but also eliminating use of paper checks as a means of paying bills from home and for obtaining cash. Many of the information functions of the check apply in each of those situations as well. Services from the home must also provide expanded information capabilities, which also must provide links to the remittance and information systems of the recipients of those checks. The flexibility and strength of the check is that it currently works equally well in each of these situations — and is processed through a single system. Electronic systems must offer comparable flexibility and efficiency, a feat they have not yet achieved.

An integrated approach to automation recognizes that our mobile, convenience-oriented society demands greater variety in means of access to payment capabilities with increased ability to link payment information, no matter what access means is used. As an information industry that concerns itself with payments and information about funds, financial institutions are in the best position and can best maintain their position within the payment system by providing services that provide such linked information through multiple means of access.

PROJECTIONS OF HOUSEHOLD USAGE OF ELECTRONIC DELIVERY SYSTEMS

To assist in visualizing the impact of an integrated, fully automated payment system, it is useful to make some projections of the likely household usage of various familiar means of making payments given current trends in payment system automation. While there is no guarantee that exactly what is projected will happen, this is intended as speculation about the consequences of continued expansion and interconnection of electronic information systems for financial services.

For the purposes of making projections of consumer behavior in usage of electronic delivery systems for financial services in the next decade, the following discusses household usage of ATMs, telephone based payment and information services, computer based financial services, preauthorized payments, direct deposit, credit cards and debit cards and the changes likely to occur in the volume of transactions occurring through each of the various delivery systems.

Integration of access to transaction products and services through a diverse range of interlinked electronic and non-electronic delivery systems will help financial institutions to survive by offering convenient, competitive and efficient service. Various components go into such systems, including brick and mortar branches, paper checks, plastic cards and electronic services, all of which are in effect delivering or facilitating consumer transaction activity. They are a means of providing a service rather than being services themselves. This assumption differs from more common financial industry attitudes that delivery systems such as credit cards or ATMs are products, which should be marketed and realize revenues independent of other product lines.

Making projections of any kind is a risky business with no more assurance of success than predicting the course of interest rates or the stock market. Nonetheless, there are only two choices. Do nothing and face regret over what might have been forseen. Or, examine what has occurred in the past, understand what is occuring in the present and extrapolate what may occur in the future. Such extrapolations are nightmares to statisticians, who want to apply mathematical models that cleanly demonstrate the source and lineage of all of the numbers in their database. But in Lewis Carroll style logic, numbers mean just what they say and nothing more. What they mean depends on what you ask or what you want. Projections are slippery things that will stay constant only as long as the world can be made to stay constant, which as the old physicist's joke states, is only at death. And then we're not sure.

Actually, physics and mathematics in their most leading edge forms give substantial encouragement to the business of making projections. In particular, a discipline that has come to be known as chaos theory argues that any specific future event will be determined by an infinite number of variables and therefore is impossible to predict. However, in any large scale system, certain patterns appear that are likely to reappear and propogate in a fashion that can be accurately predicted. In one pattern a leaf is created, in another a flower, in another a cloud system. Furthermore, these patterns often are evident in microcosm form, meaning they can be produced from relatively very little data, so long as it is the correct data. The concept of chaos as a generator of predictable patterns is allowing weather forecasting to be taken to new heights of accuracy, it allows computer graphics to generate near-photographic images of artificial reality and it allows designers of computer systems to anticipate the flow of data traffic as if they were managing the flow of fluids. The theory argues that we may not be able to predict a specific event, but we do know what will happen.

Of course, knowing whether the data upon which the projection is based is correct may be unknowable. Catch 22. Only by seeing the pattern created do we know whether the data was appropriate. For that, we look backward at what has occurred to date and project that the trends will continue. With that confidence, we can say that electronic automation unquestionably will continue to convert our financial system to an information system.

With knowledge of trends that have occurred in usage of financial services and understanding of the impact of technological change, making projections of behavior over the last decade of the century is at least possible. The following projections expand upon a series of projections I initially made in an article published in the *PSI Monitor* in 1987 and should not be interpreted literally, but as indicators of likely directions for consumer behavior.

They are rooted in a vision of an integrated payment system in which various devices provide common access to databases of financial information. This payment system is flexible and fully automated, but it still is used by people who primarily are interested in convenience, cost and control in their financial service delivery systems. Usage of particular devices or services is driven by the ability of those devices and services to meet needs conveniently and effectively.

EXISTING SERVICES IN EVOLUTION

During the decade of the nineties—

- ATM usage will rise to 75% of all households, making machine access to cash rise from approximately 20% of all cash access transactions to as much as 50%, including obtaining cash back at the point of sale through use of ATM debit cards.
- Direct deposit, encouraged by ongoing marketing, will continue its current growth. Salary payments will be offered electronically by virtually all employers, who will have automated payroll systems or contract with third-party providers to meet the requirements of making electronic tax payments. Financial institutions will offer such services routinely as part of corporate cash management services. For a variety of reasons, however, as many as one in four salaried employees will decline direct deposit. Nonetheless, usage should nearly double current levels. With direct deposit becoming standard for government benefit payments, the low-income end of the market will routinely receive payments by direct deposit, as will the elderly who receive retirement benefits. Combined, these factors indicate that as much as three-quarters of all households will

receive at least one direct deposit, although such electronic delivery will still be used for less than half of all payments to households.

- Credit cards already are a mature product, present in virtually all households that desire them. However, there is room for expansion from the current 80% penetration level to 90% or more of households, a level comparable to current penetration of checking accounts, as such cards continue to take a growing share of transaction volume from both cash and checks at the point of sale, and as cards rival checks as the most common means of accessing a transaction account.
- Debit cards at the point of sale, bolstered by merchant issuance programs, marketing by ATM service providers and blurring of the distinctions of the card association labels for credit and debit, may be used routinely at the point of sale by 60% of households, while held by as much as 80% or more of the market. With less than 10% of households currently using debit cards at the point of sale, this represents one of the greatest areas of transaction growth. As merchants and financial institutions further recognize the various advantages this payment method provides them, they are likely to actively promote such usage.
- Automated, voice based, telephone-delivered financial services, both informational and transactional, will be far enhanced from today's offerings and commonly used by two-thirds of households, representing as much as 90% of routine, information transactions and 5% of all payment transactions, which would represent as much as 100 times today's volume of telephone based payment transactions.
- A new generation of single purpose, computer based financial service devices that incorporate telephone functions while providing a screen to display text will play a significant role in payments from the home, representing another 5% of all payment transactions, displacing checks in many upscale, gadget oriented households.
- Computer based banking will grow slowly, but steadily, to meet special cash management needs in approximately one in five households, which will primarily consist of affluent and small business-owning households. Although most households will own devices that are computer based, the majority of such devices will be special purpose tools rather than the programmable, screen and keyboard devices that are usually referred to as home or personal computers. Computer based financial service users, because they represent households with extraordinarily high levels of financial activity, could represent as much as 10% of all payment transac-

tions from the home, still far less than are conducted by paper check, but making inroads.

- Preauthorized payment alternatives for both fixed and variable amount bills also will play a larger role as financial institutions and utilities respond to prodding from automated clearinghouse associations and begin to market the capability as a convenience service that also means never again paying a late fee. While a quarter of all households currently use preauthorized payment services, the majority do so for only a single payment. It will become much more common to do so for an entire range of payments. The telephone has the potential of playing a key role, providing a convenient means of allowing consumers control over the timing or authorization of a payment that an automated debit would seem to require be relinquished. Another 10% of all payments from home may migrate to this alternative, again displacing check writing.

The following expands upon reasons for these projections.

ATMs

The electronic delivery system used directly by consumers that has experienced the greatest growth since its introduction is the Automated Teller Machine, the ATM. The acceptance and demand for the machines at times have inspired bankers to believe consumers would use any electronic delivery system. ATMs were introduced nearly 20 years ago and have evolved from novelties, to examples of effective usage of technology that created competitive advantage for the institutions providing them, to their current status, a commodity service often regarded as a cost of doing business.

Usage of ATMs remained at a plateau for much of the past decade at approximately one-third of all households. Financial institutions concerned about the investment that had been made began to seek additional ways to leverage that investment, which led to sharing of the machines. Essentially, those institutions that had machines saw greater opportunity in selling access to their machines to customers of other institutions than there was in building usage within their own transaction account base. Although usage in some institutions was well above the one-third of all accounts level, it was recognized that availability of the service was a larger factor in that high level of usage than any particular customer characteristics such as age, education or financial status.

The concept was first tested by institutions that made agreements with fellow providers of ATMs, charging each other each time a customer used an ATM belonging to the other institution. The net, in theory, was a wash. The need to find additional revenue sources caused the concept to rapidly expand to include opening ATM access to customers of institutions that had no ATMs. Such institutions quickly concluded that paying per transaction fees each time their customers used someone else's ATM was less expensive than buying and promoting usage of their own machines.

As the concept of shared ATM access was promoted within the banking industry during the mid-80s, an unexpected development occurred. Non-banks, particularly merchants such as large oil companies and supermarkets, began to explore their own forms of shared access. In Florida, the Publix supermarket chain purchased and installed its own ATMs, built a processing network and negotiated agreements with individual banks to allow their customers to use the Publix ATMs. In California, the Arco oil company developed its own processing network that allowed acceptance of ATM cards for payment of gasoline purchases, an incidental ability as the company loudly eliminated its credit card program and quietly offered a proprietary debit card as an alternative. With this new competition, financial institutions were under pressure to expand access to even greater degrees, which led to regional networks for ATMs, countering the threat that non-bank owned networks would cause ATM revenue to flow out of the banking industry.

The struggle to maintain advantage and the consequent expansion of consumer access to ATMs propelled usage growth. Rather than simply increasing the number of households using ATMs, transaction growth through networks has taken off at double-digit rates. As the Baby Boom generation, which has matured during this period of ATM usage growth, moves into its dominant role in the older age ranges that have been most resistant to using ATMs, relatively few households will favor standing in line at the teller window over standing in line at the ATM machine. Consumers younger than the Baby Boomers find it all but inconceivable that financial institutions should not offer such 24-hour access to cash, just as they expect to be offered a credit card when opening a new transaction account.

The major issues for ATM providers include deciding how much consumers will pay for access to machines now that it has become commonplace for institutions to pass through to their customers the fees that they have been charged for foreign ATM usage. Whether or where to provide ATMs is no longer a critical strategic issue, but a matter of traffic counts. More difficult questions will arise as electronic point of sale terminals at retail locations are connected to shared networks not only to allow consumers to pay for purchases with ATM cards, but also to obtain cash directly from the merchant's till. Lower per transaction fees at such retail locations already are moving transaction volume away from ATM networks in some locations, but the change so far is so small that it has largely been ignored. That is not likely to remain the case as more retailers make such online connections.

Meanwhile, ATM providers are exploring the possibilities of getting additional revenue from their standalone kiosks through other services. Statement printing, postage stamp sales and coupon dispensing are only the beginning of additional applications for ATMs, all of which indicate that usage levels will continue to grow.

Direct Deposit

As one of the most familiar and widely used of electronic financial services, direct deposit is not really new. The employer-sponsored credit union that allowed employees to directly deposit a portion of each paycheck in a savings account is perhaps the oldest form, although non-electronic. Electronic networks, particularly the automated clearinghouse system, have made such arrangements more widely available and reduced the need for close relationships such as that between an employer and an in-house credit union. The federal government nearly two decades ago recognized the advantage of direct deposit as a means of reducing the cost of making millions of transfer payments for Social Security and other benefit programs. The millions of transactions that were converted to electronic transfers by government fiat and persuasion provided a base that allowed the ACH network to grow to a point where it now markets the advantages of direct deposit directly to the public, urging employees to ask that employers offer the service.

Once again, business opportunities are driving this growth. Institutions that have processed payments for the government recognize that it is possible for such systems to work efficiently and to the advantage of both financial institutions and their customers. Electronic deposit of funds tends to make it a bit more difficult for a customer to move an account, which once required little more than walking into the door of a rival institution with the latest Social Security check in hand. Seeing the value of direct deposit in this one area alone encourages financial institutions to promote direct deposit. Secondly, fee opportunities exist in charging businesses for making the transfers while the bank reduces its expense in check processing.

The government has played a major role in educating the public to the advantages of direct deposit and is continuing that role in various areas, not only including various welfare programs, but also through automation of Internal Revenue Service payments. The electronic filing of tax returns is being encouraged with the incentive of offering faster, electronic delivery of refunds. Ironically, many consumers once again are proving willing to pay a premium for such "instant refunds," which also represent a cost-saving in reduced check costs for the entity making the payments. The government may eventually require electronic payment by all taxpayers as well, but that stick currently is only used on large corporate taxpayers, who increasingly must pay employee withholding taxes electronically as well as an increasing number of state tax payments. For consumers, the interim step is payment of tax bills by credit card, which is being tested at federal, state and local levels and probably will be expanded.

Credit Cards

At first glance, credit cards would seem to be so pervasive as to represent little opportunity for electronic transaction growth. However, as with most financial delivery systems, the true level of automation is far less than what it might seem. A variety of electronic innovations are affecting processing of credit cards, including authorizing their acceptance, clearing the transactions through the system and settling among the various institutions involved. What were once paper-based activities increasingly are conducted through electronic information exchanges, specifically managed by the giant card associations. These innovations allow greater acceptance of cards by merchants of all kinds, increasing opportunities for usage of cards as well as introducing wholly new businesses such as providing credit card authorization through broadcast radio signals.

With credit card marketing extending cards to virtually all income levels, including cards that require a corresponding deposit balance to allow issuance of cards to households that otherwise pose too great a credit risk, virtually the only households without credit cards are those who refuse to deal with financial institutions at all. The history of checking account usage suggests that will be about 15% of all households. Furthermore, consumers are proving themselves willing to hold multiple cards issued by various institutions, holding open untapped credit lines to maintain personal financial flexibility. Institutions are willing to cooperate so long as issuing such cards is justified by income from annual fees, and losses from bad debts remain as relatively minuscule as they currently are compared to overall volume. With credit services a commodity product, competition is a matter of rates and fees.

These two factors combined, greater merchant acceptance and near universal card holding, suggest the greatest increases in credit cards will come not in household penetration, but in usage behavior. Card associations are actively exploring means of shifting low-dollar transactions, ranging from parking garage fees to fast-food hamburger purchases, to credit cards. Increases in usage are encouraged by improvements in authorizations systems, which make using cards quicker, cheaper and more reliable for consumers and merchants. Those improvements are likely to accelerate as network services improve and processing capability improves at the institution's end.

No better example exists of an institution dedicated to being a complete payment system than Visa International with its global authorization, settlement and switching systems. Using high-capacity telecommunication links and sophisticated computer processing centers, Visa is making its logo on any plastic card a truly international currency. Claiming 222 million cardholders worldwide and 7.7 million merchant locations, Visa is profitably reaching as much as 75% of the population in particular countries.

Debit Cards

Competition to credit cards will come from their plastic counterpart—the card that represents an available balance rather than available credit. While "secured" credit cards, those that require a deposit balance equal to the credit line extended, might be regarded as one form of debit card, there are a huge number of cards already in public hands that represent available balances. These cards are still thought of by financial institutions and consumers as ATM cards, but in fact they are debit cards and merchants increasingly perceive them as truly being "good as cash" for payments.

Some of the largest obstacles to debit card acceptance, ironically, arise from the way in which ATM networks developed on an uncoordinated regional basis with myriad fee agreements and complicated rules as to when a transaction must be electronically routed through which switch.

Key elements of the infrastructure are in place, but the processing systems are not yet fully linked in rational form. Until they are, debit growth will rise from the existing linked and integrated systems, the ACH and the credit card processing systems.

The ACH system functions as a non-profit cooperative, reducing financial institution incentives to make use of it except when it results in cost-savings through reduced check processing. However, for the merchant, it opens access to the entire banking system and virtually all banks simply by obtaining the cooperation of a single bank willing to market its ACH services to the merchant. The merchant can retain the information business side of the transaction, while having inexpensive access to clearing and settlement services. The cost of developing and managing such programs can be considerable, which so far has limited entry to a few large, highly automated and perceptive merchants, primarily in the grocery business where credit card acceptance is relatively rare.

The credit card associations recognize the potential threat and have countered through the banking industry with an old product made new, the credit card-labeled debit card. Such cards, which carry the logo of one of the two major card associations, Visa and MasterCard, were first issued in large quantities by brokerages, non-banks that wanted to provide consumers with transaction access to money market accounts they had developed. Such cards were not truly credit cards, but to the merchant accepting them, the presence of the card logo means that all such cards must be accepted if any are. The financial industry's first response to the credit card-labeled debit card was to enter the money market account business, but in the face of possible expansion of ATM card and ACH card debit programs, the risk of cannibalizing credit card portfolios is considered necessary and many are now adding credit card-labeled debit cards to their inventory, frequently substituting them for ATM cards in an interesting marketing twist. The card functionally is still an ATM card, but it now is promoted as a Visa or MasterCard.

Telephone Based Financial Service Delivery

The telephone as an information and transaction device represents what is perhaps the next great area for growth in electronic financial services, dispensing with cards or any other physical device. Just as in making a telephone call, a consumer may need nothing more than to be able to recall a specific identification number to complete a transaction.

Given the dangers of such information being misused, such forms of security are likely to be necessary, but the ability to securely identify voice characteristics may make even the use of an identification number unnecessary.

Whether through such seemingly exotic technological advances or through the relatively mundane introduction of sophisticated telephones that offer "plug-and-play" convenience, consumer usage of the telephone for bill payment and other financial transactions could readily jump from the two percent of all household level at which it has languished since the first introduction of such services to widespread acceptance, meaning two-thirds or more of all households. Such a projection does not reflect huge growth in the current generation of telephone bill payment programs, but rather the introduction of new services and new telephone based devices, developments that already are occurring. Moreover, new systems and devices seem to converse naturally, reducing the awkwardness of their use, while allowing the ability to obtain account information and complete a transaction electronically. The current generation of devices that add small screens and keyboards to telephones is only a beginning.

The changes to come also will be enabled by the combined impact of the availability of ISDN (Integrated Services Digital Network) capabilities within telephone networks and the increased automation of merchant operations. Forerunner companies include such market leaders as American Express, which learned one of the now apocryphal lessons of using such technology — be careful what you tell the customer. The mistake AmEx initially made in using Automatic Number Identification (ANI) capability was to greet customers by name. Since it could link its own database of customer information with the number of the incoming call, customer service representatives could have a customer file on screen as they answered the phone. Cardholders were startled to be greeted familiarly before they had said who they were.

The process of reducing steps in information transactions not only makes sense in situations such as customer service, but also in handling payments. Financial institutions are likely to use the same capabilities to ease customer access to their own financial accounts. Combined with merchants that are using EDI (Electronic Data Interchange) as a means of automating their internal operations and dealings with vendors, another round of business opportunities is being introduced. Merchants that are accustomed to nearly automatic customer payment (such as utilities that have the ability to deny service if payment is not forthcoming) can obtain even greater certainty and rapidity of payment by moving to systems that allow full automation of the transaction, conveniently provided to customers through their own home telephones. Opportunities in the electronic movement of funds in such systems will grow side-by-side with the electronic exchange of information in merchant systems. Improved, reliable means of settlement make such systems more attractive to all participants.

The availability of ACH services also provides a shortcut around any financial institution that may not wish to directly cooperate in such scenarios. Third party service providers are likely to arise as middlemen, handling the information flow for both merchants and financial institutions and offering a variety of electronic payment services, whether for fixed or variable amount payments. Such automated, electronic payment services range from automatic payments that operate on a preauthorized basis to debit a consumer's account at a prearranged time, to services that allow the consumer to control the timing of the debit, perhaps as simply as by pressing a touchtone button, to fully interactive systems that allow customer initiated entry of payment items.

Computer Based Financial Service Delivery

The computer in the home is likely to be the computer in the phone. Where only a few years ago there was a rush of enthusiasm for the prospect of tapping directly into the consumer demand for home computers by providing interactive, electronic services that could be obtained by plugging that computer into a phone line through a modem, the enthusiasm often reflected the promoters' lack of understanding of home computers. Although more sophisticated and powerful than anything of its kind that had ever been offered to consumers, the home computer proved to be far more difficult to learn and use than many had expected. Games, word processing and a few other activities were and still are the primary activities for home computers.

There is a discrete, well-educated and affluent market that is willing to work its way up the learning curve to use financial services through a home or personal computer, but this market is driven by its ability to work with that data off-line, particularly with financial management software. Without the need to further manipulate the information for bookkeeping or income opportunities, the low-cost alternatives that are currently available to the average household simply are superior to financial services obtained through using a computer.

That does not mean, however, that computer based financial services have no future. Quite the contrary. Those households that have a need for computer based financial services are some of the most financially active in the market. There just are not a great many of them. They are households that also operate small businesses from home or are active investors. Without those two groups, the potential market shrinks to a handful of computer fanatics who will use the computer for anything — including finding a date.

The mass market for computer based financial services lies in households that will purchase a "plug-and-play" device, programmed at the factory, not by the consumer. Just as most owners of sophisticated video cassette recorders primarily use the machines to play prerecorded movies, household use of computer based financial services will depend on the availability of devices so simple to use that they will be considered home banking appliances and very well may be provided by a financial service provider as readily as a plastic-covered checkbook is provided today. The cost of such devices is likely to fall well within the range of the toasters that financial institutions once offered as premiums and be far more applicable to the service that is being sold.

The home banking appliance may bear some resemblance to a home computer in that it is likely to have a keyboard and a screen of some type, but it also will have a telephone handset and telephone functions. It might be called a smart telephone, but it won't be a dumb terminal. The home banking services that such devices are used to obtain also will be accessible by a variety of other such devices or personal computers with the proper software.

Preauthorized Payments

The convenience of preauthorized payments often has been overshadowed by the somewhat draconian ways in which they have been introduced to consumers. Often they are presented as the only alternative to full payment in advance and if they should cause an overdraft of an account, the consumer will pay a penalty. The process of preauthorization is an extension of the commitment the consumer makes in agreeing to pay for use of a basic service or in assuming a financial obligation such as to repay a loan. At its simplest level, it is a process of designating the account from which future payments will be made and as such represents one of the financial industry's best opportunities for cementing a long term relationship with a customer without having to encase the customer's feet in that cement.

The consumer is interested in preauthorization because of its convenience. While life is uncertain, there are more certain bills than only for death and taxes. The vast, vast majority of households manage to make those payments each month even when budgets are tight and a little juggling is necessary to make it to the next paycheck. A financial institution that has years of experience with a single customer today is often wholly unaware of the fact of that experience. Nothing is of importance except the balance in the account at this moment, without consideration of how quickly that balance appeared or how soon it will be gone. A financial institution that recognizes its information function will have access to a history of its own relationship with an individual consumer and consequently can make risk decisions literally on an individual basis rather than on the mass aggregate basis that blindly-ignores what the community banker always has known. The history of the customer is critical. Such an approach may certainly lead to discrimination, but only in the proper sense of the term, in that a decision will be made on a fair basis according to the information that is available.

In such an information service-oriented business, preauthorized payments are a natural extension of personal financial management services, merely one of many ways in which the institution can provide the consumer with convenience and greater service. A fully integrated, automated electronic financial service institution does not have to be an impersonal institution, but can use its tools to be as personal as a customer desires.

THE INTEGRATED PAYMENT SYSTEM

Perhaps a fully integrated, automated payment system produces visions of 1984 and Big Brother, but the reality is not necessarily so ominous. Controls exist through competition and regulation. Abuses of information are criminal acts and should be treated as such even when the abuse is by an institution. Determining when abuse is occurring first requires understanding what the system is capable of doing. As with most tools, an electronic payment system in itself is neutral. The good or the bad depends on how we use it.

Financial Product/Service Usage and Balances
MID-AMERICA SEGMENT

	% Own	Mean Bal/ Owner	Median Bal/ Owner	Mean Bal/ Household	Median Bal/ Household
Deposit Accounts					
Regular Checking	67%	$1,647	$750	$1,103	$503
Interest Checking	49%	$3,153	$1,500	$1,545	$735
Regular Savings	66%	$3,167	$1,500	$2,090	$990
Certificate of Deposit	30%	$29,402	$15,000	$8,821	$4,500
Money Market Deposit Account	4%	$9,822	$7,500	$393	$300
				$13,952	$7,028
Credit Products					
First Mortgage	42%	$37,845	$37,500	$15,895	$15,750
Second Mortgage/ Home Equity Loan	5%	$18,532	$12,500	$927	$625
Home Equity Line of Credit	5%	$27,383	$12,500	$1,369	$625
Automobile Loan	61%	$5,497	$3,750	$3,353	$2,288
Secured Personal Loan	16%	$3,296	$1,750	$527	$280
Unsecured Personal Loan	8%	$3,429	$1,750	$274	$140
Unsecured Personal Line of Credit	9%	$2,393	$500	$215	$45
MasterCard Credit Card	34%	$1,425	$500	$485	$170
Visa Credit Card	45%	$1,126	$500	$507	$225
Broker Margin Account	1%	$14,506	$5,000	$123	$42
				$23,675	$20,190
Investment Products					
Money Market Mutual Fund	8%	$18,339	$7,500	$1,467	$600
Stock Mutual Fund	10%	$19,554	$7,500	$1,955	$750
Bond Mutual Fund	5%	$26,090	$17,500	$1,305	$875
Other Mutual Fund	5%	$25,226	$7,500	$1,261	$375
Stocks	20%	$22,547	$7,500	$4,509	$1,500
Corporate or Municipal Bonds	3%	$36,740	$37,500	$1,102	$1,125
Government Securities	7%	$15,500	$7,500	$1,112	$538
Real Estate Investments	20%	$65,315	$37,500	$12,952	$7,436
Whole Life Insurance Policies	47%	$54,440	$37,500	$25,587	$17,625
Universal Life Insurance Policies	11%	$63,674	$62,500	$7,004	$6,875
Insurance Annuities	8%	$38,591	$37,500	$3,087	$3,000
IRAs	31%	$15,682	$7,500	$4,861	$2,325
Keogh Accounts	1%	$28,446	$17,500	$284	$175
401 (k) Savings Plans	17%	$16,554	$7,500	$2,814	$1,275
				$69,300	$44,474
Estimated Financial Net Worth				**$59,577**	**$31,312**

Source: Payment Systems, Inc. (1988)

Financial Product/Service Usage and Balances
TECHIES SEGMENT

	% Own	Mean Bal/ Owner	Median Bal/ Owner	Mean Bal/ Household	Median Bal/ Household
Deposit Accounts					
Regular Checking	54%	$1,973	$750	$1,065	$405
Interest Checking	61%	$3,610	$3,500	$2,202	$2,135
Regular Savings	67%	$2,919	$1,500	$1,956	$1,005
Certificate of Deposit	33%	$25,174	$15,000	$8,307	$4,950
Money Market Deposit Account	14%	$8,925	$7,500	$1,250	$1,050
				$14,780	$9,545
Credit Products					
First Mortgage	61%	$63,024	$37,500	$38,445	$22,875
Second Mortgage/ Home Equity Loan	9%	$26,104	$12,500	$2,349	$1,125
Home Equity Line of Credit	10%	$20,928	$12,500	$2,093	$1,250
Automobile Loan	55%	$7,587	$6,250	$4,173	$3,438
Secured Personal Loan	11%	$6,951	$6,250	$765	$688
Unsecured Personal Loan	18%	$2,703	$1,750	$487	$315
Unsecured Personal Line of Credit	19%	$2,814	$1,750	$535	$333
MasterCard Credit Card	50%	$1,784	$500	$892	$250
Visa Credit Card	65%	$1,112	$500	$723	$325
Broker Margin Account	8%	$18,294	$5,000	$1,457	$398
				$51,919	$30,997
Investment Products					
Money Market Mutual Fund	19%	$24,829	$7,500	$4,718	$1,425
Stock Mutual Fund	25%	$16,616	$7,500	$4,154	$1,875
Bond Mutual Fund	10%	$34,156	$17,500	$3,416	$1,750
Other Mutual Fund	14%	$7,787	$2,500	$1,090	$350
Stocks	38%	$28,154	$7,500	$10,699	$2,850
Corporate or Municipal Bonds	9%	$31,918	$37,500	$2,873	$3,375
Government Securities	11%	$8,809	$7,500	$935	$796
Real Estate Investments	34%	$101,490	$75,000	$34,129	$25,221
Whole Life Insurance Policies	53%	$58,274	$37,500	$30,885	$19,875
Universal Life Insurance Policies	13%	$94,917	$87,500	$12,339	$11,375
Insurance Annuities	11%	$25,248	$12,500	$2,777	$1,375
IRAs	53%	$16,632	$17,500	$8,815	$9,275
Keogh Accounts	5%	$18,758	$17,500	$938	$875
401 (k) Savings Plans	36%	$14,145	$2,500	$5,092	$900
				$122,860	$81,317
Estimated Financial Net Worth				**$85,721**	**$59,865**

Source: Payment Systems, Inc. (1988)

Financial Product/Service Usage and Balances
GADGETEERS SEGMENT

	% Own	Mean Bal/ Owner	Median Bal/ Owner	Mean Bal/ Household	Median Bal/ Household
Deposit Accounts					
Regular Checking	65%	$2,195	$1,500	$1,427	$975
Interest Checking	56%	$3,323	$1,500	$1,861	$840
Regular Savings	75%	$3,906	$2,000	$2,930	$1,500
Certificate of Deposit	30%	$30,020	$15,000	$9,006	$4,500
Money Market Deposit Account	15%	$12,466	$7,500	$1,870	$1,125
				$17,094	$8,940
Credit Products					
First Mortgage	58%	$64,361	$62,500	$37,329	$36,250
Second Mortgage/ Home Equity Loan	12%	$22,089	$12,500	$2,651	$1,500
Home Equity Line of Credit	7%	$56,930	$12,500	$3,985	$875
Automobile Loan	51%	$7,207	$6,250	$3,676	$3,188
Secured Personal Loan	18%	$4,069	$1,750	$732	$315
Unsecured Personal Loan	12%	$4,223	$3,750	$507	$450
Unsecured Personal Line of Credit	12%	$2,989	$1,750	$359	$210
MasterCard Credit Card	53%	$1,718	$500	$911	$265
Visa Credit Card	62%	$1,235	$500	$766	$310
Broker Margin Account	4%	$15,058	$5,000	$629	$209
				$51,545	$43,572
Investment Products					
Money Market Mutual Fund	12%	$14,971	$2,500	$1,797	$300
Stock Mutual Fund	14%	$17,566	$17,500	$2,459	$2,450
Bond Mutual Fund	6%	$15,057	$7,500	$903	$450
Other Mutual Fund	6%	$11,499	$7,500	$690	$450
Stocks	29%	$20,379	$7,500	$5,910	$2,175
Corporate or Municipal Bonds	3%	$32,189	$7,500	$966	$225
Government Securities	9%	$7,037	$2,500	$650	$231
Real Estate Investments	24%	$94,699	$62,500	$22,270	$14,698
Whole Life Insurance Policies	51%	$69,948	$62,500	$35,673	$31,875
Universal Life Insurance Policies	21%	$96,597	$87,500	$20,285	$18,375
Insurance Annuities	11%	$42,391	$37,500	$4,663	$4,125
IRAs	44%	$17,620	$17,500	$7,753	$7,700
Keogh Accounts	3%	$26,655	$17,500	$800	$525
401 (k) Savings Plans	26%	$14,119	$2,500	$3,671	$650
				$108,490	$84,229
Estimated Financial Net Worth				**$74,039**	**$49,597**

Source: Payment Systems, Inc. (1988)

Financial Product/Service Usage and Balances
PROCRASTINATORS SEGMENT

	% Own	Mean Bal/ Owner	Median Bal/ Owner	Mean Bal/ Household	Median Bal/ Household
Deposit Accounts					
Regular Checking	58%	$2,150	$750	$1,247	$435
Interest Checking	44%	$2,958	$1,500	$1,302	$660
Regular Savings	47%	$3,670	$1,500	$1,725	$705
Certificate of Deposit	29%	$27,234	$10,000	$7,898	$2,900
Money Market Deposit Account	16%	$11,225	$7,500	$1,796	$1,200
				$13,968	$5,900
Credit Products					
First Mortgage	34%	$38,508	$37,500	$13,093	$12,750
Second Mortgage/ Home Equity Loan	5%	$25,870	$12,500	$1,294	$625
Home Equity Line of Credit	6%	$6,447	$0	$387	$0
Automobile Loan	32%	$4,060	$1,750	$1,299	$560
Secured Personal Loan	12%	$4,744	$3,750	$569	$450
Unsecured Personal Loan	9%	$4,001	$3,750	$360	$338
Unsecured Personal Line of Credit	5%	$3,791	$500	$190	$25
MasterCard Credit Card	22%	$1,764	$500	$388	$110
Visa Credit Card	29%	$1,575	$500	$457	$145
Broker Margin Account	6%	$32,018	$5,000	$1,940	$303
				$19,977	$15,306
Investment Products					
Money Market Mutual Fund	10%	$24,824	$17,500	$2,482	$1,750
Stock Mutual Fund	11%	$29,800	$17,500	$3,278	$1,925
Bond Mutual Fund	6%	$38,157	$17,500	$2,289	$1,050
Other Mutual Fund	3%	$23,556	$17,500	$707	$525
Stocks	19%	$36,762	$10,000	$6,985	$1,900
Corporate or Municipal Bonds	5%	$46,895	$62,500	$2,345	$3,125
Government Securities	6%	$23,918	$2,500	$1,329	$139
Real Estate Investments	18%	$78,384	$62,500	$13,856	$11,048
Whole Life Insurance Policies	40%	$53,399	$37,500	$21,360	$15,000
Universal Life Insurance Policies	9%	$48,313	$12,500	$4,348	$1,125
Insurance Annuities	9%	$42,616	$12,500	$3,835	$1,125
IRAs	31%	$19,051	$17,500	$5,906	$5,425
Keogh Accounts	2%	$39,608	$17,500	$792	$350
401 (k) Savings Plans	14%	$21,325	$7,500	$2,986	$1,050
				$72,498	$45,537
Estimated Financial Net Worth				**$66,489**	**$36,131**

Source: Payment Systems, Inc. (1988)

Financial Product/Service Usage and Balances
NO-TECH SEGMENT

	% Own	Mean Bal/ Owner	Median Bal/ Owner	Mean Bal/ Household	Median Bal/ Household
Deposit Accounts					
Regular Checking	68%	$1,654	$750	$1,125	$510
Interest Checking	49%	$3,095	$1,500	$1,517	$735
Regular Savings	60%	$2,442	$750	$1,465	$450
Certificate of Deposit	34%	$27,194	$15,000	$9,246	$5,100
Money Market Deposit Account	16%	$9,844	$7,500	$1,575	$1,200
				$14,928	$7,995″
Credit Products					
First Mortgage	22%	$26,319	$12,500	$5,790	$2,750
Second Mortgage/ Home Equity Loan	2%	$9,247	$12,500	$185	$250
Home Equity Line of Credit	5%	$6,881	$0	$344	$0
Automobile Loan	13%	$4,107	$1,750	$534	$228
Secured Personal Loan	7%	$3,091	$1,750	$216	$123
Unsecured Personal Loan	3%	$3,870	$500	$116	$15
Unsecured Personal Line of Credit	5%	$2,481	$0	$124	$0
MasterCard Credit Card	25%	$1,209	$500	$302	$125
Visa Credit Card	29%	$667	$500	$193	$145
Broker Margin Account	3%	$9,586	$5,000	$275	$143
				$8,079	$3,779
Investment Products					
Money Market Mutual Fund	13%	$14,552	$2,500	$1,892	$325
Stock Mutual Fund	8%	$17,006	$5,000	$1,360	$400
Bond Mutual Fund	5%	$35,426	$17,500	$1,771	$875
Other Mutual Fund	2%	$20,686	$7,500	$414	$150
Stocks	14%	$23,044	$10,000	$3,226	$1,400
Corporate or Municipal Bonds	3%	$50,796	$62,500	$1,524	$1,875
Government Securities	6%	$12,652	$2,500	$778	$154
Real Estate Investments	10%	$35,619	$12,500	$3,649	$1,281
Whole Life Insurance Policies	35%	$39,126	$37,500	$13,694	$13,125
Universal Life Insurance Policies	3%	$61,882	$37,500	$1,856	$1,125
Insurance Annuities	6%	$35,551	$12,500	$2,133	$750
IRAs	20%	$11,422	$7,500	$2,284	$1,500
Keogh Accounts	2%	$15,990	$2,500	$320	$50
401 (k) Savings Plans	6%	$15,092	$7,500	$906	$450
				$35,807	$23,460
Estimated Financial Net Worth				**$42,656**	**$27,676**

Source: Payment Systems, Inc. (1988)

Table 1

Summary Of Demographic Characteristics

Age	Techies	Gadgeteers	Mid-America	Procrastinators	No-Tech
Less than 25	1%	6%	4%	2%	11%
25-34	23%	30%	25%	10%	12%
35-44	31%	32%	21%	15%	9%
45-54	26%	17%	14%	13%	11%
55-64	13%	10%	17%	17%	14%
65-74	6%	5%	14%	21%	19%
75 and older	1%	1%	6%	24%	23%
Median Age (years)	**44**	**41**	**45**	**61**	**61**

Income (000s)	Techies	Gadgeteers	Mid-America	Procrastinators	No-Tech
Less than $15	13%	9%	28%	40%	57%
$15-$24.9	13%	16%	20%	16%	24%
$25-$34.9	11%	14%	19%	11%	8%
$35-$49.9	26%	25%	17%	12%	5%
$50-$74.9	14%	24%	11%	13%	5%
$75 and up	23%	12%	5%	8%	2%
Median Income	**$42,500**	**$41,600**	**$26,100**	**$18,600**	**$13,100**

Education	Techies	Gadgeteers	Mid-America	Procrastinators	No-Tech
No Response	0%	0%	0%	1%	2%
Attended Grade School	0%	0%	2%	3%	2%
Graduated Grade School	0%	0%	4%	8%	3%
Attended High School	1%	6%	11%	13%	13%
Graduated High School	11%	25%	36%	30%	25%
Attended College	31%	31%	21%	19%	24%
Graduated College	22%	16%	13%	11%	18%
College Post Graduate	34%	23%	11%	16%	14%

Employment	Techies	Gadgeteers	Mid-America	Procrastinators	No-Tech
No Response	0%	1%	2%	6%	2%
Full-Time	82%	82%	63%	50%	34%
Part-Time	9%	4%	7%	3%	13%
Retired	6%	7%	21%	38%	34%
Not Employed	3%	6%	6%	3%	17%

Source: Payment Systems, Inc. (1988)

Table 2

Ownership Of Consumer Electronic Products

Touchtone Telephone	Techies	Gadgeteers	Mid-America	Procrastinators	No-Tech
Currently Own	67%	84%	64%	65%	36%
Buy Next Year	7%	5%	3%	1%	5%
No Plan to Buy	25%	11%	33%	2%	59%
No Response	1%	1%	0%	33%	1%
Personal Computer	**Techies**	**Gadgeteers**	**Mid-America**	**Procrastinators**	**No-Tech**
Currently Own	87%	49%	5%	21%	2%
Buy Next Year	11%	35%	12%	4%	9%
No Plan to Buy	2%	16%	84%	0%	90%
No Response	3%	0%	0%	75%	0%
Computer Printer	**Techies**	**Gadgeteers**	**Mid-America**	**Procrastinators**	**No-Tech**
Currently Own	85%	38%	1%	17%	0%
Buy Next Year	11%	35%	9%	2%	7%
No Plan to Buy	1%	27%	90%	0%	93%
No Response	3%	0%	0%	82%	0%
Modem	**Techies**	**Gadgeteers**	**Mid-America**	**Procrastinators**	**No-Tech**
Currently Own	70%	8%	0%	7%	0%
Buy Next Year	13%	28%	5%	1%	7%
No Plan to Buy	5%	64%	95%	0%	93%
No Response	12%	1%	0%	92%	0%
Compact Disk Player	**Techies**	**Gadgeteers**	**Mid-America**	**Procrastinators**	**No-Tech**
Currently Own	27%	9%	9%	10%	1%
Buy Next Year	17%	18%	12%	1%	9%
No Plan to Buy	53%	72%	77%	0%	90%
No Response	3%	0%	2%	89%	0%
Video Cassette Recorder (VCR)	**Techies**	**Gadgeteers**	**Mid-America**	**Procrastinators**	**No-Tech**
Currently Own	82%	92%	68%	43%	5%
Buy Next Year	7%	5%	14%	2%	8%
No Plan to Buy	11%	2%	19%	1%	87%
No Response	0%	0%	0%	55%	0%

Table 2 (Cont.)
Ownership Of Consumer Electronic Products

Video Camera	Techies	Gadgeteers	Mid-America	Procrastinators	No-Tech
Currently Own	2%	30%	2%	9%	1%
Buy Next Year	5%	34%	13%	4%	6%
No Plan to Buy	93%	30%	85%	2%	94%
No Response	0%	6%	0%	85%	0%
Telephone Answering Machine	**Techies**	**Gadgeteers**	**Mid-America**	**Procrastinators**	**No-Tech**
Currently Own	44%	50%	19%	20%	18%
Buy Next Year	9%	19%	9%	2%	6%
No Plan to Buy	46%	29%	72%	2%	75%
No Response	1%	2%	0%	77%	2%
Color Television	**Techies**	**Gadgeteers**	**Mid-America**	**Procrastinators**	**No-Tech**
Currently Own	99%	97%	99%	81%	59%
Buy Next Year	0%	1%	1%	0%	5%
No Plan to Buy	1%	1%	1%	1%	37%
No Response	0%	1%	0%	18%	0%
Microwave Oven	**Techies**	**Gadgeteers**	**Mid-America**	**Procrastinators**	**No-Tech**
Currently Own	86%	92%	88%	69%	9%
Buy Next Year	4%	4%	7%	1%	21%
No Plan to Buy	11%	3%	4%	1%	70%
No Response	0%	1%	0%	29%	0%

Source: Payment Systems, Inc. (1988)

Table 3
Familiarity With Personal Computers

Base = All Respondents

	Techies	Gadgeteers	Mid-America	Procrastinators	No-Tech
Have used a personal computer	88%	80%	45%	31%	33%
Own a personal computer	87%	49%	5%	21%	2%
Plan to buy a personal computer	11%	35%	12%	4%	9%
Have access to micro computer at work	65%	51%	36%	25%	17%

Base = Respondents who own and/or plan to buy

	Techies	Gadgeteers	Mid-America	Procrastinators	No-Tech
Value is/will be more than $1,000	72%	49%	10%	13%	9%
User is/will be male head of household	55%	35%	42%	29%	8%
User is/will be female head of household	4%	22%	16%	23%	1%
User is/will be both heads of household	25%	31%	30%	31%	77%
User is/will be someone else	16%	13%	12%	17%	14%

Source: Payment Systems, Inc. (1988)

Table 4

General Banking And Financial Behavior

Main Financial Institution	Techies	Gadgeteers	Mid-America	Procrastinators	No-Tech
Commercial Bank	59%	55%	61%	59%	51%
Savings Bank/Association	25%	28%	24%	23%	30%
Credit Union	16%	15%	13%	14%	14%
Other	0%	0%	0%	2%	3%
Use of Branch Locations	**Techies**	**Gadgeteers**	**Mid-America**	**Procrastinators**	**No-Tech**
One Only	29%	37%	42%	43%	55%
One or Two	33%	38%	33%	27%	25%
One, Spouse Another	3%	2%	5%	4%	2%
One Near Work & One Near Home	6%	5%	6%	7%	4%
Multiple Locations	11%	7%	6%	8%	6%
Prefer ATMs	15%	9%	5%	3%	5%
Use Phone and Mail	3%	2%	2%	2%	1%
Visits Per Month	**Techies**	**Gadgeteers**	**Mid-America**	**Procrastinators**	**No-Tech**
Mean	6	7	6	4	4
Median	4	7	4	4	3
Main Transaction Account	**Techies**	**Gadgeteers**	**Mid-America**	**Procrastinators**	**No-Tech**
Regular Checking	47%	52%	62%	58%	58%
Interest Checking	39%	31%	22%	18%	23%
SuperNOW	8%	9%	6%	6%	6%
Regular Savings	2%	2%	3%	3%	5%
Other	4%	3%	4%	5%	3%
None	0%	1%	3%	5%	5%
Checks Per Month	**Techies**	**Gadgeteers**	**Mid-America**	**Procrastinators**	**No-Tech**
Mean	26	27	18	9	11
Median	22	27	17	11	11
	Techies	**Gadgeteers**	**Mid-America**	**Procrastinators**	**No-Tech**
Have Written Budget	22%	30%	24%	19%	22%
Who Usually Pays Bills	**Techies**	**Gadgeteers**	**Mid-America**	**Procrastinators**	**No-Tech**
Male Head of Household	46%	30%	26%	29%	34%
Female Head of Household	40%	50%	59%	45%	54%
Both	13%	18%	14%	20%	10%
Other	1%	1%	1%	0%	1%

Table 4 (Cont.)

Sources of Cash	Techies	Gadgeteers	Mid-America	Procrastinators	No-Tech
Cash back with deposit	61%	75%	72%	63%	61%
Cash personal check at financial institution	65%	57%	57%	66%	57%
Cash third-party checks at supermarket	10%	17%	22%	23%	20%
Cash back from personal checks at supermarket	51%	46%	40%	39%	41%
Cash personal checks w/o purchase at supermarket	12%	17%	16%	16%	7%
Cash third-party checks at other retailers	6%	7%	5%	10%	5%
Cash back from personal check at other retailers	12%	11%	9%	7%	5%
Cash personal checks w/o purchase at other retailers	5%	5%	3%	3%	2%
Cash third-party check at work	2%	6%	4%	7%	8%
Cash personal check at work	15%	14%	13%	9%	9%
Receive pay in cash	2%	4%	7%	5%	6%
Obtain cash from ATMs	67%	59%	40%	37%	35%

Monthly Routine Cash Needs	Techies	Gadgeteers	Mid-America	Procrastinators	No-Tech
Mean	$420	$357	$337	$349	$253
Median	$350	$250	$250	$250	$150

Ownership of Credit Cards	Techies	Gadgeteers	Mid-America	Procrastinators	No-Tech
Department store/general merchandise accounts	85%	86%	76%	76%	60%
Gasoline company accounts	54%	60%	43%	55%	39%
Bankcard accounts	85%	85%	69%	68%	53%
Other general purpose accounts (e.g., Discover)	30%	38%	23%	29%	16%
Travel & entertainment card accounts	31%	27%	12%	21%	12%
Other card accounts	2%	4%	3%	10%	13%

Source: Payment Systems, Inc. (1988)

Table 5

Payment Medium Last Used By Shoppers In Selected Retail Outlets

Supermarket	**Techies**	**Gadgeteers**	**Mid-America**	**Procrastinators**	**No-Tech**
Cash	40%	43%	55%	55%	70%
Check	57%	57%	44%	41%	26%
Bankcard	0%	0%	0%	1%	0%
Convenience Store	**Techies**	**Gadgeteers**	**Mid-America**	**Procrastinators**	**No-Tech**
Cash	86%	89%	88%	82%	84%
Check	7%	9%	10%	10%	12%
Bankcard	2%	1%	1%	0%	1%
Department Store	**Techies**	**Gadgeteers**	**Mid-America**	**Procrastinators**	**No-Tech**
Cash	12%	19%	24%	29%	32%
Check	27%	21%	26%	25%	30%
Bankcard	22%	27%	17%	20%	10%
Other Credit Card	37%	34%	31%	24%	24%
Furniture/Appliance Store	**Techies**	**Gadgeteers**	**Mid-America**	**Procrastinators**	**No-Tech**
Cash	10%	14%	14%	24%	13%
Check	39%	31%	46%	38%	56%
Bankcard	39%	40%	23%	18%	19%
Other Credit Card	9%	10%	10%	12%	4%
Discount Department Store	**Techies**	**Gadgeteers**	**Mid-America**	**Procrastinators**	**No-Tech**
Cash	29%	37%	46%	50%	54%
Check	34%	32%	31%	22%	27%
Bankcard	28%	24%	15%	16%	5%
Other Credit Card	4%	3%	3%	5%	3%
Clothing Store	**Techies**	**Gadgeteers**	**Mid-America**	**Procrastinators**	**No-Tech**
Cash	8%	28%	30%	35%	33%
Check	39%	29%	31%	36%	39%
Bankcard	32%	31%	23%	18%	17%
Other Credit Card	14%	11%	12%	5%	8%
Drug Store	**Techies**	**Gadgeteers**	**Mid-America**	**Procrastinators**	**No-Tech**
Cash	52%	53%	56%	48%	65%
Check	31%	37%	32%	34%	24%
Bankcard	9%	5%	3%	7%	2%
Other Credit Card	3%	3%	2%	1%	1%

Table 5 (Cont.)

Gasoline Station	Techies	Gadgeteers	Mid-America	Procrastinators	No-Tech
Cash	56%	51%	63%	53%	66%
Check	9%	7%	10%	15%	8%
Bankcard	6%	11%	5%	7%	6%
Other Credit Card	27%	30%	17%	20%	16%
Local Restaurants	**Techies**	**Gadgeteers**	**Mid-America**	**Procrastinators**	**No-Tech**
Cash	57%	62%	77%	68%	85%
Check	6%	8%	8%	6%	1%
Bankcard	24%	23%	9%	8%	8%
Other Credit Card	8%	5%	2%	7%	1%
Non-Local Restaurants	**Techies**	**Gadgeteers**	**Mid-America**	**Procrastinators**	**No-Tech**
Cash	54%	52%	70%	63%	73%
Check	6%	2%	4%	5%	2%
Bankcard	29%	28%	17%	16%	13%
Other Credit Card	10%	9%	4%	8%	2%
Medical/Health Service	**Techies**	**Gadgeteers**	**Mid-America**	**Procrastinators**	**No-Tech**
Cash	16%	23%	19%	26%	21%
Check	66%	57%	65%	56%	62%
Bankcard	5%	6%	3%	2%	2%
Airline Tickets	**Techies**	**Gadgeteers**	**Mid-America**	**Procrastinators**	**No-Tech**
Cash	5%	7%	8%	22%	2%
Check	17%	15%	28%	15%	19%
Bankcard	54%	55%	45%	32%	39%
Other Credit Card	20%	21%	15%	23%	4%
Hotels/Motels	**Techies**	**Gadgeteers**	**Mid-America**	**Procrastinators**	**No-Tech**
Cash	9%	16%	25%	24%	22%
Check	8%	10%	9%	7%	6%
Bankcard	53%	50%	51%	35%	54%
Other Credit Card	15%	16%	11%	21%	19%

Source: Payment Systems, Inc. (1988)

Table 6

Weighted Average Importance Ratings For Selected Financial Institution Attributes

(Greater the number, the greater the importance of the attribute.)

	Techies	Gadgeteers	Mid-America	Procrastinators	No-Tech
Accurate bookkeeping	4.8	4.6	4.8	4.5	4.6
Reasonable service charges on checking	4.8	4.6	4.8	4.4	4.5
Easy to read statements	4.3	4.3	4.5	4.5	4.4
Courteous personnel	4.3	4.3	4.5	4.4	4.4
Branches close to home or work	4.3	4.5	4.5	4.1	4.4
Quick teller service	4.2	4.6	4.5	4.2	4.2
Friendly tellers	3.9	4.2	4.4	4.3	4.4
Highest rates on savings or CDs	4.3	4.2	4.3	4.2	4.4
Lowest rates on loans	4.1	4.2	4.2	4.1	4.0
Convenient parking	4.0	3.9	4.1	4.2	4.1
Quick answers on loan requests	3.7	3.9	4.0	3.7	3.8
Convenient drive-thru windows	3.7	4.0	3.9	4.0	3.6
Convenient ATMs	3.8	3.7	3.5	3.3	3.2
Branches all over town	3.6	3.6	3.5	3.5	3.4
Attractive facilities	2.8	2.8	3.0	3.1	3.0
Branches or offices in other states	2.8	3.0	3.0	2.9	2.9

Scale:
1.0 - 1.4 = Very unimportant
1.5 - 2.4 = Somewhat unimportant
2.5 - 3.4 = Neutral
3.5 - 4.4 = Somewhat important
4.5 - 5.0 = Very important

Source: Payment Systems, Inc. (1988)

Table 7

Weighted Average Agreement Scores For Selected Statements Concerning Financial Services And The Economy

(Larger negative number indicates greater disagreement, larger positive number indicates greater agreement.)

Statement	Techies	Gadgeteers	Mid-America	Procrastinators	No-Tech
Would pay $25/year more for basic checking service in exchange for better service.	-0.75	-0.72	-0.76	-0.67	-0.79
Would consider switching for more convenient location even if cost greater.	-0.65	-0.67	-0.71	-0.55	-0.68
Do not mind reasonable price increases for financial services.	-0.55	-0.36	-0.46	-0.39	-0.25
Prefer using ATMs.	-0.24	-0.24	-0.45	-0.47	-0.54
Deferring major purchases till economy in better condition.	-0.28	-0.24	-0.15	-0.05	-0.05
Reluctant to switch because of comfortable relationship with a staff member.	-0.12	-0.14	-0.11	+0.03	-0.13
Paying too much for financial services.	+0.02	-0.07	-0.08	+0.07	-0.18
Prefer dealing with the same individual... even if have to wait.	-0.15	-0.17	-0.07	+0.06	-0.10
Quality of service the same at all banks, S&Ls.	+0.06	-0.01	-0.02	+0.14	+0.05
Would switch financial institutions for better service at same price.	+0.15	+0.19	+0.09	+0.02	-0.09
Switching is just too much trouble.	+0.17	+0.21	+0.17	+0.21	+0.31
Need for credit overrides tax considerations.	+0.35	+0.24	+0.17	+0.14	+0.17
Now is good time to buy a house.	+0.35	+0.30	+0.20	+0.01	-0.01
Interest deductibility not a major consideration in use of credit.	+0.34	+0.22	+0.30	+0.28	+0.32
Quick banking important, provider doesn't matter.	+0.27	+0.36	+0.30	+0.37	+0.47
Comfortable with current level of debt.	+0.40	+0.34	+0.30	+0.39	+0.32
Institutions should provide lifeline services.	+0.19	+0.25	+0.36	+0.50	+0.53
Most tellers competent and well trained.	+0.45	+0.32	+0.51	+0.55	+0.55
Bank resolves errors quickly and easily.	+0.47	+0.52	+0.58	+0.59	+0.57

(Scale: -1 thru -.26 = disagree; -.25 thru .25 = neutral; .26 thru 1 = agree.)

Source: Payment Systems, Inc. (1988)

Table 8

Use Of Alternative Delivery Systems

	Techies	Gadgeteers	Mid-America	Procrastinators	No-Tech
Automated Teller Machines	67%	58%	42%	46%	42%
Point of Sale Debit Cards	17%	12%	7%	9%	10%
Direct Deposit of Salary	37%	19%	11%	7%	9%
Direct Deposit of Social Security	5%	6%	11%	20%	23%
Direct Deposit of Pension	4%	4%	5%	7%	6%
Direct Deposit of Dividends	4%	3%	3%	2%	2%
Pay by Phone	3%	3%	2%	4%	4%
Bank by Phone	14%	11%	8%	6%	4%
Automatic Bill Payment	25%	25%	22%	19%	13%
Payroll Deduction Plan	25%	17%	12%	10%	14%
Drive-In Windows	48%	55%	52%	38%	33%
Mail Deposits	26%	20%	18%	16%	17%
Home Banking by Computer	1%	0%	0%	1%	1%

Source: Payment Systems, Inc. (1988)

Table 9

Weighted Average Agreement Scores For Selected Statements Concerning Electronic Delivery Systems Concepts

(Larger negative number indicates greater disagreement, larger positive number indicates greater agreement.)

Statement	Techies	Gadgeteers	Mid-America	Procrastinators	No-Tech
Prefer to use phone for more financial transactions.	-0.04	-0.22	-0.42	-0.35	-0.44
Hard to find time for routine chores.	-0.16	+0.00	-0.32	-0.30	-0.37
Prefer to use mail for routine financial transactions.	-0.17	-0.21	-0.31	-0.21	-0.34
Familiar with electronic delivery/videotext.	-0.02	-0.17	-0.31	-0.17	-0.44
Using branches much less frequently.	-0.04	-0.07	-0.25	-0.03	-0.15
Would mind public terminal to pay bills.	+0.05	+0.00	-0.23	-0.12	-0.20
Would like levelized utility bill plan.	-0.09	+0.01	-0.10	-0.14	-0.26
Interested in service to provide periodic household income statement/balance sheet.	+0.02	+0.09	-0.08	-0.05	-0.21
More likely to use telephone bill payment if could see transactions on TV screen.	+0.14	+0.26	-0.05	+0.01	-0.21
Would like financial decision programs on public information terminals.	+0.09	+0.17	+0.04	-0.03	-0.07
Automatic payment might cause overdraft.	+0.14	+0.11	+0.10	+0.14	+0.26
Uncomfortable with computer-synthesized voices on phone.	+0.00	-0.09	+0.14	+0.17	+0.10
Don't leave messages on answering machines.	-0.21	-0.21	+0.17	+0.19	+0.07
Computerized bill-pay systems give institutions too much information.	+0.24	+0.23	+0.31	+0.30	+0.29
Dislike telephone answering machines.	+0.25	+0.10	+0.41	+0.30	+0.28

(Scale: -1 thru -.26 = disagree; -.25 thru .25 = neutral; .26 thru 1 = agree)

Source: Payment Systems, Inc. (1988)